From

From Cork to Calcutta

My Mother's Story

MILTY BOSE

zubaan

ZUBAAN
an imprint of Kali for Women
128B Shahpur Jat, 1st Floor
NEW DELHI 110 049
Email: contact@zubaanbooks.com
Website: www.zubaanbooks.com

First published by Zubaan Publishers Pvt. Ltd 2017

10 9 8 7 6 5 4 3 2 1

ISBN 978 93 84757 63 2

Zubaan is an independent feminist publishing house based in New Delhi with a strong academic and general list. It was set up as an imprint of India's first feminist publishing house, Kali for Women, and carries forward Kali's tradition of publishing world quality books to high editorial and production standards. *Zubaan* means tongue, voice, language, speech in Hindustani. Zubaan publishes in the areas of the humanities, social sciences, as well as in fiction, general non-fiction, and books for children and young adults under its Young Zubaan imprint.

Typeset in Arno Pro 12/16 by Jojy Phillip, New Delhi 110 015
Printed at Gopsons Papers Ltd

Dedicated to
Shu and Imelda Bose
and
Saury and Bina Bose
with love

PROLOGUE

Come Back to Erin

It was Wednesday, 26th February 1997. Dusk had arrived; the setting sun was slipping below the horizon, leaving behind a glorious display of pink, lilac and fuchsia clouds. The breeze brought with it the fragrance of the early blossoms: jasmine, mixed with neem and eucalyptus. The squabbling ravens had finally settled in for the night, and a peace descended over the household.

I carried a tray with tea and biscuits into my mother's room, a nightly ritual that had begun when she moved in with me. I put the tray down on the table next to her bed and made myself comfortable, tucking my toes under the edge of her quilt to keep them warm.

"Didn't finish your dinner?" I remarked lightly.

"Eat, eat, eat. Is that all you ever talk about?" she grumbled under her breath.

"And a good evening to you too, Miss Congeniality," I replied.

She ignored the sarcasm as she watched me pour the tea, making sure the colour was just right.

Tea time had always been important in our family. The art of perfect tea-making was taught to me early in my life.

The ritual began with a warmed teapot. The tea had to be the perfect blend of sixty percent Darjeeling to forty Assam, brewed for five minutes, in a pot beneath a quilted tea-cosy shaped like a rooster or similar farm animal. Meanwhile, warm milk, never ever boiling, was poured into the cup through a silver strainer. My mother always had one even teaspoon of sugar in her cup, and I always had two heaped teaspoons in mine. The pleasure was in the ritual: first the milk, then the tea, and lastly the sugar. She always shook her head at the amount of sugar I put into my cup: "It's a good thing you're not diabetic," but nowadays it was mostly, "Is this tea or piss-water?"

We talked about inconsequential matters. I told her how embarrassed my son Nikhil got when I shouted and made a fool of myself every time he had the ball during a soccer game.

"He threatened to ban me from the games if I don't behave," I chuckled.

"He must be the star of the team," she said, smiling.

"Of course he is!" I gushed.

"I have to agree with him, you do carry on a bit."

"I don't remember any complaints about Brinda. She used to run up and down the sidelines screaming like a crazy person!"

"My beautiful Brinda can do no wrong."

"Oh, so now she's your favourite, is she?"

"You are such a troublemaker. You'll never change."

We laughed, enjoying the banter.

After a few biscuits and a cup of tea, I remembered a letter I had received from my eldest daughter, Ayesha. Talking to her a few weeks earlier, I had casually mentioned that her grandmother was getting frail. She had immediately responded with a long letter, which I now picked up and waved mischievously in the air.

"Want me read it?"

"Yes darling, please do," she replied quietly.

Her eyes took on an extra sparkle whenever her grandchildren were mentioned. She had a magical bond with all of them, an unconditional acceptance of all things good or bad. I made myself comfortable on the edge of the bed and proceeded to read, occasionally glancing over to catch her reaction. She had closed her eyes, but I knew she was paying attention by the glow on her face. A tear slowly trickled into the creases that now made up that face. I concentrated on the letter for I knew I would dissolve into tears if I reacted.

Later that night, as I lay in bed reading, I felt a strange restlessness, there was something vaguely unsettling in the air. I checked on my son and made sure all the doors were locked.

I tried to encourage my dog Kirby to get up on the bed. Her reaction usually was to this one of complete joy, but this time I had to coax her before she jumped up, her ears and tail hanging limp as she looked at me with anxious eyes. I lay listening to the silence and tried to calm my racing heart. I heard the howls of street dogs, first at a distance but then closer, louder. Soon, I could hear them just below the house. I felt a sudden chill and jumped up, running instinctively to my mother's room.

She lay on her back with her head tilted sideways, her arm hanging over the edge of the bed.

As I rushed to her, a blinding light consumed me. My universe was collapsing with awful suddenness. I reached out and held on to the one person who had always been there for me. Her love was total and unconditional, and taken for granted. She was my 'wee bit of green' in the saffron landscape of India, always there with a smile and a nudge when I most needed it. I must have stayed there holding her all night, mother and daughter alone for the last time, a moment and an eternity.

In the early hours my teenage son entered, treading cautiously. Before I could react, he held up a hand. "I know."

He had been lying awake, listening to me, before he finally decided to face the inevitable. His eyes were red and swollen. He unwrapped my numb arms and gently laid my mother down. As he brushed back her hair with his fingers, his words gave my heart wings.

"Mom, be happy for Granny. She's free now… She waited so long to be free."

> I stood at the door at twilight
> And my mother I could see.
> Tears from her dear eyes falling,
> And I knew she was thinking of me.
> An old Irish tune was playing,
> An old song that always thrills.
> 'Come back to Erin,' 'twas calling her back,
> To her home in the Irish hills.

1

County Cork

As a young girl, Imelda Connor thought she had her whole life figured out. She knew she would never leave the Connor farm. Here she would live her enchanted life with the perfect husband and devote herself to her animals and her family. She loved her little paradise and she knew she was born lucky – Irish lucky.

The Connors were farmers from Kilworth, County Cork, in south-west Ireland. Their two-acre farm was set among the gentle hills of Ballincollig, an area intersected more by bubbling brooks and streams than roads and by-lanes. The region was steeped in the history of nature-worshipping druids, Viking invaders, and idolized High Kings of Ireland. Most Irish families could trace their roots back to one of these kings, so it was no wonder that Patrick Joseph Connor, Imelda's father, proudly traced his own roots back to the renowned High King Thurlough O'Connor, although the line was neither as close nor as direct as he liked to believe.

Patrick was born in Ballyroo, County Kildare, on August 28, 1876. His mother Anne Rooney married William Connor, a carpenter in the village. William, Anne and their two sons moved to the tiny village of Kilworth when Patrick was eight. Like the other farmers of the area, William continued to work at his carpentry while taking care of the small farm, slowly making additions to his stone house as the family integrated into the community.

The green hills of Ballincollig were dotted with stone and mortar farmhouses. The fields around them were separated by two-foot high dry stone walls, more to keep the sheep and cows from wandering than to define property lines. They were also convenient hurdles for horses to jump as the children raced them across the fields.

Patrick grew up in this close-knit community as one of its brasher young men. He was a tall and lanky lad with a shock of red hair and steel-blue eyes that held a glint of mischief every time his wide, contagious smile lit up his face. Affectionately known as 'Mad Lad Connor,' he ran hotter than his friends tended to acknowledge, relying more on his fists than his head. He played Gaelic football with total abandon, often leaving the field injured and always furiously protesting. If he did not break a bone or sprain an ankle, it was a good game.

Despite this hot-headedness, Patrick was a well-loved young man in the community. He was genuinely warm and friendly and had that famous Irish gift of the gab. He could often be found sprawled at the kitchen table of a neighbour's house, swapping stories and helping himself to cups of tea and warm bread. His four best friends were Sean McNairy, Peter Clancy, Michael McFadden and Joseph Callahan. They had gone through school together, performed in school plays, played football, served as altar boys and sang in the church choir.

Rarely a day went by when Patrick and his friends could not be heard hooting and hollering as they raced their horses down the narrow dirt lanes. Patrick, being one of the better riders, thought he owned the bragging rights to every race he won.

"Not one of yeh losers can beat me!" he shouted as he waded through a stream.

"Yer so full of shite," Callahan replied.

"When's the last time I got a round in, eh?" Patrick grinned, referring to their tradition of the loser buying the first round of Guinness at the local pub.

"Forgotten last week?" Callahan shot back.

"Fuckin' bastard!" Patrick clambered out of the stream, angrily shaking the water off his clothes, his face flushed red.

He had just jumped on his horse when Callahan yelled, "Yer a right eejit, Connor. The black stuff's on me – now stop this slaggin' match!"

For all his bluster and bravado, Patrick also had a gentle side. He could never listen to 'Danny Boy' or 'Mother McCrea' without tearing up, nor could he ignore the peace he felt sitting in church listening to the choir. His best-kept secret, however, was the feelings he harboured for one Kathleen Tierney, the beautiful brown-haired girl who rode her bicycle past him every morning on the way to school.

He would pretend not to notice her, and she would cycle by him as though he did not exist. He had known her family for years, their paths crossing often at various church functions. One Sunday morning, when he was serving as an altar boy, he had casually looked down over the congregation and their eyes had met. He had tried to look away, but not before she'd given him a wicked wink, eyes shining with glee.

After that, he could not get her out of his mind.

Kathleen was the absolute antithesis of Patrick. He was loud and brash and full of 'arguing', while she was quiet and gentle, ever the peacemaker. He was lean and lanky where she was soft and graceful. Patrick had unruly red hair, while Kathleen had beautiful golden-brown locks that framed her heart-shaped face. Her eyebrows gently framed the bluest eyes that Patrick had ever seen.

On the downside, she had two annoying sisters, Beatrice and Sienna, who always seemed to be hanging around her.

After their encounter, Kathleen acted as though nothing extraordinary had happened, ignoring Patrick and his friends with such nonchalance that he wondered if he had imagined the whole incident.

For months, Patrick dreamt about Kathleen, deciding that he was going to ask her to marry him as soon as he got his leaving certificate from school. He flirted with the other girls, hoping she would notice, but nothing seemed to work and he was beginning to lose heart.

This went on so long that his friends began to wonder about the new, sombre turn their friend had taken. One evening, after a few too many rounds of 'the black stuff,' a lovesick Patrick blurted out his woes. Though it was too late to stop the teasing, he tried to swear his friends to secrecy.

A few days later, as the boys hung around the school yard, jostling each other and kicking a ball around, they noticed a group of girls giggling and shooting them conspiratorial glances. Kathleen Tierney was among them.

"Patrick. Look over there," Peter Clancy muttered under his breath. "I dare yer ter talk to her."

"What wud yer give me if I did?" Patrick replied.

"I'll clean the stalls for a day."

"Nah. Not worth it."

"Bastard! Yer not doin' it fer me."

"I'll throw in a week," McNairy offered.

"You'll clean the stalls for a week? Done. Shake on it."

Laughing nervously, Patrick sauntered over to where Kathleen was standing. His palms were clammy and his heart pounded so loudly he feared she would hear it. He waited for the right moment to say something, awkwardly shifting from foot to foot.

"Kathleen Tierney! Fancy meeting you here. Brilliant," he stammered.

She looked at him steadily and said with an impish grin, "Trying to make a fool of me, Patrick Joseph Connor?"

"You know my name?" he asked, taken aback.

"I know all about yeh. So don't be flirting with me like you do the other gurls." She gave him a knowing nod.

"Well, if yeh give me a wee little kiss, maybe I'll marry you someday."

She stared at him in utter disbelief, then ran to join her older sister, her face flushed.

Patrick stood paralyzed. What had he blurted out?

His friends came rushing over, bursting with curiosity.

"I asked her t'marry me," Patrick said, his voice faint.

"*What?*"

"Shite! I asked her to marry me," he repeated.

"Are ya daft?"

"You eejit! Now yuh'll have to keep yer word."

"Shure 'tis a grand thing. Can I be best man?" said Callahan.

"Aw, shaddup the lot of yeh. I'm such an eejit. She'll never talk to me again!" Patrick moaned. "I made such an arse of meself!"

Patrick waited anxiously for Kathleen to ride by the next morning. When he saw her approaching, he was amazed at how unperturbed she appeared as she happily waved to him. He, on the other hand, was shaking like a leaf.

"Kathleen! Can yeh talk to me? Alone?"

"You don't have to apologize," she replied casually, looking straight into his eyes without a trace of anger.

"Yer not mad at me?" Patrick asked in disbelief.

"Naw, I took it as a bit of a joke: but you can carry me books if you mind yerself," she added, quietly handing them to him.

That was how their relationship began, and how it continued throughout their lives. Kathleen was always the calm at the centre of the many storms that would come their way. Nothing seemed to throw her off balance; she was the perfect foil to his intemperate outbursts, always there to stop him from taking himself too seriously. Different as they were, they made each other happy. They were high school sweethearts, accepted and loved by all those around them. That they would get married was as certain as the daily showers of Ballincollig.

After finishing school, Patrick planned to continue his education in Gowran, County Kilkenny. He promised Kathleen he would return to marry her, and after a sad farewell he went off to seek fame and fortune. In Gowran, British army recruiters offered an impressionable Patrick a distinguished career in the armed forces. Young and ambitious, he enlisted immediately and was sent to the Military Academy in Loughgall, Ulster Province.

So it was that Private Patrick Joseph Connor, a young man of eighteen with cursory military training, was shipped off to fight in the hot and inhospitable insect-infested jungles of the Transvaal, where the British Army was engaged in a brutal battle against the South African Republic and the Orange Free State for control of their gold and diamonds mines. Nothing could have prepared him for the horrors of the Boer War. For three years, every day was a fight for survival, with more young men dying from malaria, typhoid and cholera than on the battlefield.

When the war ended in 1902, Patrick was posted as Lance Corporal to Kilfenora, County Clare. Toughened by the harsh realities of war, the man who returned was not the carefree jovial lad who had left Ireland with such hope and ambition.

As soon as he was able, he asked for Kathleen's hand in marriage, and they lived in Kilfenora for a while. After the birth of their first son, they moved back to Kilworth to be closer to friends and family.

Sean McNairy now owned the hardware store; he had nuts and bolts that fit anything from a wooden gate to a horse's hoof. Peter Clancy baked his famous soda bread, lemon cake and fudge and his mother's potato bread had become a local speciality. Michael McFadden ran the local 'spirit grocery,' a pub-cum-shop where you could buy anything from a pint of Guinness to a quarter-pound of butter. Joseph Callahan owned the local pub where Patrick, Peter, Michael and a group of other regulars could be heard arguing for hours over the relative merits of rotating crops or leaving the land fallow. They all had a different opinion but they were united in blaming the British for their problems.

Nestled among the farms, the spiral steeple of the parish church could be seen from every corner of Kilworth. On Sundays, the bells rang out every hour on the hour and there wasn't a lady who didn't cross herself when the chimes began. Everyone contributed to the pot used to maintain the church and its priests; a good pot meant they looked after their own. The church was the social centre of the community. All town meetings were held in its back rooms and though local politicians ran for election, in reality the power rested with the Bishop and parish priests.

The nuns ran the girls' school in one section of the church, while the boys had their own classes run by the priests at the opposite end. Girls and boys shared the sport fields, where the nuns kept eye on them. There was a peaceful timelessness about the place.

Kathleen and Patrick settled into their small farm with their two boys: Gerald Patrick, born in 1905 and named after his grandfather, and Cyril Patrick, born a year later. A third boy, Patrick Joseph, was born in 1907, followed the next year by Francis Joseph. Four boys in five years.

Francis had barely turned three when Kathleen became pregnant again. On a warm morning in June, Kathleen began to feel the first pangs of labour. Arrangements had been made with her younger sister Sienna to take care of the four boys. Beatrice, her eldest sister, came over early and took charge. Her first order of business was to send Patrick to the pub to get a 'long' drink.

"I have a wee bit of advice for you," she said, looking him straight in the eyes. "'Tis time to keep yer whistle in yer pocket, if you know what I mean."

"I'd be mindin' me own business if I were you," Frank retorted as he walked away.

"And you better get yer ugly mug back here by five," Beatrice continued, unafraid, "an' don't be showin' up skuttered, if you know what's good fer yer!"

Beatrice kept an eye on how far apart the contractions were, snapping directions at the midwife. "For the love of God, do I have to do it all meself? Did you send for that good-for-nothing doctor?" She had sent two messages for the doctor to be there by four, figuring the baby would not arrive until later on that evening.

"I need to walk, Bea, I don't think the baby can wait for the doctor," Kathleen pleaded between moans and shallow breaths. "I feel the pushing urge!"

"Someone get the fuckin' doctor!" Beatrice yelled at the top of her voice, adding, "Forgive me, Jesus!" as she crossed herself.

"Oh Beatrice!" Kathleen smiled weakly. "Are those the first words you want my baby to hear?" The midwife took over, helping her to lie in the birthing position.

"'Tis coming! I see a head. I see red hair. Come on, girl, take a deep breath and push."

Beatrice had other thoughts on her mind. "I'll fuckin' kill that doctor when he gets here."

On June 19, 1911, at exactly 4.45 pm, Imelda Mary Josephine Connor made her début into the world.

A short while later, Patrick walked in, pale and humbled. He rushed to Kathleen and kissed her tenderly on the forehead.

"Is me darlin' all right? 'Tis the last one for sure." He shot a glance at Beatrice.

Kathleen handed him the little pink bundle. "Here's yer wee angel, Patrick. Here's our wee bitty baby girl."

Patrick looked at the baby and melted. He sobbed as he held her. He had always been a proud father, but this tiny child felt so different. She has stolen his heart the instant he set eyes on her.

2

West Bengal

Many miles away from the Irish shore, protected by the Himalayan mountains and nurtured by the river Ganges, lay the subcontinent of India. The river ended its laborious journey through the country by empting into the Bay of Bengal, creating a fertile delta that hosted the largest mangrove forest on earth. There in the heart of the delta, in the district of Midnapur, lay the village of Rajnagar.

Gadadhar Bose was one of Rajnagar's most prominent residents. He was the patriarch of a well-established zamindar family, and ran his estate with the help of his three sons. The youngest, Prasanna Kumar Bose, was a mild man who was content to live quietly with his wife Piyali. They lived in a two-storey house built around a courtyard, next door to the homes of his brothers and parents.

Gadadhar was a progressive man, instilling the values of education in his grandchildren. He insisted his sons marry girls who had gone to school. Piyali was youngest daughter-in-law, and was his pride and joy. She had been to school until the tenth standard, which was unusual for girls since book-learning was considered a distraction from their future roles as mothers and housekeepers.

Piyali took a deep interest in the schooling of her three children, specially her youngest son Amarendra Nath. He was different from the rest of the family, shy and withdrawn, happy to stay in his room and read books on philosophy, art and history. It was Piyali who had the greatest impact on young Amarendra's life. She loved to sit in the corner of his room and listen to him read, often confusing him with questions.

"Oh Ma, you ask too many questions! Go watch the birds. That stork with the bent wing arrived yesterday. She would not stop squawking till I went out and welcomed her."

"She did the same thing with me. The silly bird is building her nest right over the gharials mating pond again. I'll have to make sure the nets are still in place."

Piyali used to watch the birds for hours from her veranda. She recognized many of the migrating birds, gave them names, and talked incessantly about them to Amarendra. The two of them made logs of the birds and kept an inventory of their surviving chicks.

For one of her birthdays, Amarendra decided to get his mother a parrot. He took Ashu, his childhood companion, to the market and bought the most striking and talented parrot he could find.

Ashu was the fourth son of the family's cook. At the age of five he had been brought into the household to be a playmate for Amarendra. As he grew older, his father was paid a small stipend for his work, which was to keep Amarendra company. Piyali tried to get Ashu to study, but he had absolutely no interest in books.

Piyali was touched when she was given the parrot, but told the boys she couldn't keep the poor bird caged. Not realizing its wings had been clipped, she took it to the edge of the garden and let it go. The surprised bird tried to take off, only to plunge into the stream. As it struggled in the water a couple of gharials swam towards it. Amarendra immediately jumped into the water, followed by Ashu, to save the bird as the startled gharials scattered.

After that, the bird never left the vicinity. So began Amarendra's life-long love affair with parrots.

As he grew older, Amarendra's moodiness often worried his parents. He was bored with school, and complained about knowing more than his teacher. He was a dark, lanky boy with a very serious demeanour. He was studious to a fault, reading late into the night by candlelight. He was interested in logic, astronomy, metaphysics and philosophy. Voltaire and Bacon were his favourite writers, Socrates his philosopher of choice.

Birds, however, were his obsession.

He would wake up before sunrise to watch the Siberian whooping cranes, and the painted storks with their black and pink plumage gracefully sweep onto the treetops. His logbook not only included species but minute details about missing tail-feathers, nicks on the beak, and other distinguishing marks.

Calcutta was the country's capital city, and English was the official language of government. Amarendra was well aware that if he wanted to get ahead in his career he would have to make his way there, which required him to be fluent in English. So, determined to get a better education, he applied to a private school in Calcutta. The competition was fierce but he won his

place, and Prasanna and Piyali reluctantly supported their son's
decision to move to the city.

And so, at the age of sixteen, Amarendra Nath set out to
meet his destiny in the most exhilarating city in the world. His
aptitude for learning was immediately recognized and within
three months he was transferred to one of the most elite schools
in Calcutta. Amarendra decided he would be a lawyer; he saw
the opportunities this profession had to offer with the changing
laws and challenges of the new government.

By the time he was twenty-two, he was well on the way to
becoming a well-known and respected lawyer. He was of 'a
good marriageable age' and his family cautiously began to look
for a pretty bride, from a bhodro Bengali family. They finally
found the perfect match with the Mitras. The father was a well-
established lawyer and could be a great help to Amarendra.
They had a son named Dhiren, and two daughters, Charulata
and Pankajini. The younger daughter, Pankajini, was educated
and beautiful. At fourteen, she would be a young bride, but
the families decided that the couple would live together only
after Pankajini's schooling was complete, by which time she
would be seventeen. The marriage was arranged with joyful
anticipation.

On their wedding night, Amarendra was appalled to discover
that his bride could barely speak English. He immediately
made arrangements for an English tutor who was given strict
instructions to teach Pankajini to speak English well and
introduce her to the classics: Shakespeare, Dickens, Milton,
Shelly, Keats and the Bronte sisters. Every evening, Amarendra
quizzed her about what she had read.

Pankajini, for her part, was equally unimpressed with her

new husband, and especially disappointed in his appearance. She had been told he was brilliant, well-read and a little older, but so smart she would not even notice the age difference. She fantasized about a handsome young man who would sweep her off her feet.

She was indignant that he questioned her like she was a schoolgirl, not giving her credit for her knowledge of Bengali literature. She had studied English, and could read and understand it well, but was shy and didn't like speaking it in public. "I can dance, sing, and recite classical Bengali poetry, but all this husband wants to know is what Hamlet means when he says 'to be or not to be'?" she grumbled to her sister. "One of these days I just might tell him what I really think!"

3

County Cork

After his daughter was born, Patrick was a changed man. He sang her lullabies, hymns and even songs of the revolution. Imelda was his pride and joy, the centre of his universe. As she grew up, she knew exactly how to keep 'her Da' happy. She'd clap her hands and dance the jig with squeals of delight, her red hair falling across her face. She had him wrapped around her little finger. When she was old enough, he traded a calf to get her a colt named Toby. He watched with pride as she mounted the horse and sat erect and proud in the saddle.

"That's me best gurl!" he bellowed, clapping his hands in joy.

Imelda flourished as the spoilt sister of four older brothers, but all this changed with the birth of Connors' last child, another girl. Patrick took one look at the baby and declared her Kathleen Marie Mulberry Connor. She was the image of her mother, with large iridescent blue eyes, a turned-up nose, two dimples and a smile that could melt your heart. As he rocked her in his arms he would gently touch her nose with his finger, "Yer a lucky wee one, Kathy, almost as beautiful as yer Ma."

Kathleen Marie became the darling of the family, competing with Imelda for the limelight. At first Imelda was jealous, but soon fell in love with her gurgling, bouncy little sister. Kathy became Imelda's shadow, and Imelda would take her everywhere. With six children to raise, a farm to run, and her health frail, their mother was happy to let Imelda take Kathy under her wing.

Patrick Connor was a military man; he liked discipline and order and ran his home the way he ran his brigade. Like most Irish patriarchs, his word was law. Supper had to be on the table by six, the children washed and tidy, and all the animals fed and cleaned at precisely the same time every day. The farm ran like clockwork, with chores fairly distributed among the family. Every child was accountable for their share of the work.

Patrick was a large man with strong wide shoulders, holding himself erect like the professional soldier he was. He had a magnificent moustache over his wide smile and large white teeth. His boisterous laugh softened his stern face instantly, his eyes taking on the mischievous twinkle that all his children had inherited. His resonant baritone could be heard at the local pub, leading a noisy choir through rousing fighting songs about King Thurlough O'Connor and Kevin Barry.

Working for the British Armed Forces, Patrick's position was precarious for he, like most of the Irish population, wanted Ireland to be independent, yet his livelihood depended on the British Government. The more militant leaders of the IRA were gaining support in the growing power struggle. The bully tactics of these new members appalled Patrick. He had seen death and terror in the Transvaal, and did not want to relive that horror in his homeland. He voiced his anger and frustration at both the

Irish and British politicians, and those close to him worried that his outbursts could have dangerous consequences. Kathleen worried as she quietly watched him drink too much and get carried away singing songs that 'seared the soul, and fired the heart'.

"We come from a glorious line of Kings, don't yuh be forgetting that!" he roared to all who could hear.

Patrick, Kathleen and their six children lived in a two-storey farmhouse built of stone and mortar. It had a roof of slate mined from the local quarries of Knightsbridge. The house was built around the kitchen where the large dining-table took centre stage. Here a cast-iron pot often hung over the fire warming a stew or broth made from chicken, ham or lamb. The enticing aroma of soda bread would fill the morning air. In the back yard was a smoker, where the ham would be smoked for days. It was the oldest son Gerald's job to keep the oak chips damp and smouldering, and the butter churned in the barrel.

The children often brought home apples from neighbouring farms and, in the summer, raspberries and blackberries from the bushes lining the streams. Berries or baked apples, sprinkled with sugar and smothered in cream, were a favourite dessert.

In family-farming, the line between family and farm is indistinguishable. The children had chores to complete before they got dressed to go to school. The troughs had to be filled for the pigs, the cowshed mucked out, cows milked, horses walked, sheep fed and stalls cleaned. By the age of five, Kathleen had her own special chores: feeding the chickens and geese, and collecting the eggs. She knew the right mix of corn and grain, and exactly how much would be enough.

With four brothers to cope with, life on the farm was not

easy for Imelda. Gerald, Cyril, Patrick and Frank were not only much older, but taller and stronger. They were constantly challenging each other to wrestling or boxing matches where Imelda had to intervene, chastising them or threatening to tell their father.

Imelda could hold her own, however, when it came to horse-riding. She would challenge her brothers and their friends to race the horses through the fields, over the boundary walls down to the stream, and she always won. It was a beautiful sight to see her streaming across the fields with her red hair flying behind her, her body taut as she guided Toby, smooth as silk, over the stone walls.

She could milk the cows faster than anyone on the farm. The brown sugar she fed them helped, she was also fond of the animals and lingered among them long after her chores were done. It was where she was happiest: out in the fields, feeding a lamb or playing with the piglets, with little Kathy as her constant companion.

Kathleen never seemed to recover fully after the birth of her last child. The strain of supervising six children, running the farm, looking after the household and her husband's high demands completely wore her out. Women, at that time, aged quickly and died young. The community recognized this, and the church had a large group of volunteers who were sent out to help struggling families with the cooking and cleaning. The nuns from the parish were also on hand to lend an ear or make a roast.

Imelda was protective not only of her elder brothers and sister, but also of her mother. When Patrick was impatient with his wife, it was left to Imelda to speak up for her mother, preventing him from crossing the line between being harsh and being cruel. She sometimes took the blame for unfinished tasks, for she knew her father would never raise his voice at her.

Mornings were always chaotic: lines outside the two outhouses, the children pushing and shoving before they stumbled downstairs, all washed and dressed in their school uniforms. Kathleen greeted each one of them with a cheerful, "And a good mornin' to yer."

A slice of bread, a glass of warm milk, and off to school they would go. And at the end of the day, Kathleen would always be waiting for them at the top of the lane when they returned.

Kathy usually saw her mother first and would run to her squealing with joy.

"How's me baby?" Kathleen would ask lovingly, and Kathy would launch into her usual routine.

"Mother Josephine said I was the best girl in class today."

"Mother Josephine doesn't know ya then, does she?" Imelda added sarcastically.

"I drew this picture for you, Ma," Kathy continued, pointedly ignoring Imelda.

"Oh, 'tis so beautiful!" Kathleen gushed.

"Kathy's your favourite," Imelda pouted. "Everything she does is 'soooo beautiful!'"

"Now don't be sayin' that, Mel," Kathleen replied, affectionately reaching for Imelda's hand. "What would I do without you, eh? She's still a baby and needs more mindin', that's all."

"She's not the sweet wee baby she pretends t'be," Imelda protested. "She's been tellin' all me friends that she saw me kiss Shaun Callahan. And whenever she sees Shaun she runs up t'him and starts singing, 'Imelda loves Shaun,' that too in front of all the other lads. 'Tis an embarrassment, it is!"

Kathy cut in. "But I did so see her kiss Shaun, right behind the barn; she kisses all the boys behind the barn. 'Tis a special kissing place! I saw Cyril kiss Josephine there too."

"Shut yer beak, you little liar! I'll not walk you to school ever again." Imelda angrily stalked off.

"Shame on you, Kathy! You know fine well this foolishness has to stop," Kathleen said sternly. "You go right inside and say sorry t'yer sister."

"But 'tis true! I did so see her kiss Shaun."

"One more word and t'will be bed before supper."

Imelda was especially tense that day. That evening, Father O'Reilly was coming to their house for supper. The parish priest was invited to share a meal with the Connors at least once a month. Imelda thought he was the most handsome man in the entire world, and so did her friends. Whenever they got together all they would ever do was talk about Father O'Reilly's piercing blue eyes. It did not go unnoticed that the teenage attendance at the church had increased considerably since he was assigned to the parish. Even the nuns had an extra bounce in their step since his arrival.

Imelda got up regularly for six o'clock Mass every Sunday, her hair neatly plaited, lips bitten and cheeks pinched pink as she eagerly awaited his sermon. She felt he looked at her more often than at the other girls, and blushed quietly when she thought he was secretly addressing her. Even Patrick noticed his daughter's newly awakened interest in church life.

"Now don't be carryin' on about that priest," he yelled after her many a morning as she happily skipped down the lane.

"Did you hear that Father O'Reilly was an orphan, and forced to take the cloth?" she nonchalantly mentioned to her mother as she helped her take out the special linen.

"No, I heard he got the calling before he got his leaving certificate. 'Tis a grand thing. Now pass me the white napkins and don't worry your mind about it."

"If only he could marry and such."

"Imelda! You know fine well he chose not 'to marry and such'! Get me the glasses and put yer mind to better use."

"'Tis not only me, Ma. I've even seen Mother Superior flirt with him."

"Holy Mother, he'll be here any minute. Hurry and get Kathy ready. Be sure to give her face a quick wipe."

Patrick came home each day at five-thirty sharp. He would change out of his uniform before doing his routine inspection. He was a hard taskmaster with little patience for incomplete assignments.

Hidden from him was a dizzying burst of underground activity. The minute he left the house, pigs were sneaked out of bedrooms, kittens, chicks, lambs, and an assortment of baby animals quickly returned to their pens. All this was done under the watchful eye of Kathleen, who let the children occasionally sneak in their adopted pets.

There was one time when Patrick was concerned about one of the piglets in a large litter. He thought it was not going to survive. Imelda begged him to give it to her. She kept it in a basket in her closet, feeding it every few hours for a couple of weeks. She named the piglet Turnip, and he soon became Imelda's second shadow along with Kathy, following her everywhere. When Turnip had outgrown the basket, she slept on a blanket, refusing to stay in the pig pen. She even fought the family dogs for scraps from the kitchen table.

The children were ready for bed by eight. On special occasions they joined Patrick and Kathleen in front of the fireplace. Here they told stories, read aloud, played silly games and teased each other mercilessly. Impromptu sing-a-longs signalled the evening was coming to an end, the younger ones clamouring for "just one more song" to delay bedtime. They knelt by their beds to say their prayers before being tucked in for the night.

Every night Patrick walked past the bedrooms after all the children had gone to bed. He would stick his head in the door to say, "Good night and God bless."

Turnip and the assortment of kittens hidden in the closet instinctively kept very still until the house was quiet and it was safe to move. Peace descended on the house at nightfall. Sometimes Patrick and Kathleen would go hand in hand for a short 'dander'; or walk to the pub for 'a wee join' with their friends.

Kathleen's health seemed to become more precarious as the children grew older. There were weeks when she was too weak to get out of bed, and then she would be fine for a few months before becoming bedridden again. Imelda was now approaching her teens, and took over many of the chores that were too strenuous for Kathleen. Nuns from the parish took over the laundry and cleaning, and a stream of friends made sure the family was supplied with freshly-baked bread and pies for supper.

Kathleen's sisters, Sienna and Beatrice, were over often during these times, doing all the special little things that

Kathleen would have loved to do for her family. They would make delicious lemon rolls, jam tarts and gooseberry jam; but their most important task was to keep their sister's spirit up.

Everything seemed to be going along smoothly until one morning when a neighbour came looking for Kathleen. Getting no answer from the doorway, she walked around the back of the house to find Kathleen lying in a heap next to a basket of wet clothes.

Imelda had just been setting up her easel for her art class when Mother Bernadine tiptoed in and whispered in Mother Joseph Michael's ear. Their faces were somber. Then Mother Bernadine came over to Imelda and said quietly, "Imelda, will you come with me?"

"Come with you where? Is something wrong?" Imelda asked, startled.

"We have t'go home. I already have Kathy outside, and Father O'Brian has taken the boys home."

"Has something bad happened?" Imelda asked anxiously.

Outside, little Kathy was skipping around, singing happily, oblivious to the tension around her.

"Please tell me nothing has happened to me Ma! Just tell me that, please?" Imelda pleaded.

Tears were rolling down Mother Bernadine's face. "Let us pray she is all right. I know God will hear us." They knelt together by the side of the road, next to the stirring fern, for a moment of intense prayer. Imelda got off her knees with a smile on her face.

"She is going t'be all right; I just told Jesus if he harms me Ma, I will never go to church again. He would never let that happen."

When they neared the farm they could see bicycles, buggies and horses outside. Imelda left Mother Bernadine's tight grip and went running wildly into the house. Everyone she had ever known was there. She felt a dark foreboding.

Kathleen was lying on the bed, her head raised on pillows, her long hair framing her pale face. She had her eyes closed. Sienna and Beatrice were slumped at her feet, their faces red and swollen. Patrick was standing back with closed eyes as Father O'Reilly held on to him.

Imelda ran to her mother's side and buried her face in her neck. "I'm home Ma, yer goin t'be all right now," she murmured.

She felt her mother's hand quiver slightly, tenderly touching the back of her head, light as an angel's wing.

"My Mel, my darling child," she whispered, "I'm so sorry!"

"Oh Ma! Don't say that!" Imelda cried.

"Darling Mel, take care of the wee one fer me."

4

Calcutta

As Amarendra's reputation grew, and his stature as a lawyer rose, he and Pankajini moved to 84 Harish Mukherjee Road. The house was located in Bhowanipur, a well-heeled district a few miles south of Calcutta's most celebrated landmark, the Victoria Memorial.

Amarendra had selected an Italian architect to design his home. He wanted the house to reflect the grandeur of the stately homes he had visited on a trip to Tuscany. The floors were of imported Italian marble, the chandeliers of Belgian crystal, and the hallways adorned with statues of Venus, the seductress Beatrice, serene angels, laughing cherubs, swans and birds in flight.

As the house grew, so did the Bose family. Pankajini had her first son, Himanshu, when she was eighteen. He was a quiet and serious boy, much like his father. Two years later she had a daughter, Menu. Then came Subranshu, nicknamed Shu, and thirteen months later his brother Sauranshu, called Saury. Finally, there was a beautiful daughter named Swaha. She was the baby, so was appropriately called Chotto, the little one.

The big break in Amarendra's career came when Nripendra Narayan, the Maharaja of Cooch Behar, asked him to represent his state in reclaiming land that the British had requisitioned from his kingdom. It was a landmark case: an Indian king fighting the British Government to get back land it had taken over by force. The presiding judge was British, and to the astonishment of both the British and Indian judicial community, he ruled in favour of the Maharaja. The victory placed Amarendra Bose firmly in the annals of Indian history. The Maharaja, overwhelmed with gratitude, was willing to generously reward him. Amarendra demurred, but recalled the Maharaja telling him about a black panther he had accidentally shot, only to discover she had two little cubs. Amarendra had been deeply touched by that story and when he found out they were alive, he asked for them instead of payment.

The next day, the cubs arrived in a velvet-lined box. Along with the cubs was a sateen pouch with an attached note from Maharani Sunita Devi. She wanted to show her appreciation with a gift for Amarendra's wife. Inside the pouch was a diamond star strung on a necklace of solitaire diamonds.

This was Pankajini's first big gift. It was brilliant and beautiful but too ostentatious for a Bhodro lady, so she would take it out, put in on and look longingly at herself in the mirror, then return it to the vault.

Next to the beautiful marble fountain, Amarendra built an outhouse containing two sturdy cages. It was disguised with bougainvillea, but still it was an eyesore. Amarendra could not be persuaded to move the cubs to the back of the house because the cows and calf had their shed there. He promised to move them to a large enclosure he would build for them at the Calcutta Zoo.

As his stature in the community grew, Amarendra indulged his passion and accumulated a large menagerie of tropical birds. There was the Umbrella Cockatoo named Shona, his absolute favourite, a gift from his mother; an African Grey parrot named Smoky who could talk up a storm; a second Rose-breasted Cockatoo, named Rosie; a mischievous Scarlet Macaw called Rani and a couple of large Indian ring-necked talking parrots. When his car would drive through the gate, Shona would start yelling, "Ashoo! Ashoo! Boro sahib is here." She would not quieten until Amarendra took her off her perch and into his bedroom where she watched him change. She actually answered the questions he would ask her.

"Shona, were you a good bird today?"

"Shona good bird. Ashoo, get my slippers."

Amarendra's birds were his passion. His daily ritual was to come home, change and then relax on the open porch with the birds. Ashu would lay out his tea, a plate of fruit and a snack. A masseur would give his feet a massage, while each bird took its turn to perch on his arm. Shona presided, sitting on his shoulder. He could be heard laughing with great pleasure whenever the birds picked up a new word or phrase.

After the tea and massage, the panthers Kālu and Bhālu were let out of their cages to romp with him in the garden. They were like tame cats, purring loudly as they rubbed up against his legs. All the while there would be a constant chatter of birds repeating what they had been taught.

"Good morning, Amar!"

"Have a nice day."

"Ashu, bring the tea."

The children, however, had taught them a different vocabulary.

"Shu is a foo-ool!"

"Chotto is a *motto* (fattie)!"

"Bloody bird won't shut up!" and the notorious "Chee! Chee!"

It was unusual the way all the birds would repeat "Chee! Chee!" whenever Pankajini appeared. She was convinced it was Ashu who encouraged them. She was petrified of the panthers, and the birds she found disgusting. Their constant squawking and defecating made her ill. She even believed Ashu stole the best fruit from the kitchen for the birds, and was endlessly trying to spy on what he kept aside for them.

"The birds eat better than his own children," she complained to her sister once. "I've never seen his lordship ask to examine my food, but God forbid the birds gets a bad nut. And that worm, Ashu? I know who does the eating."

Amarendra and Pankajini maintained a united facade at all the family gatherings. They went on vacations together, and treated each other with respect. But at home, they led separate lives. The children knew they could never show disrespect to either parent, even in front of Ashu. Ashu had no fear of anyone. The only physical discipline the boys had ever received was from him.

The head of the household staff was the baboochi, the cook; the most temperamental of employees. He decided the menu for the day with Pankajini, who was respectfully called Boroma. He would suggest the fresh fish of the day, and keep her informed about the vegetables and fruit that would arrive daily from the farm. The baboochi was assisted by a helper, a young woman. Her work usually entailed grinding all the fresh spices, cleaning the fish or chicken, and cutting the vegetables. The baboochi did all the cooking, leaving the rest of the kitchen work to the other employees, who scoured the pots with ashes and helped Ashu with the feeding of the birds and the panthers.

Pankajini had her own personal maid, who had the thankless task of being harassed by her employer all day long. She was constantly berated for not putting out the correct blouse or the proper pair of shoes for the day. Pankajini would follow her around criticizing everything she did, from making the bed to arranging the hairpins in a straight line.

The other helpers were not an integral part of the household. There was the milkman who took care of the two cows and one calf. There were two drivers, and the gardener. The garden, the courtyard, the animals and the exterior of the mansion were all Amarendra's domain. There was a butler and a bearer. The bearer was in charge of Shu and Saury, who were growing up to be quite a handful.

The two boys were inseparable. They went to school together, played football and cricket together, and had a British lady come over twice a week to teach them to speak English the 'proper' way. All the children learnt classical Bengali music on Saturday mornings, and on Sunday afternoons the family would take a boat ride down the Hooghly and spend the evening at the farmhouse. It was on the banks of the river, so they could swim and row a small dilapidated boat that was kept there for them. Occasionally they would be joined by Dhiren Mitra, Pankajini's brother, his wife, and his two daughters Lotika and Bashi. Lotika, or Monu, was everyone's favourite cousin.

Shu and Saury were generally viewed as the 'evil twins' by the household. They were constantly in the planning stages of pranks they were going to execute on some hapless victim. Poor Ashu was often the prey. On one occasion they hid on top of a cupboard waiting to ambush him. As Ashu walked by they pounced on him, breaking the antique mirror he was carrying into a thousand pieces. Enraged, Ashu dragged the two by their ears into their father's office.

Amarendra gave his customary speech, then asked them what punishment befitted the crime. The boys hated that, because they had to give themselves extreme penalties to prove their judicial neutrality. A couple of weeks later, they were back in the office. This time they had been trying to teach Ashu how to box when Shu accidentally hit him squarely in the face. After the blood was cleaned, and the nose permanently re-shaped, they faced a very angry Amarendra.

"It's your fault! We repeated 'protect your face' a million times. Such a sissy, I barely touched him!" Shu protested.

"Am I Goddess Durga, with eight hands? How can I protect my face and chest and stomach?"

"You hit *Ashu*… in the *face*… with your *fist*?" Amarendra repeated slowly, emphasizing every third word, his lips curled in disgust.

"Of course not!" Shu replied, horrified. "I just jabbed him, I thought the boxing gloves would soften the blow. I told him over and over again to protect his face. Saury will verify that."

Saury nodded vigorously.

"Boxing gloves? Where did they come from?"

There was an awkward silence as both the boys looked at Ashu.

"Okay! Okay! I made a mistake," he blurted out.

"Get rid of the gloves, take Ashu to the doctor, and when you return, finish his chores. I will inspect the panther cage myself. The two of you are a grave disappointment to me."

Neither boy ever forgot the look of disapproval in his eyes.

But it was only a week later when there was yet another incident. This time, it involved the dhobi's daughter. Shu and Saury had noticed the pretty girl delivering clothes to the house. They made their plans carefully, breathlessly waiting under Boroma's bed till the tiny jingle of her anklets came close to the bed where she was laying out the clothes. When she was close enough, they grabbed her ankles with growling howls.

"Bachao, bachao! Help me!" she screamed. Clothes flew all over the floor as she tried to whip them with a towel, jumping up and down to get her ankles free of their grabbing hands. Shu and Saury were in hysterics under the bed until they heard their mother came in. Then there was silence.

"Aushobo shameful boys, giving our family a bad name. Chee-chee! What will the neighbours say? Ruining our reputation! I will talk to your father. No cricket this month. Ashu, remember, no cricket for the boys. You're the one teaching them all this aushobo behaviour!"

"Yes, yes, always my fault," Ashu mumbled angrily.

The problem with this sort of delegated reprimand was that it was never implemented. Shu and Saury were seldom personally blamed – it was always Ashu, or the other person in charge. A few days later, Boroma saw the boys getting ready to play cricket.

"Ashu? Didn't I say no cricket?" she demanded angrily.

"Today is boro cricket match with Bow Bazaar fellows. Cannot miss," Ashu replied.

"Boro match cannot miss! Ki Engleesh!" Boroma imitated Ashu with disgust.

Shu and Saury played cricket in the park across from their house. The teams were loosely made of the boys from Harish Mukherjee Road, and from the street bordering the other side of the park, Garden Reach. A continual problem was getting twelve players for each team. The regulars of the Harish Mukherjee Road team were Shu, Saury, Robin Mitra, Bappa Mallik, Dilip Lahiri, Mithun Biswas and Nikhil Chowdury. The rest they got by enlisting the gardener's sons, the milkman's sons and Ashu. Ashu was crucial to the scheme. Being part of the team, he would never follow up on the punishments of 'no cricket'. He was either a hero or villain of the match. If he caught a ball, which was seldom, he was carried off on their shoulders, and if he missed a catch, he was abused mercilessly.

"What the hell is the matter with you? The bloody ball went right through your hands!" Saury shouted.

"Bloody ball bloody hard!" Ashu protested.

"You have a bloody sieve for hands!" Shu added.

"Don't mind them," Robin Mitra consoled, patting him on his back. "You did a great job! Just don't let Boro-sahib hear you curse like that."

Surprisingly, Ashu was the most contentious of players. He could never graciously accept being bowled out.

"No Owzet! Ball not hit wicket."

"Ashu, if Biswas calls you out, you're out," Nikhil tried to reason with him. "Biswas is on our team."

"We won't let you play with us," Shu warned.

"Does the old fool not understand the fundamentals of the game?" Abijit Bose from the Garden Reach team exclaimed.

"Me not old fool! You fool, bastard!" Ashu would scream obscenities he had picked up from the boys. The argument had to be settled by the cooler heads of the 'arbitration committee.'

Shu and Saury always critiqued each other's play. Saury even critiqued himself after every shot.

"Took my eye off the ball."

"That ball skid just as I was about to hit it."

"Didn't bend my knees enough."

"That bloody ball was a googly if I ever saw one…"

After every match the two brothers would walk off the field, arms around each other, and thrash out every run scored and every ball bowled. They would analyze and criticize every mistake the other had made. The arguments would never get out of hand, just a little heated. One thing they both agreed on was that it was impossible to teach Ashu the finesse of good sportsmanship.

Their older brother Himanshu was cut from a different cloth. During one of their many arguments they decided to let him be the judge. His decision, they agreed, was final. Without a second thought, Himanshu ordered both of his brothers to be locked in separate bathrooms for two hours. That was the end of his judicial career with his brothers.

As they grew older, they became increasingly aware of the almost formal relationship their parents had developed. Saury, the more sensitive of the two, was his mother's favourite, often helping her write Bengali poems and articles in a small monthly newsletter she helped publish. He was acutely aware of the emotional distance their father kept from his wife. When their grandmother Piyali visited, Amarendra would spend the evening with her down in his library or garden. Boroma only joined them at meals.

"Baba just isn't personally invested in us," Saury grumbled.

"Something as personal as punishment he leaves to that psychotic Ashu. It's bloody bullshit. Wouldn't it be better if he got mad and shouted, like Ma?"

"I can't even visualize that," Shu agreed somberly. "He doesn't like confrontation; he has enough of that at work. He wants us to think about what we are doing, you know – appeal to our higher senses."

"You always stand up for him; he wants to distance himself from us. Have you ever heard him raise his voice?"

"Of course I've heard him raise his voice. Haven't you heard him shout when the panther's cages are not clean? He won't yell or scream at us, that's not his style. He gets upset with us over some of our antics. How involved do you want him to be? He always talks about our future, our goals…"

"That's not what I mean. I can't explain it, but I can't get him to show any real passion. You know how you punch me, when you're mad? *That* kind of emotion. I've never heard him raise his voice at Ma either. Can't you feel the distance?" Saury's eyes filled with tears.

"Why are you getting so upset? So Father doesn't get provoked over minor matters. I have seen him very passionate about freedom for the country and rights for Indians. I've been told he is very passionate in court. You want to see emotion, tell him one of the birds is dead! He's different, he's a thinker; you know that, and he expects great things from us."

"That's too easy. Poor Ma has such a lonely life," Saury mused.

"Lonely? She is never alone! If she is not harassing the servants, she's on the phone with her sister or Dhola kaka. She is not interested in anything Baba does. I actually feel sorry for

Baba; if anyone is alone, it's him. All Ma does is babble about mundane household events."

"She's a very intelligent woman; she could teach you a thing or two about Tagore. Baba is always up in his ivory tower. Ashu is the only person who can be honest with him, the only one. You're scared shitless when he calls you to his office."

"Nonsense. I can discuss anything with him," Shu protested.

"Really. Then why don't you tell him you smoke?"

"Let's change the subject, Mr. Big Ears is here," Shu interrupted, when Ashu walked in with glasses of lemonade.

"Beeg eyars!" he shook his head from side to side as they all burst out laughing.

Religion did not play an important part in Amarendra's daily life, so it was left to Pankajini to follow the traditional religious celebrations of Durga, Sarasvati and Kali Puja.

Durga Puja is the most auspicious festival in West Bengal. It is a time of great joy and celebration. The festivities include shopping for new outfits, buying gifts for friends and family and visiting their homes laden with sweets and food. Shu and Saury's favourite part was when the clay image of the goddess Durga was taken out of the home to be submerged in the river. They would follow a rag-tag band with their friends and neighbours dancing like drunken sailors as they made their way down to the Hooghly.

In the early years Amarendra and his family used to travel to their ancestral home in Midnapur for Durga Puja, but as the children grew into their teens the family celebrated the festivities at home.

The other important festival was Kali Puja. The Goddess

Kali is the antithesis of the beautiful Goddess Durga. She is dark, bloodthirsty and fierce.

During Kali Puja, families would traditionally appease the goddess Kali's demands for blood by sacrificing goats at her temples. The Bose family distanced themselves from any animal sacrifice. However, they were involved in feeding hundreds of poor families who would arrive for the feast. Special cooks and servers had to be hired for this occasion, and they would serve the meals from big steel buckets. All the members of the family would assist serving their guests, making sure when they left they had gorged enough to give the meal a two-belch validation.

5

County Cork

The church where Kathleen Tierney Connor had worshipped all her life overflowed with friends and family. Aunts and uncles with cousins and grandchildren arrived from unknown places to mourn with the family. The Connor children were bewildered, their eyes dull with shock. Their mother's sudden collapse and death had plunged them into deep despair. Kathleen, in her quiet way, had been the glue that had held them together. The boys were not expected to cry, and Patrick stood, disoriented and hollow-eyed, in the front row of the church. His back was straight, his head held high, as he held on to the two older boys, Gerald and Cyril. The six children, their heads bowed, tried not to show the fear that engulfed them. Imelda, who had just turned twelve, held on to little Kathy's trembling hand.

She was angry with God, angry at the people intruding on her grief, and angry most of all with her mother for leaving. When the choir began to sing 'Ave Maria', Kathleen's favourite hymn, Imelda felt her heart would burst. She leapt to her feet, her hands over her ears, and ran. She ran past the overflowing pews and the stunned faces, past the familiar oak church doors with their carved panels, not stopping until she collapsed in the field behind the farm. Alone, she sobbed uncontrollably. She was crying – not for Kathy, her father or her brothers – for herself now.

Patrick found her in the field, face down under the sprawling maple tree. He had seen his wife sitting under that tree so often that he instinctively scanned the field for her. Heavy-hearted, he sat down beside Imelda and tenderly put his arms around her. "Ma's in a better place; God took her 'cause He needs her."

"Tis a mean, mean God who took Mother. What are we goin t'do? What are you goin' t'do? Ma just died and left us and now we have nothing."

"What d'you mean, nothing? We have each other! She will always be with us, no one can take that away."

Imelda looked up and believed him. Then he fumbled inside his shirt and pulled out an envelope, took Imelda's hand and gently placed it in her palm, firmly folding her fingers over it.

"Tis yours, keep it safe for us all."

Imelda opened the envelope and found inside the heart-shaped locket Patrick had given to Kathleen when he left for the Military Academy. On the front were two entwined roses, and on the back the inscription 'PC loves KT'.

"Why did yeh take it off Ma's neck?" Imelda gasped. "'Tis hers!"

"I wanted to leave it on her, but Mother Bernadine insisted yer Ma would want you to have it. I had no mind to take it."

He was sobbing so hard that his whole body was shaking. When all the tears were spent they sat there, drained, quietly gazing into space. They knew they would need all their strength to face the reality of what had happened.

The farm was never the same. Their lives had been broken into a million little pieces, and yet, they had to continue as though nothing had changed. Each family member concentrated on his or her assigned task. They seldom smiled, resolute on completing the job on hand, consciously avoiding eye contact.

Imelda watched over the family with fierce determination. Even though she was the fifth child and not yet in her teens, she took over running the household as though that was her destiny. Her aunts, Beatrice and Sienna, tried to help with Kathy, but she would have none of it. She would howl at the top of her lungs, throwing the most terrifying tantrums whenever they suggested Kathy could spend a few days with them.

Being the youngest and most vulnerable, Kathy was afraid to let Imelda her out of her sight. She would wait outside the bathroom door when Imelda washed her hands. She insisted on sleeping in the same bed even though Imelda had pulled their two cots together. The boys also kept a close watch over their younger sisters.

Sometimes when the responsibility overwhelmed her, the one place Imelda could find solace was inside her mother's closet. She would sit on the floor with her knees against her chest and breathe in the scent of a frock or sweater. At times she fell asleep, for here she felt a calmness descend over her. One night Kathy was searching for Imelda and saw her coming out of the closet.

"Are you kissing Shaun in there?" she asked, full of curiosity.

"Don't be an idiot," Imelda said roughly. "Why aren't you in bed?"

"I can't get t'sleep without you," Kathy whined. Imelda took her back to bed. As they lay there, Imelda said very carefully, "I go in the closet t'be close to Ma; you must let me do that for a wee while."

"Is Ma in the closet?" Kathy asked, bolting straight up.

"No, Kathleen. Ma's in Heaven. You know that she's up among the stars watching everything we do. She's happy when we're happy and sad when we're sad."

"I wouldn't want ter make her sad," Kathy said tearfully.

"I know, so when you feel sad, just act like she is here and talk to her. Tell her you miss her, and love her. Tell her whatever you want. That will take the sadness away."

"Nothing will take my sadness away."

"Hush with that. You know yerself 'tis not true. How many times have I told you that Ma did not leave us? God took her away. Ma would never leave us. Now close yer eyes and mind what you think."

She gave her little sister a tight hug and a few pats to put her back to sleep.

The Connor household was run by a series of women who took turns making meals, looking after the children, and keeping the house in order. Among them was a young women in her twenties named Nancy Evans. She had recently arrived from England to visit her family and had offered to help out when she heard the story of the six children and the poor widower. Since she was an outsider, rumours began to circulate that Patrick had previously met her on one of his frequent trips to England.

Nancy took over the cooking and cleaning. She made sure the children were fed and their clothes washed. She knew

Patrick wanted the house spotless and organized. Imelda, at first glad to have help, soon had a change of heart. She saw Nancy as a threat, a rival for her father's affection. She wanted to keep her mother's memory alive, and the very thought that her father could shift his attention to another woman filled her with rage. She began questioning aloud how the two of them met, how Nancy had very conveniently showed up in Kilworth just around the time her mother died.

She had noticed a distinct change in her father's behaviour. He would leave for days without telling them where he was going. He would sneak out at night after they were all in bed and return in the early hours just as they were waking up. There were sometimes secret meetings in the house late at night. A few times Imelda woke up to hear strange whispering in the kitchen. With her creative imagination she blamed all this on Nancy and complained constantly to her aunts.

"A girl young enough to be his daughter!" Beatrice huffed, disgusted at the thought.

"Me poor sister, bless her soul. She'd be turnin' in her grave," Sienna sighed.

"But where does he go?" Imelda asked anxiously. "I know Nancy stays in the house to mind us."

"Imelda, don't you be minding his goings-on, 'tis a dangerous world we live in," Beatrice warned.

But that did not stop Imelda wondering about her father's strange behaviour. She discreetly set up barriers between Nancy and the family. When Nancy would suggest a meal she would pointedly differ.

"On Wednesdays Mother would like us t'have lamb stew."

"But I've made the chicken," protested Nancy.

If Patrick so much as said a kind word to Nancy, Imelda would become red-faced and sullen. The chasm between them continued to deepen as Nancy tried desperately to be part of the family. She saw Imelda as the only real obstacle to Patrick's heart; he adored his daughter, and would never let anything come between them.

Imelda was also vigilant about protecting Kathy from any disciplinary action from Nancy. She put her foot down when Kathy was asked to help with the simplest of household chores.

"Tis not your business t'be telling Kathy what to do," she reprimanded Nancy.

"Well who's goin' ter tell her?" Nancy replied sharply.

"Why, me, of course! I would think you knew that."

"I have to answer t'yer Father, not you," Nancy insisted.

"We'll see about that," Imelda huffed, walking away.

Nancy started staying late, and joining the family for dinner. She worked from morning to evening trying to please everyone, and liked to eat with them once in a while. This infuriated Imelda.

"Why d'yeh want her to eat with us?" Imelda screamed at her father. "She's not one of us. She's not even from round here!"

"Imelda," Patrick reasoned, "yer Ma's not here anymore, we need help, that's all, Nancy would never take her place."

"I hope not, what with her bein' half your age! I think she has a liking for Frank," she added, mischief in her eyes.

Patrick was conflicted. He could see the tension building up between the children and Nancy, but he was lonely and enjoyed the conversations he had with her. Kathleen's death had left his heart empty, and Nancy was always eager to listen to his stories and cheer him up.

Nancy was from a family of thirteen siblings and patience came easily to her. Even though Patrick was two decades older, she genuinely enjoyed his storytelling and knowledge of Irish history, and he was flattered that a young woman would pay attention to him. The trouble was that poor Nancy could do no right in the eyes of the children: they were just not ready for a stepmother.

One morning at breakfast Imelda noticed that Nancy was wearing her mother's shoes. Shocked, she ran upstairs to check the closet; there was not one, but three pairs of shoes missing.

She ran downstairs, screaming at the top of her lungs.

"How dare you wear Ma's shoes? Take them off this minute, you piggin' bitch." She rushed to grab them off Nancy's feet.

Taken back by the ferocity of the attack, Nancy threw the shoes at Imelda as she scrambled out the door.

"You'll be sorry! Callin' me a bitch," she screamed back at her. "You're the Devil, y'are! After all I've done fer yuh! Oh, you'll be very sorry when yer father hears about this."

For the next week, there was a quiet simmering anger in Patrick's demeanour and Nancy was nowhere to be found. Beatrice and Sienna were there every day to make sure the house was functioning, and the parish sent over another woman to help. Rumour had it that Nancy had returned to England. Distraught, Patrick began drinking even more heavily; he would either be too drunk to talk, or not come home at all.

Two weeks after the shoe incident, Patrick disappeared for a few days, saying he had to report to the army headquarters in Aldershot. The children were helping clean up after supper one day when they heard a shuffling outside.

Imelda opened the door. There stood Patrick, all dressed up

in a suit. Kathleen rushed into his arms but Imelda held back. He seemed unusually nervous, and after a quick greeting he gathered the other children around, and told them he had a surprise for them. He went outside and returned with Nancy on his arm. She had her hair up and was formally dressed. Her eyes held a victorious glint as she looked down at Imelda.

"I've an important announcement to make," Patrick stammered. "Nancy and I have just returned from England where she has done me the honour of becoming me wife. Meet me new wife, Nancy Connor."

At that moment Imelda hated her father, and a little bit of that anger would stay buried in a corner of her heart for the rest of her life. She saw his marrying Nancy as a monumental betrayal of her trust. It dishonoured the memory of her mother, something she could never forgive.

"She will never take Ma's place as long as I live," she shouted and stalked out the door. Harnessing her horse, she rode to her Aunt Beatrice's farm. There she told a stunned Beatrice about her father and Nancy.

"Holy Mother of God! Me sister's not been gone a year and he's got himself another wife. May his soul rot in Hell." She crossed herself to ward off the curse.

"She'll be using all Ma's clothes and shoes," added Imelda, sobbing inconsolably.

"Over my dead body she will! Come on Mel, we'll get Sienna and get Kathleen's things out of there."

The three of them marched into the kitchen where Patrick was sitting.

"I'm a wee bit skuttered, but have you heard the news?" he asked meekly.

"Out of me way, yeh bastard," Beatrice said as she pushed past him. "I'm here ter take me sister's things. And heaven strike me dead if I ever step foot in this house again!"

"I'll explain," Patrick pleaded, "Listen to me, we're family…"

"Not any more, we aren't. Me sister, bless her soul, not gone a year, and you? Yeh rotten bastard, gone and got yerself another wife! Should be ashamed of yerself."

"Could yeh at least give me a chance to explain?" Patrick pleaded.

"Who married you? Not Father O'Brian. I'd chase him out of Kilworth meself if he did."

Beatrice and Sienna pushed past Patrick and his new wife, giving them dark stares as they went to recover their sister's belongings.

Much as Imelda hated living in the same house as Nancy and Patrick, her responsibilities on the farm could not be avoided. The animals needed tending, and she had four brothers and a sister who relied on her. A tense truce was established in the Connor household, where Nancy and Imelda did their best to avoid each other. Nancy had her hands full with a family of indignant children and a farm to run. She kept conversations with the children to a minimum, especially with Kathleen, who would rush to Imelda if asked to put so much as a teaspoon away.

Imelda, with the help of her aunts, did everything she could to make Nancy's life difficult. One way to get under her skin was to keep her mother's presence alive. Every tradition her mother loved was continued with much enthusiasm and support from all the children.

One of their favourites was the annual ritual of making fresh Bridget crosses. These crosses were made from wild rushes growing by the streams, threaded through with brambles and wildflowers and tied together to form a cross. The cross symbolized the powerful mythological figure Bridget who roamed freely among the streams and woodlands and was believed to come to the aid of farmers. No Irish farmhouse was without one. The crosses, they decided, were to protect them from Nancy.

The children continued to treat their stepmother with contempt – even though she was pregnant with their father's child – and Patrick was caught in the crossfire. The marriage and the child he had hoped would fix everything had only made matters worse. He stayed away from the constant confrontations, spending most evenings at Callahan's Bar. Although he defended his wife in public, at home he always stood up for the children, especially Imelda.

Imelda, ever protective of her younger sister, felt Kathy was vulnerable. She never left her alone in the house with Nancy, making sure there was always a cousin or brother around. Imelda's hostility towards Nancy grew as her teenage years advanced. She never allowed herself to respond to Nancy's occasional friendly gestures, and her aunts and cousins kept the pot simmering.

In school, studying Irish history, she was learning about the dreaded cursing stones of Feaghna. The Druids of Ireland had been known to win many battles, not by their warring skills, but by the powerful curses they put on their enemies. Imelda decided to have her own stone-cursing ceremony. She gathered up Kathleen and her younger cousin Paddy and led them to the back of the farm. They knelt next to the dogs' graves as Imelda sprinkled a little holy water on them.

"'Tis a powerful curse, so we have to pay close attention. Paddy, put on the hat and stand in the centre."

"Nah! 'Tis a girl's hat."

"'Tis a cursing hat. Now just do as I say. I'm the witch here, you don't want me t'be cursing you too, do yeh?"

"If yer the witch, *you* wear the hat. 'Tis a witch's hat!" He crossed his arms stubbornly.

"Give me the hat then, yeh idiot." Imelda grabbed the hat from him. "Let us begin the cursing. Shut your eyes, take slow breaths, and listen to every word I say: I have the cursing stones of Feaghna here."

She showed them a few small gray pebbles, the size of acorns. As they looked at the stones with fearful eyes, Imelda slowly walked around them, her arms spread like an eagle ready to fly.

"Now Kathy, spit on the stones. Paddy, you too, just a wee spit."

Imelda spat on them as well.

"Now walk round me with yer hands in the air and repeat, 'May the cat eat you, and may the devil eat the cat.'"

"Are we cursing the cats too?" an alarmed Kathleen asked.

"Hush, Kathy. You're breaking the spell. 'Tis the witch's cat, yeh idiot!"

Imelda knelt in the centre, crushing the small stones with a pestle and mortar as the other two went around her in a circle chanting, "May the cat eat you, and may the devil eat the cat. May the cat eat you, and may the devil eat the cat."

"Now we must bury the stones under a leprechaun's bed." They looked under all the bushes until Paddy found a mound of leaves that looked slept-on.

"I found the bed!" Paddy shouted.

"Shush! You want ter wake him up?" Imelda carefully put the crushed stones under the mound.

"Not a word about the curse. 'Tis our secret," she told them as they walked back to the barn.

"What curse did we put on her?" Kathy asked nervously.

"The stones put the curse. Now shut yer beak, or all our work will be for nothin.'"

They studied Nancy's every move for the next few days. If she said she had a headache, they would exchange knowing glances. If she sneezed, they knew it was working. Along with the curse, Imelda used her charm on her father to create as much tension as possible between Nancy and him. She relished their fights. She would leave the room when the arguments grew heated, and listen with her ear against the wall with a look of serene satisfaction.

Patrick adored his daughter, despite the fights and tension she created with Nancy. He loved the gutsy way she always stood up for her brothers when he reprimanded them. He knew she was contemptuous of his new wife but he could no sooner tame a wild colt than control Imelda. Her wild red curls matched her fiery personality, and she would explode if Nancy so much as scowled at Kathy. Her poor stepmother was terrified of her. She could rally the Connor clan into a feisty group at a moment's notice and reward them with fierce loyalty and a good word in her father's ear. One evening, she came home to find Kathleen crying.

"What's the matter?" she asked.

"Nancy says I can't have pudding at supper!"

"Oh she does, does she? I'll see about that." Imelda stomped downstairs.

"Did yuh tell Kathleen she couldn't have pudding?" she demanded.

Expecting the tirade, Nancy replied in a silken voice, "I asked her to set the table for supper, and she refused. Yer father said I can ask for help."

"He meant you can ask me," Imelda replied.

"Well, *you* were out riding; Kathy's quite old enough to help. She'd be helping yer ma, now wouldn't she?"

"But yer not our mother! Don't y'dare compare yerself to her. You aren't even related to us, yer just an old biddy here to do the housework – the maid! So don't yuh be telling me sister to do anything."

"Don't you be raisin' yer voice at me, young lady! I'm yer father's wife whether you like it or not!"

"You wicked ol' witch, trying to take our Ma's place! Couldn't find a man in England, could ya? So you sneak in here and flirt with a man old enough t'be yer father," Imelda spat, her anger bursting out of her.

"I don't have to listen to this! You … yer pure evil."

"Call me evil, you ugly piece of shite? Have you looked in the mirror? Have you seen yerself? Couldn't find you in hell with a lantern! Just do yer maid's job."

"Call me the maid, ya big glipe!"

"Yes, maid, you pug-faced bitch."

"You big idiot maid!" Kathy yelled, eager to join in.

Shocked, Nancy swirled around and slapped Kathy across

the face. As she stood there stunned, Imelda grabbed a chair and hurled it at her stepmother.

"You piggin' bitch! Touch me sister again and I'll kill yeh!"

Nancy ducked. The chair narrowly missed her and landed on Kathy, knocking her out cold.

"Holy Mother of God! Look what you made me do," a distraught Imelda screamed as she ran to her sister. Kathleen would need ten stitches across the back of her head.

Nancy, who by now had a son named George, realized that the only way her marriage to Patrick would survive was if Imelda were of the house. Beatrice and Sienna were worried that something terrible could happen, not only to Patrick, during one of his drunken incoherent outbursts, but to the children.

In the south of Ireland, the IRA was secretly recruiting young men for 'the cause' that was being enthusiastically embraced by the local population, causing unspoken concern. Army personnel like Patrick were at risk. Even though they supported an independent Ireland, they had invested too many years in the service of the British government to give up their livelihood for a cause they supported, but did not necessarily want to die for. The older generation understood this, but the new recruits had little patience with what they thought was treasonable behaviour.

The boys were caught up in the fervour of revolutionary rhetoric. They joined marches and rallies, shouting anti-British slogans, and were surprised that Patrick never tried to stop them. Instead, he encouraged them to join the more radical cells, keeping a close eye on their activity.

Patrick showed a bravado that baffled his friends. Never afraid of the bullies who demanded he resign, he felt he was as Irish as the best of them. And more than that, he had a deep abiding faith that the Irish would never kill their own.

With an uncertain future and a tension-filled home environment, Beatrice and Sienna started making discreet enquiries about sending Imelda away to a Catholic boarding school in England. They contacted a cousin, Edna O'Brian, who had married and moved to London a decade earlier. Edna was delighted. She had two daughters of her own, and thought it would be wonderful for them to get to know their Irish cousins. When all the arrangements were completed, it was time to break the news to Imelda.

To everyone's surprise, Imelda agreed immediately. She was miserable at home, anxious and tense. She had dreamt of going away with her sister to a place where they could find happiness again. She agreed on one condition: that Kathleen would go with her.

"But yer too young to look after yer sister," her father reasoned with her.

"You know yourself Kathleen wouldn't stay here without me," she pointed out. "'Tis a miserable life fer us."

"But how will I live without me two angels?"

Imelda looked at her father and saw a broken old man. She put her arms around him as tears spilled down her cheeks.

"I want you t'be happy, Mel. I want us all to be happy again," he wept as he hugged her.

"I know, Da. We all want that, but..."

Patrick had no choice but to let the girls go. He was heartbroken. Imelda was his very soul, and he saw in her that fiery Irish spirit he so admired. He, too, once had that fire, but now he struggled with demons he could no longer control. Then there was his little Kathy, gentle and sweet, soft-spoken and loving. He would catch sight of the twinkle in her eyes, the shy smile and deep dimples, and he would see his wife.

Arrangements were made for the girls to move to London. From there they would be transferred to a Catholic boarding school near Rugby.

Beatrice and Sienna spent weeks sewing outfits for the girls. The nuns at the parish helped by having modern patterns shipped from English magazines. They wanted Imelda and Kathleen to outshine their British counterparts. Their 'mammy' would have be so proud of them, they whispered quietly to each other. Along with the many outfits there was plenty of advice.

"Yer Irish; never forget that."

"Only go to places that have Irish in 'em."

"Careful of those Brits, they're sneaky little buggers."

"No emotions at all!"

"Cold as a slab of cod!"

"Cold-hearted bastards. Have yer wits about when they're around."

"'Tis ice-water runnin' through their veins."

"Stay far away from them limies."

Imelda rode Toby over to her Aunt Sienna's house. Her cousin Laura was going to look after him for her. Realizing that it would be the last time she would be seeing her beloved horse, she bent over and wrapped her arms around his neck. She couldn't remember a time when Toby wasn't by her side when she needed him. Her chest was so tight she could barely breathe.

"I think me heart's burstin'," she gasped as she steered him towards the cemetery.

Toby carefully made his way to the grave. He had taken her there many times. As she hung on to his neck she began to feel her throat ease and soon she could breathe again. She watched her tears trickle and roll along his neck hair in tiny rivulets, each tear choosing its own path. Finally, exhausted, she slid off the horse and lay face down on the grass by the grave.

"You're right, Ma, you always said I was yer drama queen."

For a long while she lay there, telling her mother all about her fears, and how scared she really was. She had been putting on a brave face not only for Kathy, but also for Beatrice and Sienna. She left with a bitter-sweet prayer. "Please, Ma, stay close to me and Kathy, for 'tis too much for our hearts to bear alone." Then carefully she plucked a few strands of grass from around the grave and put them in the locket she had never taken off, and quietly rode to Aunt Sienna's farm.

Laura, her cousin, was waiting for her. Imelda handed the reins over.

"You better take care of me horse: I'll be watching you, ya little skitter," she said, trying sound cheerful.

"He's the best horse in County Cork, I will love him forever. Thank you, smelly Melly," Laura giggled.

"He's the best horse in the world. Don't forget the turnips and the parsnips. He loves his turnips in the morning." Imelda gave Toby one last hug then turned and left without looking back.

It was Beatrice and Sienna who put them on the boat on a cold and rainy morning. Their suitcases were bulging. They had matching tan coats and white knit caps and gloves. Both the girls were somber as they held tight to their aunts' hands. "Remember nothing can harm you. Yer Ma and guardian angels are watching over you. Never forget that."

"You always, always have a home with us," Beatrice went on, wrought with emotion.

"Divide the money and keep it separate," Sienna added, drying her eyes.

"Jesus and Mother Mary, keep an eye on me children!" Beatrice burst into uncontrollable sobs. She had always been her sister's keeper, and Imelda and Kathleen were like her own.

"I'll take good care of Toby," Sienna added softly. "Be safe, my darlings. God speed and may the blessings of Saint Patrick go with you."

The boat set sail under dismal weather conditions. The biting air swirled and blew rain into every nook and corner. Clinging to each other, the sisters waved till their arms hurt, watching the Irish coast slowly recede into the ghostly mist.

"Are we far from Ireland now?" Kathy asked in a tiny voice.

"Yes, too far to swim back. If you squint real hard you can still see a wee bit over there."

"When d'you think we'll be back?" Kathy asked bleakly as she looked at Imelda with tear-rimmed eyes.

"Remember what Mother Bernadine told us? Worst comes to worst, we can come right back and become nuns."

"But she also said, 'Heaven help us if you do!'"

Imelda smiled, giving her head a quick shake to hide the tears building up in her eyes.

"Give me hand a hard squeeze. We're together on a new journey. Take a deep breath and feel Ma with us: she'll make us brave and strong and free."

6

Calcutta

The children of the Bose household were growing up fast. Himanshu Bose was in his final year at Presidency College and planned to follow his father's footsteps by studying law. Arrangements were being made for him to take the bar at Lincoln's Inn College, London.

Before his departure there was a flurry of activity to find and marry him to a suitable girl. His family did not want their young and vulnerable son to be influenced by foreign women that he would meet while in London. Himanshu, recognizing this, did not put up much resistance to his arranged marriage to Maya Mitra.

Maya Mitra seemed to be perfect. She was part of the illustrious Bengali family of Raja Digambar Mitra. Her father, Manmatha Kumar Mitra, continued the family's political traditions as the sheriff of Calcutta and was an active member of the Indian National Congress. Maya was the youngest of eleven children, and lived in a large mansion in Jhamapukur.

Shu and Saury were enthralled with the phrase "our *bou* (wife) from Jhamapukur." The wedding had all the trappings of a princely affair and the two teenagers being married sat bewildered amid all the pomp and ceremony. Maya, known affectionately as Dhebu, sat with her sari over her face and cried throughout. She was fourteen years old and Himanshu was nineteen.

After the wedding, the bride arrived at the Bose's residence decked in a red and gold sari, the rubies on her necklace so big that Boroma actually gasped out loud. She brought with her sixteen boxes of clothes and household goods, and her own maid. The maid had looked after her since she was born and was like a surrogate mother.

Dhebu had large, brown swan-like eyes that looked straight at you when she spoke, even though Bengali brides were rumoured to be meek and shy. The one unexpected habit she had was that of chewing paan – a heart-shaped green leaf that held supari nuts and chunna, a mild drug. Dhebu always carried her paan container with her. It was refilled several times a day. She was a vegetarian and had special meals made for her by her maid. She wanted her meals to be cooked in a detached kitchen, in separate utensils, as she did not want eggs, fish or meat from the main kitchen to contaminate them.

All this had been clarified and agreed to before the marriage was finalized. Boroma had agreed readily, thinking Dhebu was young enough to be molded into an obedient daughter-in-law once she came to live in the Bose household. She was to stay with the family while Himanshu was abroad completing his legal studies. In the meantime, the family was going to educate her in English and prepare her to become a little Bengali Memsahib.

The trouble started the first month after Dhebu had settled in. Boroma took her a box filled with various expensive whitening creams and different lotions which she had carefully saved for the new bride. Dhebu listened quietly, saying nothing, but the next day when Boroma asked her why she was not wearing any of the make-up, she replied casually, "Oh, I threw it all away."

"You... threw it... away?" Boroma was barely able to get the words out.

"Yes. I'm allergic to it."

"You... threw away the beautiful boxes too?"

Boroma was speechless and had to lie down for the rest of the day. She would talk about those expensive creams and their beautiful boxes till her dying day.

Having lived with seven brothers, Dhebu knew how to handle the boys. She immediately won over both Shu and Saury who were fascinated with her strong opinions, so different from theirs. After three months of continual battles, Boroma was distraught. "Even her English teacher says she is stubborn as a mule," she said. Dhebu refused to speak in English. Every English tutor quit after a couple of weeks. She just sat with her arms crossed, chewing her paan, and refused to answer any questions.

"Why should I learn English? I'm Bengali. If you want to talk to me, speak Bengali," she would say. "Don't spout your *haw-haw* gibberish to me."

"My Bengali is as good as yours," Shu replied, a little defensive, "and my English is much better. One does not preclude the other. There's a big world out there, Boudi, where Bengali isn't spoken."

She became the rebel sister. Chotto and Menu were astonished to meet a girl who did not care about her looks. They watched from a safe distance the turmoil the new bride brought into the household. She did not care what other people thought. She seldom wore her heavy jewellery or fancy saris. With her two brother-in-laws, she was full of mischief and loved playing hide-and-seek with them. "Okay Boudi, catch us if you can!" they teased, as she chased them, tucking her sari between her legs.

Most egregious of all was her refusal to eat fish or chicken. "You cannot be a Bengali and not eat fish," Boroma stated categorically.

The family was constantly shaped by cliques and the forging and breaking of alliances. Himanshu was different. Serious, aloof, studious, and detached from the bickering and arguments, he was like his father, watching from a distance without muddying himself by getting involved. Shu and Saury, on the other hand, were troublemakers. They bickered relentlessly, yet could not be kept apart.

"Has Mama's boy written an ode to his mother this week?" Shu would ask sarcastically.

"Have you any more derisive comments to make?" Saury asked.

"Maybe I could write about the twenty ways to prime a cricket bat? Would that be good enough for your publication?"

Shu was constantly taking digs at Saury's attention to detail. Saury was a perfectionist, and would become obsessive about the most insignificant tasks. Every item on his desk had its designated place. He was also the more insightful and thoughtful of the two brothers. Not only did he have an intuitive understanding of his mother's lonely life, but he had a soft spot for his younger sister, Chotto. She had grown into a beautiful teenager, with large doe-like eyes, an aquiline nose and a beautiful smile.

Shu, on the other hand, shared the same natural exuberance as his middle sister, Menu. She was funny, very smart and laughed hysterically at all his jokes. There was not a mean bone in her body and she loved to listen to the stories her father and grandmother told her about the birds and wildlife in the nearby woods.

Shu's bond with her grew stronger when both of them fell dangerously ill with typhoid. They were isolated in a room for three weeks, and the prognosis was dire. One night, the doctors called an emergency meeting to tell the family to prepare for the worst. It was the third day that Menu's fever had not broken. She lay wrapped in cold damp towels, drifting in and out of consciousness. Shu, lying in the bed next to her, felt their spirits were connected.

"Menu," he said quietly, "if you promise you won't die tonight, I promise I won't either. Give me your hand: we are stronger together." He put out his skinny hand and held on to her hot, sweaty palm.

"I'll try, dada," she replied feebly.

"If you die, I will too. You have to do this for me."

"I will try."

"That's not good enough. Say 'I will not die'. You have to promise."

"I will not die," she repeated, barely above a whisper.

They survived that night, but both were marked for life. Menu had lapses in her memory and Shu lost the hearing in his left ear.

Both Menu and Chotto were growing up and Boroma became more and more concerned about their complexions. Whenever there was company, she would make them sit close to a light so they would appear fairer. "If only you were a little more *phorsha*," she would say to Chotto, "then you could marry a prince." She was so fixated on their colour that she experimenting with all sorts of powders and whitening creams. One morning, Chotto came in looking white as a ghost.

"What has happened to you?" an astonished Saury asked.

"Ma says I look more beautiful like this," she replied sadly, a tear making its way through the white paste.

"Let me talk to her." He walked angrily into his mothers' room. "Ma, what have you put on Chotto's face?"

"I just put some oil in the talcum powder to see what it does, that's all," she replied.

"She looks like a ghost," he shouted. "A bloody *bhoot*."

"Why are you raising your voice?" she asked, bewildered.

"Chotto, take it off immediately, don't let Ma put anything on you again."

Boroma sat down, taken aback by Saury's outburst.

"I'm only doing this for her," she said meekly.

"No, Ma, you have a problem. Chotto and Menu are such beauties yet all you talk about is how dark they are. I have a good mind to talk to Baba."

"Talk, talk, talk! You men are all the same, full of talk. But when you look for a bride you will ask for a fair and slim girl."

"Why do I waste my time?" Saury walked away, exasperated.

7

London

Arriving in London was a shock for both Imelda and Kathleen. Their Aunt Edna had two daughters, Joyce and Maureen, who were about the same age as Imelda. They had been born in London, spoke with a posh accent and dressed in fashionable English attire. The Irish sisters felt like country bumpkins, awkward and self-conscious in their old-fashioned frocks with Peter Pan collars and wide sashes.

"Did you hear them sniggering at our shoes?" Kathleen whispered later that night to Imelda. "They talk so funny! Did you understand them?"

"Nah! I just nod along. For 'me' they say 'my'. This is MY sister, MY room, MY hat; Can YEW please pass MY book; that is FOUR the cat; I could hardly keep from laughing meself," Imelda chuckled. "When Maureen said, 'Oh my, that collar is immense,' I said, 'Thank you kindly.' She looked so surprised. I think she was bein' sarcastic."

"What language do they speak here? Their English is different fer sure! I hate them. I want to go home," Kathleen said.

"London is a big city, Kathleen," Imelda explained patiently to her scared little sister. "'Tis even larger than Dublin. I thought it quite peculiar meself; no fields, no sheep, no horses, or even cows… But go back home? Never. I would never give the witch the satisfaction. Don't forget, we're safe from those IRA bullies here. You wait and see, in six months Joyce and Maureen will be wanting to borrow our clothes. I'll make sure of that."

With that delicious thought the girls drifted into a peaceful sleep.

They were up bright and early at the breakfast table the next day.

"What language do you speak in your country?" their cousin Maureen asked sweetly.

"We speak mostly Irish in our country," Imelda replied, "and Gaelic."

"Well then, I must say your English is rather good. My mother says we should apologize for laughing at you, but we couldn't understand some of your words," Joyce explained.

"Now, now, girls. I used to talk like Imelda and Kathleen when I came over. We speak the same language, we just say words differently," Aunt Edna interrupted. "I have enrolled both of you in English speaking classes. I don't want children laughing at you at school."

"English speaking classes? What language do we speak now?" Imelda gasped.

"Of course you speak English," Edna said. "But you do want your classmates to understand you, don't you?" She looked amused at their astonished expressions.

At their elocution classes they met people from Ireland, Scotland, Wales, Spain, Germany and Portugal, all being taught how to speak the King's English. As soon as they realized they were not as bad as some of the others, they began enjoying the lessons.

"The Spanish lady keeps saying 'si', instead of 'yes'," Kathleen said.

"She is too old to be learnin' how to speak. What did she do her whole life?"

"She spoke Spanish, idiot!"

"It's pronounced 'id-ee-yot,'" Kathleen said, saying the word as they had been taught in class recently.

"We can understand English, 'tis the talking we can't do. Alright, let's practice. I'll ask you questions. What is boot-ter?"

"Why, 'tis butt-tah!" Kathleen replied gleefully.

"No! Wrong, Miss Kathleen. Not ''tis butt-tah'. You reply in a full sentence … 'It is butt-tah.' 'Please pass the butt-tah.'"

"Thank you very much," Kathleen replied in a mock-English accent.

"Say, 'May I have the butt-tah please?' Not 'Can I have a wee bit o' boot-ter?'" The girls burst into peals of laughter.

"Wee bit? Dahling, 'wee' is not a word to be used in polite company. It is indiscreet!" Imelda imitated their elocution teacher, giggling.

Imelda soon got busy with the sewing machine. She shortened the hems and reshaped the collars of their 'hand-made' dresses, making them look almost store-bought. Edna helped them get acquainted with the boarding school, where the Irish nuns immediately took a liking to the two girls.

The first major problem was Kathleen having to sleep with the younger girls in a separate dormitory. Imelda went to the Mother Superior and recounted her story of woe. The two sisters had lost their mother, and their father had turned to drink. She had single-handedly kept the family together when their father suddenly married an evil English woman, she had sent them far away from home. Imelda was afraid that if her little sister was forced to sleep away from her, her recurring nightmares and epileptic seizures may return.

"Oh, Mother of Mercy, we were not told of her condition. She may have to be sent home."

"We don't have a home anymore. I think we're orphans," Imelda said, her eyes filling with tears.

"No Imelda, you are not orphans. Tell me, what do you think will help Kathleen?"

"I could sleep next to her, and help Mother Camilla monitor the girls in her dormitory."

"That's against the rules, Imelda," Mother Superior replied.

"Only fer a short while. She'll be fine when she gets used to the place."

"Very well. I will allow you you sleep there for a month or two. You are wise beyond your years, and a very good sister."

"Thank you, Mother Superior."

"Mind your English, Imelda. I noticed you say 'tis' and 'fer'. That is not acceptable here, so your assignment is to write 'it is' and 'for' a hundred times in your language notebook. Repeat 'for,' like the number 'four', ten times."

Life's a bitch, thought Imelda as she muttered 'four-four-four-four' through clenched teeth.

Back home in Ireland, Patrick Connor had become desolate after Imelda and Kathleen left. The girls' departure was just the beginning of many other hardships that would come his way.

He soon found out that his new marriage made him socially unacceptable among his inner circle of friends. Nancy was an outsider, almost two decades younger than him. It might have been forgiven had they waited a decent amount of time before getting married, but disrespecting the dead was an unforgivable offence. The same friends who had encouraged Patrick to befriend Nancy "fer the good of the young 'uns" now averted their eyes whenever she entered a room. "He'll not have a day's peace, if there's a God above."

Patrick often noticed a look of pity in the eyes of his friends. There were embarrassed glances, and a slow shuffling of feet as friends would join him at the bar and the women slowly move away, leaving Nancy isolated. She began staying home with their son George, and Patrick bristled with bitter resentment. But far more dangerous than the mutterings about his personal life were the insidious rumours circulating about his political connections.

By the early twenties the majority of the Irish citizenry were loosely divided into two camps: the Unionists, allied to the British, and the Nationalists, demanding immediate Home Rule. There was turmoil and confusion as its people waged bloody war not only against the British, but against each other. Secret assassination squads were sent out to kill police or army personnel, or anyone deemed an enemy of the State. Mutilated bodies were dumped on the roadside as a warning to others. Fear and suspicion stalked the once peaceful countryside.

Patrick realized his days in Ireland were numbered. His friends were worried about the rumours circulating about him, and warned him about the hot-headed young IRA newcomers who were quickly moving into leadership positions. Traditional family ties or community affiliations counted for nothing there – either you were with them, or branded a traitor. Patrick was indignant that a bunch of young, swaggering hoodlums dared to question his loyalty to the Republic of Ireland.

One evening the Captain of the Kilworth Division of the IRA paid him a visit with a dozen armed soldiers. Patrick, Nancy and the boys had just finished supper when there was a loud knock on the door.

"Don't answer that," Gerald said in a low voice.

"I'm not afraid to open me own front door," Patrick replied as he rose to go.

"Please, Dad, don't," Frank begged.

"Open the fuckin' door or we'll blast it open," came a voice from outside.

"Go hide upstairs. Not a sound from the lot of you." Patrick motioned to Nancy and the boys with his finger on his lips. He opened the door slowly.

"Well, lads, what can I do fer yeh?"

The men stood with their guns pointed at Patrick. They wore black army fatigues, their faces hidden behind black hoods with holes cut out for their eyes. The only unmasked person was the captain.

"Put ya fuckin' hands up and get out here," he barked at Patrick.

"Does Liam Lynch know you idiots are here?" Patrick asked, cool as steel. "I would talk to headquarters before I did anything stupid."

He saw an flicker of apprehension in the eyes of the captain.

"Playin' games, are yeh? We don't take orders from Lynch or Barry."

"Go ahead an' shoot then, I'm not afraid of a bunch of cowards," he replied without a hint of fear.

"Dad! Shut up," Cyril screamed as he and Gerald barrelled down the stairs.

"Get back there!" the dark-eyed assassin yelled as he poked the rifle butt into Patrick's shoulder, directing him outside, towards the back of the yard. "Put yer fuckin' hands up and keep walkin' or I'll blow yer fuckin' brains out, right here in front of yer fuckin' sons."

"Please don't kill him, he's proud Irish like us! I swear on Mother Mary! Please." Cyril was on his knees, sobbing.

"Get up off yer knees, don't yuh be beggin fer me life. Let them kill me; I'm not afraid to die fer Ireland. Every last one of them will be shot for this."

He looked back at the masked boys who stood with their guns trained at him.

"Go ahead, shoot, yeh stupid bastards. Make yehselves proud."

Gerald, weeping and breathless, also fell to his knees. "Fer the love of God show a bit of mercy, he's an ol' man. I swear he's one of us. He has a wee baby. Please. I'm beggin' you."

Patrick looked unafraid as his young assailants shifted nervously and looked anxiously for direction.

"Well, what are yeh waiting fer? Call yerself Irish?" he shouted defiantly.

"Dad! Shut ya mouth," Frank sobbed, still crouched sobbing on the ground.

"Should I take him out now?" said one of the young men, was his arm though shaking.

"Wait," said the captain. The men lowered their guns. "I'll be back tomorrow, and you'd better be here. We will be watchin' this fuckin' farm. Try any shite and we will hunt you down and string you up like animals. Every one of you." He turned and stalked away, followed by his band of teenage soldiers.

The Connors stood at the bottom of the garden, all five of them, the boys trembling and crying, while Nancy comforted the baby inside the house.

"You should've let them shoot me. 'Tis better bein' dead than forced to leave Ireland," Patrick said steadily. "I'm a professional soldier. Those fuckin' bastards don't scare me."

"Don't be tellin' us what scares you. You'd be dead now, if we didn't beg fer yer life," Gerald shot back at him, " an' they'll be back tomorrow to kill us all."

That dark and terrifying night, the family disappeared from Kilworth. At daylight, there was no sign of any of them. Their meager possessions were packed and cleared out, their animals gone. The village was abuzz with speculation. Some swore the IRA had wiped out the whole family because Patrick was a British spy, while others wondered if Patrick was really an IRA informer and had been playing both sides.

The real story is that they were given a new alias and relocated to the army barracks at Aldershot, southwest of London. Here they were confined to the base for six months with no outside communications and the family name was changed from Connor to O'Connor. For the next few years, Patrick's whereabouts were shrouded in mystery. He was moved from one secure military accommodation to another on the outskirts of London, and at one point even provided a low-profile job at the villa of an Italian Count. Finally Patrick was granted early retirement with full benefits. After that, he and Nancy moved to a small cottage in the village of Putney Green in Herefordshire.

Nancy happily settled into her new life. Here she was Mrs. Patrick O'Connor, not the distrusted young woman from England who married the widower. She concentrated on raising her son George, and made a tentative peace with Patrick's children. Frank and Cyril joined the British army while Gerald and Patrick did construction work. Once or twice a month they would have Sunday supper with Frank and Nancy.

While Nancy felt at home in England, Patrick pined for his homeland and the friends he had left behind. He felt lost and uprooted, spending long drunken evenings among strangers at one of the many Irish pubs scattered throughout the area which had become sanctuaries for lonely expatriate Irish men and women.

8

Calcutta

Amarendra Nath Bose was at the top of his profession and widely respected at the Calcutta High Court by both his British and Indian colleagues. He was a strong advocate of the English education system, and saw it as the only way for Indians to get ahead in British India. Amarendra was determined his sons would receive the best education money could buy. His eldest, Himanshu, had returned from England a barrister and was already a junior advocate in the court. Shu had been accepted at the School of Engineering at Faraday House, London. His third and youngest son, Saury, was enrolled at the Institute of Chartered Accountants of England and Wales, also located in London.

Shu and Saury did not follow the frugal example of their brother Himanshu, who lived an exemplary and modest lifestyle in London. The younger brothers knew that money would never be a problem, so alongside their education they choose a lavish lifestyle that few could afford.

Shu had gone to London a year ahead of Saury, and had initially set himself extremely high standards. He vowed to concentrate only on his studies and not be distracted by other temptations. His three best friends, Bappa Mallik, Nikhil Chowdury and Robin Mitter were in England at the same time, Nikhil and Bappa at Cambridge and Robin at Oxford. During the summer break, Shu took classes in literature, poetry and anthropology at Kings College, Cambridge.

He had the good fortune to arrive in London during the time that his uncle Dhiren Mitra was posted as the legal advisor to the British High Commissioner. Dhiren Mitra was the first Indian ever selected for the post. He would go on to be appointed the first Indian Solicitor General of Her Majesty's Government, and later be honoured by a knighthood. His wife Sachindra, a quiet diminutive woman, welcomed Shu, as did her daughters Lotika and Bashi.

The first order of business on Dhiren and Sachindra Mitra's list for their nephew was to take a course in English social etiquette. He had to acquire the *savoir faire* required to mingle with ease at the elegant social events they hosted. Shu was required to read and order from a menu written in French and give pithy introductory speeches.

After three months, Shu moved out of the Mitra residence and shifted to a small flat on Somerset Street. He borrowed most of the furniture from his Uncle's home. His extracurricular activities were confined to tennis and the theatre. Saury arrived a year later, and planned to stay with Shu until his classes began. It did not take long for the conflict to begin, and it was over a cup of tea.

"Did you pick these cups up off the pavement?"

"Not fancy enough for you?" Shu replied.

"Fancy? I'm talking about taste. Where are the matching saucers? Your lifestyle certainly does not reflect your upbringing."

"I happen to have more important matters on my mind," Shu replied, bristling.

The next day, Saury went to Harrods and bought an eight-piece dining set of fine English bone china, in crème and etched with gold, and a matching tea set. He bought hand towels and tea cloths, a tea cozy, pot holders, and an assortment of measuring spoons and pot stirrers.

"How did you dry the dishes?" he asked Shu on another occasion.

"The old-fashioned way: fresh air. And since I have the odious task of managing our finances I don't have the time to micromanage your expenses."

"Ma gave me some cash she had stashed away for me, from the publication."

"I don't believe it!" Shu replied derisively. "If I remember correctly, you couldn't give that rag away. The years of brown-nosing are finally paying off."

Saury was a perfectionist. He would spend hours puttering around, straightening pictures, re-arranging and organizing drawers, until Shu would explode.

He had a ritual for everything. The morning 'cuppa' started by pouring hot water into an empty teapot, swishing it around, pouring it out, and instantly putting in the tea leaves. The water, on its first boil, had to be poured onto the tea leaves, and covered immediately by a tea cozy. It took him half an hour to make the perfect cup of tea, a task Shu completed in two minutes and once timed to prove his point.

"Two minutes," Saury scoffed. "Even the most uninformed knows you have to leave it to brew for five."

"I could set up a gourmet buffet in the time you take to make one bloody cup of tea."

Saury's martinis were a similar affair, and Shu's perennial joke was his brother's martinis were only ever ready after the last guest had gone. Mixed in with this humour was an underlying touch of envy. The brothers had a close but complicated relationship. Fiercely competitive, they enjoyed baiting each other, and their quick repartee was egged on by their friends. This competitive behaviour spilled into other areas – in their academics, on the tennis courts and, of course, with women.

Shu was the more serious of the two, occasionally trying to play big brother. He had a holistic outlook and focused on the consequences of every decision. He had inherited his father's tendencies to mull over his actions with an objective overview, and had his feet firmly planted on the ground. Saury, on the other hand, was led by his emotions. A hopeless romantic, he wore his heart on his sleeve, invariably leading to heartbreak. He was also extravagant, and unthinkingly flaunted his privileged background.

He moved into a new flat in a posh part of the city and bought himself a Lagonda coupé. To be invited on a drive was a honour bestowed only on a select few. One of the hidden stipulations was the understanding that the colour of the invitee's outfit would not clash with that of the car: forest green, never to be confused with emerald green, sage green or apple green. The obvious absurdity of the situation annoyed Shu to exasperation. Jokingly, he had suggested Saury buy a neutral-coloured coat for all the girls to wear.

To further their playboy image, they took tango lessons. Their teacher was a fabulously sensual dancer from Argentina. They kept re-enrolling in the classes until they were politely asked not to register for the next session.

To round off their impeccable credentials, a good game of tennis was a prerequisite. Learning to jump the net gracefully split many tennis shorts. For Saury, form was everything. It was important to look good when you hit the ball. Sweating was something he did not enjoy, and he always had a small towel on hand.

"There! You did it again. You didn't bend your knees or turn your shoulder when you hit the ball."

"I hit the ball, isn't that the point?" Shu replied.

"The goal is to hit the ball *correctly*."

"We only have the court for an hour, so shut up and hit the goddamn ball."

"All I'm going to say is that some of your line calls showed a complete lack of integrity." Saury muttered. They always left the courts swearing they would never play together again.

For all their bluff sportiness, there was a fussy side to both the brothers. At home in India, they were rubbed down with soothing herbal oils after a game of cricket or soccer. They used moisturizers and lotions to keep their face and hands from drying in the frigid English weather. To take the shine off, they would use a dab of face powder. Their friend Robin Mitter would call them 'the powder-puff Boses' behind their backs.

Despite all his extracurricular activities, Shu managed to be a brilliant student. His range of interests was eclectic. He had been captivated by the work of a German anthropologist, Professor Carl Schultz. The professor had lived among the nomadic Masai tribes and his thesis was on their survival. To be able to converse with him, Shu had enlisted in a series of summer lectures on African tribalism. During those classes he got friendly with the twin daughters of the professor, Clara and Ada Schultz. Within a few months, he moved into their spacious flat in Knightsbridge. The arrangement was ideal: Shu lived rent-free and the girls had a man to help with their social obligations.

Both Clara and Ada had travelled to Africa to spend their vacations with their father, and they would entertain Shu and his friends with tales of their adventures there.

"I'm taking the advanced course of Anthropology at Kings College." Shu informed Saury one day.

"Could it be because Clara and Ada Schultz recommend it? You do know that professional and personal relationships should not mix?"

"Why not? Suits all three of us. The twins have a nice place for me to hang my hat and they have me to do my bit on the home front. It's an intellectual relationship, no one gets emotionally involved. Got to run. Watch your letters home, I don't want Ma coming to London to check up on her sickly son."

To maintain the lifestyle they wanted, both Shu and Saury had to find innovative ways to squeeze more money out of their parents. Saury had discovered he could write to his mother and tell her he had succumbed to the latest epidemic in London, and in a week he would receive a large cheque. Saury needed Shu's cooperation to sustain a steady flow of cash. It was more lucrative to buy Shu's silence with a twenty per cent cut than send fake doctors' reports with long explanations.

Shu had acquired a circle of close friends at Cambridge. He had taken a year off from Faraday House to get a degree in literature. He spent many summer evenings imbibing in pink gin and rowing along the lazy river. Cambridge offered a change from the hectic activities in London. They played cricket and tennis at the club, leisurely drinking Pimms or champagne under the umbrellas set up for its mollycoddled members. Clara was a frequent visitor. After hours, they would hang out at the many bars and cafés or go party-hopping for weekends of revelry.

9

London

Like most Irish immigrants, Imelda and Kathleen felt isolated and lonely in London. It was difficult to get used to mainstream British life. Imelda got her school leaving certificate and took Kathleen out of school to live with her in London. Initially they stayed in a family member's flat, contributing by doing the housework and daily chores. Patrick and Nancy had been absent from their lives for some time, and Imelda missed her father. The family seemed scattered and disconnected.

Imelda did what most of the Irish did: she frequented the many Irish pubs in the city. There was O'Reilly's, McNally's, The McCoy, The Cavanaugh, Donahue's, O'Leary's and McFadden's. These had become places where homesick Irish men and women gathered to drink a pint of stout, sing songs and feel comfortable. Having to support both Kathleen and herself, Imelda quickly became resourceful at making money. She got a job modelling clothes for a small distinguished designer. In the evenings, she bartended at a pub called The Green Hog, where she and Kathleen would also get a free supper. Old man Brenaugh, the owner of the pub, took the two girls under his wing and even paid Kathleen to help with the dishes. The girls were on first-name basis with all the patrons, often challenging them to games of darts or checkers. At this time, Irish people coming over, escaping the terror and chaos of daily bombings and political killings.

Imelda discovered that in England, one had to be connected to royalty or else be very rich to belong to any of London's riding clubs. Melton Riding Club, in Leicestershire, was the most distinguished. It had an riding school where the lords and ladies of the royal court practiced dressage and show jumping. Its polo club hosted international teams and it was well-known for its horse shows, riding trails and foxhunts. Melton boasted a large stable of horses and was constantly on the lookout for trained help.

Imelda was single-minded in her determination to find a job at the club. She made the hour-long train journey to Melton and rang the bell at the imposing wood and beveled glass door. The club had the air of exclusivity, with its perfectly manicured lawns and grand entrance, lined with flawless conically-shaped trees.

A doorman dressed in a red and tan uniform looked down at her with disdain and snapped, "Go to the servant's entrance, around the back."

"Why? I'm not a servant," she replied defiantly.

"Are you a member of the club, Madam?" he asked, nose pointing to the heavens.

"No, but I'm not a servant either. I have come to meet the horse-master."

"As I said before: round the back." He slammed the door in her face.

She was about to let loose a few choice words, but bit her tongue and instead walked up the gracefully curved walkway behind the clubhouse. The scene took her breath away. Meadows full of wildflowers gave way to emerald-green pastures with mist-covered hills in the distance. Lush fields edged with white fencing held the most magnificent horses she had ever seen.

She walked across the grass to the outer fence and stood mesmerized by the tranquility of the place. She felt at peace crossing the small field to get closer to the horses. A mare and her colt came trotting up to her, the mare proudly showing off her shiny new baby, who frolicked and played next to her. Imelda stood by the white fence quietly talking to the mare, occasionally glancing at the arrogant stallion prancing haughtily in the next field along.

"May I help you, young lady?" a raspy voice startled her.

"Oh! I'm so sorry, am I trespassing?" she asked, suddenly aware of her grand surroundings.

"That depends on why you're here," the man replied, his eyes half-closing as his face crinkled into a smile.

"I came to meet the horse-master to ask about a job, but these beautiful horses made me forget everything. That one reminds me of my own horse, Toby. He's so proud! Just look at the way he holds his head."

"That's our star stallion, Amber. Which part of Ireland are you from?" the man asked as he leaned against the fence.

"Kilworth, County Cork. My father owned a small farm there."

"Pure Cork! I could tell. I come from County Clare, but I've been here a while. What kind of work are you looking for?"

"Any job, as long as I work with horses. I'm very good with animals. Do you know if the horse-master is in?"

The man let out a loud belly-laugh. "You're talking to him. It must take a lot of nerve to walk right in to the most exclusive riding club and ask for a job. We do have a screening process. Just being good with animals won't get you far, I can tell you that."

"I know all about horses, I've had a horse since I was a wee girl. We had to do all the looking-after ourselves. We even took in four horses to stable. I know how to groom them, clip their hooves, file their teeth and use a hoof pick. I know the difference between the dandy brush and the stiff brush. I can tell if a horse is sick, feel their moods, feed them, ride them, train them. Please, Mr. –" She stopped, turning red with embarrassment. "I'm sorry, I didn't get your name…?"

"Liam Connolly. A pleasure. And your name?"

"I'm Imelda Connor."

"How old are you, Imelda?"

"I'm going to be eighteen soon, well, in about eleven months. Please give me a chance. I'll work for nothing."

"You don't need the money?" he asked, surprised.

"I need the money, but I would love to work here, more than any other place in the world."

"How well can you ride?" he asked. "And can you jump?"

"Can I jump? Better than all the lads in Ballincollig. And bareback too. I can show you."

"Let me take you back to the stable. I'll watch you saddle the new horse that just came in. Wait here for me."

When Liam Connolly returned, he walked with her to a stable with twelve stalls. Imelda's eyes were huge as she walked passed the beautiful thoroughbred horses. Each stall had a brass plate with the horse's name etched on it; everything was polished to a rich golden glow.

"A little overwhelming?" Liam joked.

"I've never seen anything so fancy in my life," Imelda replied softly. "Do they wear golden breeches to ride in?"

"It always comes down to basics, Imelda. It's all about connecting with a horse, and how it reacts to you. You either have it, or you don't, and I can already tell you do. That's Starburst over there. He came in two days ago and is a bit skittish, so be careful. I won't give you any directions; I want you to show me how you'd saddle him."

"Do you have sugar cubes?" Imelda asked anxiously.

Liam laughed and he showed her where the sugar cubes and carrots were kept.

For a while, Imelda watched the beautiful brown horse with the large white star on his forehead. She talked to him gently in a hushed whisper from a short distance. After he had got used to her, she slowly moved closer and offered him a lump of sugar. As he ate, she patted his neck, talking all the while. In half an hour, she had him saddled and riding around the paddock. Liam Connolly smiled broadly.

"Imelda, that was nothing short of brilliant. Give me a few days to figure out how I can fit you in. It's very hard work, but I know you'll be happy."

And so she was. Imelda was now holding down two jobs – one at the stables, the other bar-tending at a local pub – and Kathleen made money helping two sisters run their small boutique. She and Kathleen moved into a small one-bedroom flat with lace curtains sent by Aunt Beatrice. One evening, when Imelda was tending the bar, a tall, handsome brown-haired man walked in. He had the rugged looks of an athlete, was clearly Irish, and his wide open smile had a familiar look to it. He stared at her for an instant and let out a loud yell.

"Imelda Connor!"

"Shaun Callahan? What in the world are you doing here?"

"This is the luckiest day in my life!" Shaun told the amused patrons. "I spent my entire childhood jumping over boulders trying to catch this red-haired wench." He laughed out loud as he lifted her off her feet.

"Put me down Shaun, you'll have me fired. What are you doing in London?"

"I'm at Cambridge. I can't believe you've been here all the time. Where have all your freckles gone? Is this the brat who terrorized me?"

Imelda turned to Kathy, who had just walked in. "Kathy, remember Shaun?"

"The boy you kissed behind the barn?" Kathleen replied cheekily.

Shaun had a huge crush on Imelda, and when she was about ten years old she would stand on the rock boundary between their farms and promise him a wee little kiss if he could catch her. He never did. He was now studying at King's College, Cambridge.

They came from the same place, dreamed the same dreams, and thought so much alike that when one began a sentence, the other would complete it. The two soon were soon inseparable, and after six months decided to get engaged. Shaun got Imelda a small diamond ring that she would polish every day. She would drive up to Cambridge every other Saturday to watch his rugby matches. She hung around with the girlfriends of the other players, becoming part of a tight-knit group that travelled together to cheer on their men. She was content with the way she had navigated her way into this perfect life. The shattered pieces of her heart were finally beginning to heal.

10

Cambridge

It was a rollicking party with a live band, plenty of champagne, and an enthusiastic crowd. When Shu and Clara made an entrance the carousing was already in full swing.

"What's going on?" Shu asked Robin Mitter.

"The football season is over! We won the championship, beat Oxford by two. Great game. Where the hell were you?"

"Slept in. What a bloody rowdy bunch. Are all the players here?"

"Yes, Nikhil is friends with Peter Cunliffe, the captain. He invited the entire team to celebrate." Shu waved to Nikhil, who was whooping it up with a bunch of players.

As Shu surveyed the scene, a beautiful red-haired girl caught his eye. She was dancing with joyful abandon, was clearly the centre of attention and seemed to be loving every minute of it. He watched her for a few seconds before he turned to Clara.

"Come on Clara, let's hit the floor!"

"I haven't had my first drink yet," Clara complained as he jostled her onto the dance floor. He and Clara were busy jitterbugging when he accidentally collided with the exuberant redhead.

"Pardon me. My fault," he apologized, as he turned to face her.

"It sure is," she laughed, her blue eyes twinkling mischievously.

Imelda had noticed Shu the minute he had walked into the room. He was stunningly handsome, with an arrogant self-confidence she could feel from across the room. She also caught him slyly looking at her as she danced. He had his back to her, as she slowly edged her way over to his side. "You're full of the blade tonight!," Shaun remarked as he went to get them a drink.

What should have been a fairly perfunctory introduction turned out to be a moment neither of them would forget. On impulse, Imelda turned to Shu and said, "Haven't seen you around here. You new maybe?"

Taken aback, Shu replied, "By 'new' do you mean something new and shiny?"

"I meant, where do you come from?" Imelda replied, a little flustered.

"I've been pondering that quite a bit lately. I'm presently taking a summer course at Cambridge. I am a student at Faraday House, and I come to you all the way from Calcutta."

He bowed as he took her hand and kissed it, and then looked straight into her eyes.

"Ooh! Cal-coo-tah, that's even further away than Cork!" she replied, bursting into peals of laughter. She had an impish expression, and as she returned his direct gaze, he felt something stir within him. He stood there shuffling his feet, feeling extremely uncomfortable at the obvious enjoyment she was having at his expense. She had dismissed him and his attempts to be grand with a laugh, and it seemed to come so naturally to her. Just then Clara returned with a drink for him. She eyed Imelda suspiciously while the normally unperturbed Shu mumbled something and whisked her away.

Shu was unprepared for the impact that Imelda had on him. With that devilish sparkle in her eyes, she seemed to see right through all the bravado with which he had armed himself. He was so distracted he could not concentrate on what Clara was saying. He did not want to make conversation, but to watch the girl with the laughing blue eyes and flaming red hair.

Imelda's hand was trembling as Shaun led her away. She wanted to know more about this stranger. He stood apart from all the others with his dark eyebrows and intense black eyes; he held his head with a slightly self-conscious deprecating look, but it was the directness of his stare that ruffled her most. Throughout the evening she was aware of being followed by those eyes. Whenever she casually glanced in his direction he immediately looked away. He left before she could talk to him again.

That night she couldn't keep the handsome stranger out of her thoughts. He was so indifferent to her flirting, so separate from that raucous crowd. She could not wait to return to London to tell Kathleen about him.

"Oh Kath," she gushed, "he is the most gorgeous man I have ever met. He has dark eyes and dark hair just like Valentino."

"Valentino? Did his hair shine?"

"He did. Well, he kind of glowed. I can't explain. He had deep black eyes that look right into you."

"Black eyes – only the Devil has black eyes."

"Don't be silly. Oh, and his splendid smile. Did I tell you about…"

"What about Shaun? Does he know?"

"Of course not! I don't have to tell him everything," Imelda reacted defensively.

"I thought you loved him?"

"Of course I love him. I'm going to marry him, but maybe you can love two people at the same time…"

"Not if it's true love," a distressed Kathleen moaned.

"Look. I've only met him for a second; who knows if we'll ever meet again. Shaun's my love forever."

She looked at her ring, giving it a quick shine to reassure herself.

"Did I mention he has a German girlfriend?"

"A German?" Kathleen shrieked. "A spy?"

"There was something very odd about her. She had a furry little thing with a mouth clipped on to its tail around her shoulder. It was disgusting."

"Was she pretty?"

"No. Too perfect. I don't want to think about her…"

Over the following weeks, Imelda could not get Shu out of her mind. She combed every bookstore and café in Cambridge hoping to catch a glimpse of that jet-black hair, that aquiline profile.

Shaun, meanwhile, was getting tired of Imelda's desire to go to different restaurants and pubs every time they went out. He liked to go to the same place and feel comfortable among his friends.

"I don't know what's come over you. This is the third pub we've been to and you want to leave? I've had it."

"All you do is talk about soccer and rugby. I want a change once in a while, is there something wrong with that?"

"I liked things the way they were. We don't have fun anymore. I'm not going to another pub. I'll be at The Greens if you change your mind."

Eventually Imelda recognized that she and Shaun had drifted apart. She could not understand her own erratic behaviour, so hardly expected any sympathy from him.

"He must have hypnotized me, like they do the cobras," she confided to Kathleen afterwards.

"I know," Kathleen agreed sullenly. "And you broke up with Shaun, I'll never forgive you."

"I can't forgive myself. I still miss Shaun, it felt so good to wear a ring and let the whole world know I was his girl. I just want to be happy, to laugh like Mum and Dad."

"You mean when they got drunk, and sang loudly?"

"They were happy and made each other laugh," Imelda smiled, her face softening. "I can't explain what happened. But one thing I know for sure, there are times you just have to listen to your heart."

11

London

Shu was making a spectacle of himself. The Irish girl with the dazzling smile and bright blue eyes had him bewitched. He made discreet inquiries about her, but to no avail. He decided to talk to Nikhil, who was captain of the cricket team and hung out at the sports club and gym with the other athletes.

"You remember the red-haired girl with those soccer goons?" Shu asked casually.

"Why?" Nikhil replied suspiciously.

"Just curious. She was a great dancer. Seemed a little out of place with that crowd," Shu continued.

"She's very much part of that Catholic clique," Nikhil said.

"Does Catholic clique mean the same as Indian clique?"

"No! Catholic clique has more of the Pope/church dynamic. Sunday Mass, confession, communion... Shall I go on?"

"Quite scathing. Do you always stereotype so easily?"

"I'm just a cynic warning you to tread carefully. Anyway, she's with one of the chaps."

"What does 'with one of the chaps' mean?"

"It means the same as 'Shu's with Clara.'"

"That could mean anything."

"Have you lost your bloody mind? She's as good as married. Are you and Clara having issues?" Nikhil asked, suddenly serious.

"Life is meaningless without issues," Shu replied morosely.

"Dumb bastard! You think you can bullshit me?" Nikhil laughed.

"Thanks, Nick. You're a hell of a friend."

It happened just like it does in the storybooks. Dateless and feeling sorry for her miserable existence, Imelda asked Kathleen to go to a movie with her. As they settled into their seats, Kathleen heard a sharp gasp from Imelda

"It's him, over there," Imelda whispered, pointing surreptitiously over her shoulder.

"Who? Oh HIM," replied Kathleen as she strained her neck comically to look. "The one sitting next to the blonde? Must be his wife by now."

"Stop it Kath," Imelda groaned, "It's not funny. Let's leave."

"We are staying. You forced me to come to see Greta Garbo."

"Only 'cos people say I look like her."

"People also say you're an idiot!" Kathleen shot back. " We are not wasting our money, we are staying."

When the movie ended Imelda shut her eyes. When she opened them, he was gone. Kathleen had shamelessly stared at Clara and Shu as they walked right past her.

"Do you think he saw me?" Imelda breathed.

"Nope! He only had eyes for her. *Ze spy.*"

"It's good I saw them, I know for sure it's hopeless." Imelda said sadly as they waited until everyone had left. She felt deflated, as though the joy had been sucked out of her. She walked out, shoulders drooped, holding back tears.

Then she felt a slight tap on her shoulder. There stood Shu, with a beaming smile on his face. He seemed genuinely happy to see her as he held out his hand.

"Shu Bose, we met at Nikhil Chowdury's party in Cambridge."

Imelda gaped at him, turning bright pink and feeling the world spin around her. Embarrassed, he continued. "You remember, that man from Cal-coo-tah?"

"Of… of course. Hello again, I'm Imelda."

"Ah yes! Imelda. Imelda who?"

"Imelda Connor. And this is my sister Kathleen. Kath, this is Shu and…?"

"Clara, dahling." The blonde 'spy' held out a hand.

"Care to join us for a drink?" said Shu eagerly.

"Thank you, but we can't tonight. We're meeting friends at the Black Hog," Imelda replied.

"Well, listen Imelda, if you ever need a ride up to Cambridge give me a hum on the phone. I go up practically every weekend, and am always looking for company. Here's my number. I'll wait to hear from you." He smiled his splendid smile as he handed her a scrap of paper.

She felt paralyzed clutching the note as he turned and walked away. "A hum on the phone!" she finally burst out. "I've never heard that before, have you Kath? Isn't he just gorgeous?"

She saw Shu turn around and wave to her. He too wanted to reassure himself that it was not an illusion.

"And did you hear his accent? Funniest thing ever!"

Over the following days, Imelda felt like she was walking on air. She endlessly rehearsed what she would say to Shu. The problem was that she had always gone to Cambridge with Shaun, and all their friends were his friends. She would have to come up with a cast-iron reason for taking a trip without him. As for Clara, well, hadn't Shu invited her right in front of her? They must have a platonic relationship, Imelda rationalized to herself.

"I have to think of something that doesn't make me sound too eager or dim-witted," she confided to Kathleen.

"Good luck with that," her sister replied, with a dark look.

"Well, I can't have him thinking I'm going up to Cambridge just to be with him, now can I? You wouldn't understand…" Imelda smiled dreamily. "How about: 'Hello Shu, this is Imelda.' Nah! too ordinary. Or, 'Good morning, guess who?' What do you think? Or should I go for a lower voice?"

"I can't take it any more! If he likes idiots, he'll love *you*."

Shu was sure that Imelda would call the next day – but there was silence. Every time the phone rang he lunged for it. He wondered if he should have taken her number. That would have been the smart thing to do. She may have lost the scrap of paper. Why was he so anxious to meet that ridiculous girl? She was a country bumpkin from Ireland, with an atrocious accent – and yet he felt nervous and faint whenever he thought of her.

Just then the phone rang, and a hesitant voice said, "Hello, this is Imelda." At first there was a deathly silence, but then both of them said hello together and burst out laughing. They agreed to go up Cambridge the following Saturday, both pretending they had been invited to a party they just could not miss.

"Shall I pick you up at around nine?" Shu asked.

"I could meet you at the station. It would be easier for you," Imelda replied, trying to keep her voice steady.

"No, your place is better, that way I'll find out where you live and you won't be able to hide from me," Shu flirted.

"If you insist. Wear a red carnation so I'll able to recognize you," Imelda giggled.

"I will be there early."

"Don't forget the carnation," Imelda laughed. She hung up, shuddered involuntarily, and ran in a few exhilarated circles around the room. Then the thought suddenly struck her: what on earth was she going to wear?

Kath came in a little later to find her sister sitting on the floor with every bit of clothing she owned strewn around her.

"I don't have a damn thing to wear," Imelda declared dramatically.

"Well, what's all this?" an exasperated Kath exclaimed.

"We have to go shopping. If I can't find the right dress, I can't go."

After three days of intensive shopping they located the perfect dress, a simple A-line with a shirt collar and vertical stripes of blue and green. Imelda modelled the dress for the other customers, dancing and pirouetting, until they all told her the dress was *made* just for her.

Meanwhile, Shu had some fast thinking to do. He told Clara he had to see his English professor about the thesis he had submitted.

"Oh! Was that the call you were waiting for so anxiously?" she asked innocently.

"No, I was also expecting a call from my uncle," Shu replied evenly.

"I could drive up with you," she offered.

"Unfortunately, Tulu and Robin are driving up with me; we thought we would make it an all-boys adventure." His palms were sweating: now he would have to remember to ask Tulu and Robin to lie for him.

He then did the unthinkable: he asked Saury if he could borrow his Lagonda coupé. He knew the car came with a hefty price tag. Saury would rather walk than be seen in Shu's car, so swapping cars was out. The negotiated price a dinner at the Moulin Rouge.

Shu arrived to pick up Imelda dressed in his best cream slacks and navy blazer. He had on a silk cravat, and remembered the carnation. Overdressed for the occasion, but looking debonair and handsome, he saw Imelda at a distance waiting for him. Once they had got over their initial self-consciousness, they started to enjoy themselves.

"So, you lived on a farm? Who did all the hard work?" Shu asked.

"We did – my family. It was hard work, but we really loved the animals. Did you have any pets in India?"

"Yes, my father is the animal lover in our family. Over there, we have people to do all the dirty work."

"Working with animals is never dirty work. I'd love to live on a farm again," she added wistfully.

"And shovel that stuff? I love horses, do you ride?"

"Of course I can ride! I ride bareback too."

"Maybe you could ride an elephant bareback," Shu laughed.

Later, neither Shu nor Imelda could remember what was said on the way up to Cambridge. They did not attend any of the parties, content to spend the time together, laughing at every silly incident, playing off each other's humour, totally immersed in each other.

They were so different: Imelda an extrovert, warm and trusting, and optimistic; Shu an introvert, cautious, restrained and in control of his emotions. His wit was urbane, with a cutting edge and a twist of sarcasm. He did not intimidate Imelda with his erudite quotations, nor did he impress her with his sophistication. She was naturally funny, seeing humour in little things he would normally not even notice. But most of all she made him laugh at himself.

They went rowing on the river, Imelda helping with one oar, splashing him playfully, daring to get his spotless pants wet. They browsed in the little bookshops, where Shu found a small book about Nanavati, an Irish missionary who had worked in India. He bought it for Imelda.

They found a grassy bank for their picnic, and Shu carefully lay down a blanket before he sat down, placing the picnic basket next to him.

"Why do you have to lie on a blanket? Do you not like the feel of the grass?" asked Imelda.

"It's a habit I acquired in India; one never knows what lies hidden in the grass. Could be a cobra. Or a scorpion…"

"Nice try. You're just scared of getting stains on your pants."

"That too. Grass stains are impossible to get out. You already have me pegged," Shu laughed.

Imelda lay on the grass plucking the petals off a daisy. "He loves me, he loves me not, he loves me…" she chanted softly.

"I'm curious," said Shu. "Who is 'he'?"

"You'll never know," she said, then looked at him intently. "Now tell me about that blond girl I've seen you with." She had her face on her hands and looked straight into his eyes.

"Clara? Well…" he cleared his throat, taken aback by the directness of her question. "Clara Schultz and her sister Ada and I share a flat in Knightsbridge."

"Share a flat? You all pay rent?"

"Well, their father owns the flat, but we all share the expenses. They are so alike, honestly, sometimes I can't tell them apart." He laughed dryly.

"I think she has a thing for you."

"Now, can I help it if women have a 'thing' for me? I'm just irresistible, don't you think?"

"I think you are very conceited."

"And I think you are very beautiful."

"Are you flirting with me?"

"I thought you'd never notice."

That night, they strolled along the river holding hands, exchanging stories about their incredibly different lives. Shu felt himself drawn inexplicably to Imelda. Later, when he asked her to dance, she melted into his arms, and it seemed as if they had danced together their whole lives.

The weekend flew by much too quickly. On the drive back to London, Shu was careful not to get too close to Imelda. When he didn't give her a goodbye kiss, and rather formally thanked her for an incredible time, Imelda spontaneously threw her arms around his neck and gave him a warm, passionate kiss on the lips.

"Thank you, I've had the most wonderful time. I hope to see you again. Give me a hum on the phone!" She laughed and turned to went inside.

Shu sat in his car for a few minutes. He put his fingers to his lips in a daze. His knees felt weak. He was utterly and hopelessly in love. Sudden panic tightened the muscles of his throat and he could barely swallow.

Spending the weekend with Imelda had not been a good idea. All his instincts had warned him against it. He had never wanted a relationship with a deep commitment. He had not even thought about love. Imelda coming into his life complicated his carefully planned lifestyle. His life was now in total disarray. What about the twins? The one thing they had all demanded was honesty.

All he could think was when he would see her again. He needed to talk to someone. Saury was the only person with whom he could be totally honest – and besides, he did have to return the car. He knocked tentatively on Saury's door. His brother opened the door dressed in his navy and red silk Chinese robe.

"Christ, look at you. All dressed up and nowhere to go," Shu chuckled.

"Is big brother checking on me?"

"Of course not! I've just come to return the car, thank you, and…" he took a deep breath, "and maybe ask for some advice."

"Is everything alright?" Saury asked.

"I'm so confused," Shu replied glumly.

Saury smiled, enjoying the moment.

"Let me guess. You need another hand-out from the old man?"

"Wish it was so simple. I won't beat about the bush, Saury. I've met a girl. Well, you know that. After all, you're the extortionist with the car."

"This is about a girl?"

"I'm in a bloody mess."

"She's pregnant. Oh God. Let me get you a drink. God knows, I need one…"

"What an outrageous thing to say. I'm not an irresponsible cad, but it's worse than that."

"What could be worse? She's pregnant and loves opera? By the way, you look like hell. Your hair's a mess, and there's grass on your pants."

"I feel like hell too. I do need a drink, a strong one. Got any brandy?"

"Always. Maybe we'll break in my new snifters. The ring to the glass is unbelievable…"

"I'm buggered, that's for sure," said Shu morosely as Saury handed him his drink. "I don't know what to do. I have to tell the twins. Although… technically, I don't owe Clara any explanation, do I? We don't have any binding commitments."

"This is sobering. Take a deep breath; a long slow sip of the brandy; and now go through the scenario one step at a time. You've met this girl – name?"

"Imelda Connor. She's Irish."

"Irrelevant. How long have you known her?"

"One weekend. Well, not really. I met her six months ago at Nikhil's, and she made quite an impression. The Irish part is not irrelevant."

"Then you met her again? You spent one weekend together and you think you are in love?"

"Something like that. Insane, isn't it?"

"Absolutely! Don't do anything drastic yet, you really don't know too much about her. I mean, what's the attraction? Brilliant mind or biting wit?"

"Neither. She's funny in a different sort of way, not the wit we're used to."

"Hmmm, that's disturbing. Let me start at the other end of the spectrum. Would you say she's the brightest bulb on the tree?"

"Why don't you come straight out and ask if she is stupid? Well, she is not. She's beautiful, genuine, happy, funny, authentic. Authentic: that's what she is."

"Authentic? That is not a word I associate with you and women. Has your whole life been a lie? You always said it was the intellect that attracted you to women. You know *nothing* about this girl."

"Enough to want to spend the rest of my life with her. God! How can I be such a fool? I had everything planned. I only have a year left at Faraday House. What am I going to do?" Shu said miserably, lifting his glass for a refill. "This is going to ruin my reputation."

"*Your* reputation? What about *mine*? Our reputations are irrevocably linked – not that that's ever been of any benefit to me, may I add."

Both Shu and Saury were getting drunk.

"Just go with the flow," said Saury. "You're too pragmatic, always wanting to be in control. I think maybe life is offering you a great lesson."

"What lesson?" Shu asked, even more despondent.

"Sometimes things happen that are beyond your control."

"I'll never be smug again. Who would have thought? A girl I just met. Knows nothing about India, anthropology, engineering, the world… Nothing is right here, nothing makes any sense. You know how she says Calcutta? 'Cal-coo-tah'! Really quite endearing. I've lost my bloody mind. I should leave."

He tried to get up but staggered back into the chair.

"I may have to spend the night. I'm in no condition to drive."

"Especially in that shoddy car of yours."

Saury picked up the bottle and sat down on the floor next to Shu.

"There may be no tomorrows, enjoy the moment while it lasts,

'Here with a loaf of bread beneath the bough

A jug of wine, a book of verse – and thou

Besides me – singing in the wilderness.'"

They drank and sang melancholy Bengali songs, until there was a loud banging on the door. "Will you shut the fuck up? It's three o'clock in the fucking morning," Saury's neighbour bellowed as he pounded the door.

"Care to join us?" Shu answered in his inebriated state.

"Bloody Indians!"

"Did you hear that? That bastard called us Indians," Shu exclaimed loudly. "We're Bengalis, you stupid son-of-a-bitch."

"Sorry, Jeffrey. Didn't realize how late it was," Saury cut in quickly.

"We're Bongs, you idiot! Here a Bong, there a Bong, everywhere a Bong-Bong!" Shu rolled around on the floor, laughing at his joke.

"Shut up, Shu. You'll get me evicted," Saury hissed at him.

"Noise? I'll show him real noise," Shu said, making mock boxing movements in the air.

"Just go to sleep," Saury said wearily and threw a blanket over him.

The next morning, a subdued Shu helped clean up.

"Sorry about last night. Who was that crazy bastard at the door?"

"That was Jeffrey Kline. Actually quite a nice chap, lives across the corridor in flat 8. I didn't know drinking made you so belligerent."

"I'm no fool. I knew there was a locked door between us," Shu replied. "I'm Gandhian: none of this eye-for-an-eye bullshit. But can you check the hall to see if Mr. Kline is lying in wait for me?"

12

London

Imelda and Shu's relationship intensified as they spent all their spare time together. They barely noticed the disapproving glances strangers would throw their way. Shu introduced Saury to Kathleen and the four of them often went out dancing, occasionally joined by Leslie, Saury's girlfriend.

Shu had often boasted of his equestrian skills, so Imelda thought it would be fun for the four of them to spend an afternoon riding at the club. It was a beautiful spring day when Shu and Saury arrived, dressed in khaki jodhpurs, brown leather riding boots, britches, high-cut black riding jackets with tails, and black velvet riding hats.

"You better be bloody good riders dressed like that," Imelda commented.

"Riding is in our blood. Our Maharajas played polo long before it became the rage here," Saury replied condescendingly.

"All I'm saying is: you better be bloody good riders to go out dressed like that."

"Sir Lawrence Bigelow asked if they were members of the equestrian team from Argentina," Kathleen told Imelda.

"And?"

"Before I could say a thing, Saury went over and shook his hand, introducing himself as 'Captain Saur-ree, team Argentina.' I was too mortified to speak."

"Holy Jesus! What if the Argentinian team shows up?"

"Don't worry, we'll do Argentina proud," said Saury. "I told Sir Lawrence I was very impressed by the club, and complemented the magnificent grounds. Fine fellow! I even invited him to Buenos Aires."

"I repeat," Imelda hissed through her teeth, "you better be damn good riders."

Shu had different concerns, and Saury's joviality was not helping the situation. He was mumbling about the horses being larger than the ones back in Darjeeling.

"I haven't ridden in years," he muttered.

Saury dismissed his worries with a wave of the hand. "Horses are horses. It's like swimming, once you learn how to swim, it doesn't matter how deep the water is."

Shu gallantly led the two larger horses over to Imelda and Kathleen.

"Black velvet riding hats." Imelda rolled her eyes at her sister.

Without much fanfare they got on, Imelda's apprehensions growing as Saury repeated, "I'll need to practice my trot and half-trot. Then I'll go for a twenty minute canter, and only after that shall I fearlessly go for the full gallop." The others rode silently.

"Just relax and enjoy yourself," Kathleen said calmly, sensing Shu's anxiety.

"Watch out for low-hanging branches, and don't for the life of you clench your knees too tight or the horse will bolt. Just do the controlling with the reins," Imelda instructed as they rode into the wooded section of the trails.

To any passing riders, Saury would exclaim "Viva Argentina!" loudly.

"English riders don't like so much exuberance, Saury," Imelda repeated.

Shu was heard intermittently huffing "bloody big horses" while Saury was euphoric. "Deportment is key to good riding. I say, these woods brings out the poet in me. I could have been a Browning." He kept up a constant commentary until Imelda called out, "There are a lot of low branches. We need to look out for them."

"Sorry, what?" Saury said, turning round in his saddle.

"Watch out!" Kathleen yelled, but it was too late.

A large branch hit him and knocked him right off the horse. He landed in the middle of some red flowering azalea bushes. For an instant there was deathly silence, then an explosion of laughter from Shu. Which startled his own horse. Which promptly bolted.

"Let go of the reins," Imelda screamed, "you'll hurt the horse."

"Hurt the bloody horse?" Shu gasped as he clung to the underbelly, finally letting go when the horse slowed down, landing in a pile of rotting leaves.

There they were, the equestrian champions of Argentina, one in an azalea bush, the other in a pile of damp leaves. It was a comical sight, and one that Kathleen and Imelda would never forget, tears streaming down their cheeks as they watched.

"That bloody horse ambushed me," said Saury as he brushed the dirt off his pants.

"Let's go back to the club house and get a drink," said Shu.

"A drink? We have to return the horses to the stables, cool and wipe them down and feed them first. Shouldn't take more than a couple of hours," pointed out Imelda.

"Don't you have people for that?" Saury asked astounded.

"Yes, we do. You're looking at them."

"But Sir Lawrence invited me to join him at the Rafters. I accepted for all of us," Saury persisted.

"I think he assumed you were on a visiting equestrian team," Imelda added, her voice shrill.

"For a moment, so did I," Saury mused.

As the months rolled by, Shu knew he had to face up to the twins' growing suspicions. He had been avoiding them, trying to put off the inevitable confrontation. They bided their time, watching him squirm in his lies. Clara knew, of course; she sensed it from the minute she saw Imelda and Shu together on the dance floor.

She also knew that Shu was a pragmatist. He would not jeopardize his high-living lifestyle for a girl who hadn't even been to college. She was well-primed when Shu left a note saying he wanted to discuss a few important matters with her and her sister. The meeting was exactly what he expected – awkward and embarrassing. They sat around the formal dining table not looking at each other, making stilted conversation with tight-lipped smiles.

"Maybe we could talk in the library," suggested Shu.

"That would be nice; we haven't had an intimate talk for ages. Would you care for a liqueur, darling?" said Clara, as she took his hand to lead him into the library.

"I'll get straight to the point. I guess lately, I have not been entirely honest with you."

"Not honest with us?" Clara said, her voice a couple of decibels higher than usual, as she exchanged exaggerated glances with Ada. They were not going to make it easy for him. Where was that smooth raconteur now?

"I realize that our relationship didn't seriously matter," he stumbled on.

"That's not true," Clara whispered, her face cracking into an ugly grimace.

"Well, I was feeling slightly confused about the situation between us, and then I met a girl."

"A girl? So that's what this whole thing is about. And I was with you when you met the girl, you lying bastard," Clara shot back.

"I met a girl, and I've fallen in love with her. I didn't mean to deceive you. It happened so fast. I just didn't know how to handle it. I hated every minute of the lying, it was bloody awful."

"Then don't do it," Clara suddenly blurted. "You cannot possibly give up everything for an unsophisticated girl like that."

"I won't try to explain. I probably couldn't anyway."

"You should have been honest. I thought we were friends," Ada said as Clara rushed out of the room, sobbing.

"I'm sorry; I didn't want it to come to this."

"We knew it inevitable, especially when our formal gowns were mysteriously moving in and out of our closets." Ada came over and gave Shu a hug.

"You must think I'm a rotten bastard," Shu said quietly. "I hope you can forgive me over time."

"You're already forgiven, Shu. I envy what you have, and so does Clara. We sensed this a long time ago. Clara was hoping it would all go away. Let me go and check on her. Take care, darling Shu, we will miss you terribly…"

13

London

Shu had put his life in order and now Imelda knew it was time for her to do the same. After having had no contact with her father and stepmother for over four years, she finally agreed to go to a Sunday supper at their new cottage at Putney Green. It had small rooms for the children to stay in when they visited. All her brothers were now working except for George. Imelda seldom visited, but when she did she stayed up late talking to her father, always reminiscing about the past. She was the only one who was not afraid to talk to him about her mother, make him repeat their love story and sing her favourite songs. She felt so close to him at those times, and the visits from his favourite child were the only thing he looked forward to in his retirement.

She realized Patrick would resist meeting Shu if he knew he was from India. She had heard him criticise the British for sending their men to a country that, to him, was uncivilised and had only typhoid and malaria to offer.

Imelda would bristle when he would make these blanket statements, but Patrick would shout back:

"You know nothing about people! I've lived and fought in the jungles of the Transvaal, hand to hand, and believe me, those savages would have eaten me alive if they got the chance."

His mind was coloured by his own experiences, and nothing Imelda said could change his belief that all brown- or black-skinned people were dangerous and were to be avoided.

Imelda rarely talked politics at home, and would listen quietly to her father and brothers talk about the atrocities carried out by both sides in Ireland, Patrick's dreams of returning slowly fading. In her naivety, Imelda believed that once her father met Shu, his prejudices would fall away. He would see him through her eyes. With great trepidation, she asked Patrick if she could bring over a special guest for Sunday supper.

Imelda had butterflies in her stomach when she woke upon the day of the visit, not only thinking about her father's response to Shu, but of Shu's reaction to her family. Shu might be at home conversing with professors and intellectuals, but it was the small talk that worried her.

"First there is Gerald. He is a machinist and loves Gaelic football. Cyril is in the British army, wants to be deployed to Ireland to fight against the IRA. He plays Gaelic football. Next is Patrick – Paddy – he's the real star of the family, plays for the Gaelic football league, and is a bartender at O'Leary's, and lastly there is Frank. Also in the army. Plays rugby for his squadron. Got all that?"

The O'Connors came from such a different world to Shu. He began to read up on all things Irish: Gaelic football and Irish rugby teams, their fans and star players. He frequented illegal gambling dens, betting on boxing, and winning twenty quid on a dog named 'Mel's Glory'. He was eager to share this new wealth of information with his friends.

"What the fuck is Gaelic football?" was Nikhil's reaction.

"It's like rugby," Shu replied.

"That's a game for hooligans, idiot!"

"I've discovered a new tribe, and none of my friends give a shit," Shu complained to his brother.

"Stop this Irish bullshit," Saury retorted, "enough is enough! You're making a complete arse of yourself. Have all your years at Faraday House and Cambridge come to this? I can't even laugh at you anymore. Just be yourself, or try to be like me."

On the fateful day, Shu dressed with care. A navy pinstripe suit with a red cravat. He checked himself in the mirror – and was horrified. He couldn't arrive for a family dinner dressed like this! All his clothes were far too smart and natty. In desperation, he called Tulu: his friend always managed to pull off the 'shabby casual' look; he would know what to do. Tulu's English wife, Barbara, picked up. Barbara had had her own share of problems from her family when she decided to marry an Indian. She listened to Shu's litany of woes and then burst out laughing.

"Shu, you are an idiot. Just wear your corduroys and relax. They aren't going to love you anyway. Believe me, clothes are the least of your problems."

Shu changed into fawn corduroys, a casual shirt, and a brown wool tweed jacket. On his way over he picked up a bottle of an expensive Irish whiskey for Patrick and a bunch of flowers for Nancy. He even borrowed Saury's car.

The minute Imelda introduced Shu to her family she realised

things were not going to go the way she had hoped. Patrick O'Connor glowered, his face red with suppressed rage. He was grim and silent throughout the meal, while Kathleen and Imelda babbled on giddily, trying to cover up their embarrassment.

"Father, did you know Shu came first in his class at Cambridge?" Kathleen exclaimed earnestly.

"He's an engineer at Faraday House," Imelda added.

"Well, 'tis a lucky day fer us he's here, isn't it?" Patrick retorted sarcastically.

"Paddy," Shu started, turning to one of the brothers, "I hear you are quite a star in the Gaelic football league. Do you have to be Irish to join?"

"It helps, but we let good players in from Scotland, Wales and England."

"Aren't Antrim the league leaders…?"

"Paddy, pass the brussel sprouts," Patrick cut in sharply, ending any semblance of a conversation.

Poor Shu, all his gallant efforts failed. There was so much distrust and anger at the table. Imelda was furious at her father's behaviour; she decided to speak to him.

After a quick thank you, Shu was glad to get outside and breathe freely. He took Imelda's hands, slowly pulled her to him and put his arms around her.

"Everything is going to be alright, just give the old man time. He's never met an Indian before."

"I'm so embarrassed I could die." Imelda's eyes filled with tears.

"Don't worry, darling. It will work itself out. Why don't you come back to London with me?"

"No, Shu. I have to stay here."

"Did you notice I ate a brussel sprout? What I do for you."

"I love you too," she murmured as she kissed him. Kathleen came outside to tell Imelda that her father wanted to talk to her.

"I have a few words for him," she replied angrily.

"Imelda, please let me drive you back to your flat..." Shu pleaded.

"He's right. Dad's in a frightful temper," Kathleen whispered, her voice trembling,

"I'm not afraid of my own father. I want to talk to him." Imelda replied defiantly.

Shu hugged her once and she watched him drive away.

Her heart was beating fast as she walked back. She was not going to let her father insult Shu. He did not scare her with his bully tactics.

Patrick had thrown everyone out of the room and was pacing back and forth like a caged animal. He would move heaven and earth before he let a 'native' make his way into his daughter's heart. He couldn't believe that he was so brazen. Dressed like a toff, talking like a Brit, acting like that. As though he was entitled to be treated as an equal. The nerve of it.

Kathleen had raced upstairs to the bedroom, and put a pillow over her head. She knew Imelda was fearless and would not shut up. She was right.

Downstairs, Imelda faced her father squarely, and got right to the point.

"I don't think you were very gentlemanly, Dad. Shu was a guest in our house, and you did not treat him right," she said angrily as she entered.

"Guest? You've got nerve bringing that sort of person here," he snapped back.

"What sort of person do you mean?"

"A bloody native! Bringin' a fuckin' uncivilised savage who thinks he's bloody British into MY house. Jesus! Next you'll be bringing in a fuckin' wog."

"Name-calling, that's all you ever do! 'Tis so easy to call different people names; you know there're names for people like you too. Ignorant is one."

"Are yeh calling your own father ignorant?" he bellowed.

"Yes! Ignorant and a racist! What right do you have to call him an uncivilised savage? You don't know him, do you? Did you give him a chance? Did you say one polite word to him, or thank him for the gifts he brought? Do you even care how he feels about your daughter, your own flesh and blood, huh? D'you care about how I feel about him?" Hot tears streamed down Imelda's face as she broke into sobs. "Do you care about anything other than your hate, father? What has he done except love me? He is more civilised than the lot of you and I…"

With that, Imelda felt the full force of Patrick's wrath. He slapped her across the face so hard that she was lifted off her feet and came crashing down on the floor, hitting her head on the wooden floorboard.

"Bloody son-of-a-bitch thinks he's fuckin' British just 'cause he's been to Cambridge? I forbid you from seeing him again, understand? Yer never to see that Indian bastard again! Never!" he screamed, his face scarlet, the veins on his neck throbbing like they were about to burst.

"But Da," she sobbed, as she held her hand to her burning cheek, "I love him."

She heard the front door slam as Patrick stalked out the house. He had never hit any of his children as adults. As she lay slumped on the floor, her head and face throbbing with pain, she heard quiet footsteps approach and felt, Kathleen's arms around her.

"Why don't you ever listen, Mel? Now look what he's gone and done," Kathleen admonished her, her own face swollen and red from weeping.

"I hate him. I hate all of them. I wish Ma was here, she'd have never let him do this to me. I know why God took her away, he did not deserve her," Imelda blubbered between sobs.

"He'll go to hell, for sure," Kathleen added, as she pressed a cold wet towel to Imelda's face.

"They can all go to hell. After all I've done for them, not one of my brothers said a word to protect me, not one!" She screamed loudly for them to hear.

"They're afraid of Dad too, Mel. We all are, when he gets into a rage."

"Well I'm not. I can stand up to him anytime. Let's see what he can do to me. I don't care anymore, he is an ignorant man. An adulterer. That's what they all said, and now I believe them. He made Ma sick, he made our Mother die. She sobbed as Kathleen led her to her room. "I would have done anything for him. Anything!"

"I think leaving Ireland did that. He left his heart in Kilworth," Kathleen said sadly, trying to calm Imelda.

"Heart? He has no heart. His heart is a hole filled with ugly hate. Why didn't they just shoot him? Him and my gutless brothers."

Exhausted, she threw herself down on the bed.

"I'm going to keep seeing Shu. He mustn't know what happened. Kathleen will you take a letter to him tomorrow? I'll tell him I can't see him for a few days."

"You won't be able to. Have you see your face?" Kathleen brought a mirror for Imelda to look into.

"Oh my God."

"I'll get some more cold water for your head."

The O'Connor household was very quiet for the next few days. No one had seen the full fury of Patrick's rage before; they were all terrified to say anything that might set him off again.

Patrick was inconsolable, out drinking every night, sharing his angst with strangers. At home, he was unrelenting, forbidding Imelda from leaving the house until she apologized and swore never to see 'that Indian' again.

But Imelda was as strong-headed as her father. Defiantly, she stayed in her room with that mutinous expression on her face. Last time he'd seen that, Patrick recalled, was when he demanded she call his new wife, 'Mrs. O'Connor'. He'd lost that battle.

Shu was subdued and introspective: he was becoming increasingly aware of the sacrifices they both would have to make if they were to stay together. Imelda, he knew, could be very obstinate and he couldn't see her compromising to suit the expectations of his conservative family. He loved her and what he loved most was her spontaneity. She brought with her an exuberance and honesty that could not be contained: something that would not go over well with his mother. She would expect deference and compliance from her daughter-in-law… but for the moment, Shu's thoughts were consumed only with Imelda. He felt helpless against the primitive outbursts of her father. He cautioned her to remain calm, and try to maintain a little bit of order over their world, which was rapidly spinning out of their control.

For a few days, Kathleen acted as messenger, taking their passionate letters back and forth. But what Shu didn't realise was that Imelda was house-bound not only because of her father's threats, but due to her face: her right eye, in particular, was swollen and bruised.

"I feel that being incarcerated because of your relationship with me is too big a price to pay. Maybe a serious reconsideration of our situation is the realistic path to follow. It's unbearable to be the cause of your pain," he wrote.

On the third day, Kathleen and Shu were coming out of a pub and heading towards the underground when suddenly a group of thugs jumped out of an alleyway, knocking Shu to the ground. They pummelled him with kicks and punches, until he fell, unconscious, to the ground. By the time Kathleen's screams attracted a crowd, they had fled.

Shu was rushed to the hospital and immediately put into intensive care, where he drifted in and out of consciousness. When he awoke he was in a white room surrounded by a worried family. Every inch of his body ached.

"Am I dead?" he whispered, in pain.

Shu didn't remember much: just Kathleen's scream.

"You were attacked by a gang of hoodlums," Sir Dhiren informed him. "Don't worry, the police chief has assured me the perpetrators will be brought to justice. Did you recognize any of the assailants?"

"It was so fast," Shu replied feebly.

"Rest now. I have sent a telegram to your parents telling them you will be moving in with me. These roaming gangs are getting out of hand. But no nephew of mine is going to be attacked on the streets of London without severe consequences." He left with the police chief and an entourage of guards.

The doctor listed Shu's injuries: concussion, two cracked ribs (one of which had punctured his lung), and some internal bleeding and bruises in the stomach and on the legs. A few days in the hospital for observation were ordered.

"You took quite a beating, young man."

Saury was fuming and could hardly contain himself.

"This was not a random act. Kathleen called me in hysterics. She's sure it was her brothers who attacked you."

"They ambushed us from behind. How could she see?" Shu replied half-heartedly.

"Bullshit! She's not worth it, Shu, you have to end it. We can't associate with people like that."

"We'll discuss this later. I don't want Mama babu to know. God, don't make me talk," he moaned.

A few days later Nikhil, Bappa, Robin and Tulu Sen came to visit. They were quiet and apprehensive.

"What the shit happened?" Bappa asked in astonishment.

"Can't remember a thing. Felt like Chicken Little – 'The sky is falling, the sky is falling!' Saw real stars though. Bloody hilarious," said Shu.

"If only I had been there," Saury added seriously.

"Please don't make me laugh," Shu groaned.

"Did you get a shot in?" Nikhil asked half-kidding. "Obviously your tango moves didn't help much."

"Bastard! I crumbled like a cream puff and hit the ground before the first blow." They all had a hearty laugh.

Shu stayed in the hospital a few days before moving into his uncle's mansion in Aldwych. He was interviewed by the police chief a couple of times, and each time he insisted he knew nothing.

It had been over a week since he had been in contact with Imelda. He saw the reality of what would happen to her if she continued their relationship. He had four months left before he had to leave for India, and he was beginning think all his dreams would soon unravel.

During her interview with the police, Kathleen had collapsed in shock. Confused and dazed as she was, she could still clearly recall a voice from the chaos that had surrounded Shu's beating; her brother Paddy's voice.

She could not tell Imelda. That would be the final straw. When she returned to the house she told Imelda some fictitious tale about Shu having to rush to Cambridge.

As the days wore on Imelda began to get more and more despondent.

"He has abandoned me. He would never not write for one whole week," Imelda sobbed. "I think something bad has happened."

Kathleen decided she could not do this to her sister. She sat Imelda down and told her the whole story, blow by blow.

"How could you let them do that to Shu?" she screamed at Kathleen.

"It was over in the blink of an eye."

"All this time you knew he was hurt?"

Imelda immediately blamed Patrick and Nancy as the instigators.

She refused to eat. She hated her whole family. She should

have been at Shu's side. Silently, she packed her few belongings and went to bed. In the middle of the night, she woke up a sleepy Kathleen.

"Kathy, I'm leaving, I'm never coming back." She wept inconsolably, for if there was one person she loved most in the whole world, it was her little sister.

"Please don't leave me, Mel," a frightened Kathleen pleaded.

"I have to go to Shu, I just have to." She hugged her, holding her close.

"You are not leaving without me," said Kathleen. And there was no talking her out of it.

"We'll slip out the window," whispered Imelda. "I feel much better now that you're coming."

Imelda wrote a note to her father telling him she knew what he had done, and that she was never going to forgive him.

"Even though I hate you with all my heart, and will never see you and your wicked wife again, I pray God forgives you and saves your evil soul."

She and Kathleen made a rope out of the sheets and tied it to the foot of the bed. Imelda let Kathleen down first, and Kathleen landed in the rosebush under the window. As Kathleen was untangling herself Imelda threw the two small suitcases out the window, hitting her sister and knocking her over. She lay there waiting breathlessly as Imelda slid down – straight into the same bush. Kathleen could barely breathe from laughing.

"Idiot! I could have killed myself! I'm all scratched and bleeding, and I've torn my favourite frock," hissed Imelda angrily.

"I could have been killed too," Kathleen protested.

"You know it's your fault. Ouch! Help me take out these bloody thorns.

They waited breathlessly to see if any lights came on, then slowly picked up their bags and hobbled quietly up the gravel pathway toward the Underground.

As they waited at the station for the first train, Imelda said, "You know Kath, we've had a lot of wretchedness in our lives. We lost our mother, now our dad, our brothers, our animals, our farm. I remember we were all so happy once. Where did all that happiness go?"

"It left with Ma." Kathleen said sadly.

"But we have each other," Imelda said firmly as she put her arm over Kathleen's shoulder, drawing her close. "And Ma is an angel watching over us. If you believe that with all your heart nothing can ever harm you."

14

London

Imelda arrived at the Solicitor General's mansion looking a ghost of her former self. Outside the gate she put her suitcase down, straightened her back, patted down her dress, ran her fingers through her hair and looked at Kathleen nervously.

"Do I look alright? My stomach is so full of butterflies."

Kathleen looked at her sister's scratched arms and legs, her red puffy eyes, her swollen jaw and her torn dress. "You look grand," she said as she moved Imelda's dress around to hide the ripped side.

"The worst thing that can happen is Shu will tell me he can't see me anymore, and we will turn around and leave. That won't be too difficult."

A guard escorted them through the courtyard and rang the doorbell. A servant answered and led them into a little enclave at the side of the entrance hallway.

Shu had been brooding the night before in his room, writing and rewriting a letter to tell Imelda it was over. He and Saury were in complete agreement that this relationship was no longer viable. His mood had been dark and ominous since the incident, and he had retreated from his friends. He was still in bed when informed that a young lady was waiting to see him. Gingerly, he came down the steps.

He noticed the hat in her hand, and then the suitcases by the entrance. Her red hair was dishevelled and her dress was in tatters. There were scratches up and down her arms and legs. Her face was ghostly white, and her normally sparkling eyes were filled with dread. As they stood facing each other, a strange thing happened. Shu, bruised and bandaged, depressed and full of apprehensions, suddenly felt the weight of the world being lifted off his shoulders. He had no more decisions to make. Just seeing Imelda had, in one instant, wiped away every shred of doubt he ever had. He broke into a wide smile that lit up his entire face. He knew then that he and Imelda were going to be together for the rest of their lives. Imelda hesitated for a second, then let out a yell so joyous that even Kathleen, standing a few feet behind, with all her fears, felt as though life was going to be alright. Imelda and Shu slowly stepped into each other's arms, knowing they belonged together.

This was the defining moment of Shu and Imelda's lives. They both knew that there was no turning back. They just stood there holding each other close, not saying a word.

Finally, he unfolded his arms and led her to a large chair.

"Darling, what have they done to you?"

She was so relieved to be in his presence, she collapsed into the chair, her body racked with sobs. She tried to explain what had happened, but she was incoherent as her words just tumbled out, making no sense. Shu simply held her: there was no need to say anything. Imelda's life as she knew it was over. Realising she had given up everything she considered important to be with him overwhelmed Shu.

When Sir Dhiren came down for breakfast, he found them asleep on the chair, with Kathleen sleeping nearby. Imelda was on Shu's lap, her head nestled against his shoulder. They both looked so young and vulnerable that it touched his heart.

Shu confided in his uncle and aunt, telling them he and Imelda had decided to get married. Sir Dhiren listened and questioned them, cleaning and refilling his pipe a few times. Mrs. Mitra, Saury and their cousins Monu and Bashi joined them, while Kathleen stood by.

"Imelda, how old are you?" Sir Dhiren asked Imelda.

"I'm going to be eighteen in a few months."

"Good, then you'll be of age, and we won't have legal problems," he said.

His wife, on the other hand, was taken aback that Imelda was so young. "O Ma, she's still a bachha. Too young to have to make such big decisions."

Nevertheless, she left the room and when she returned it was with a big smile on her face. She took Imelda's hand in hers and placed a couple of gold bangles in it.

"This is a small gift for you. Welcome to our family." She gently touched Imelda under the chin and kissed her forehead.

"They're so beautiful," breathed Kathleen.

"They better not be from my dowry," Monu cried in mock dismay.

"Shu, I don't remember you asking me to marry you… I thought you had to talk to your parents first," Imelda said.

"I am worried about Ma," Shu replied, suddenly serious.

"Don't worry. I know my sister," Sir Dhiren reassured

Imelda. "After a grand show of resistance, you will be welcomed into our family."

"What about his father?" Imelda asked meekly.

"Amarendra? Don't let his crusty exterior fool you, he's a pussycat. Just tell him his birds are the smartest in the British Empire and you'll have him eating out of your hand. Shu is glib enough to get around him."

"For my renowned superficiality, glibness and general ability to win over anyone, I have my grand old uncle to thank," Shu said raising his imaginary glass.

Mrs. Mitra had a few thin bangles on her arm; she took two off, and motioned to a glum Kathleen. "Come here, let me put these on you. They may be a bit small, but I will squeeze them on."

"Oh no, I didn't mean I wanted one," Kathleen exclaimed.

"You're my youngest daughter now, so start listening," she said lightheartedly.

Sir Dhiren turned to the Nepali housekeeper serving them.

"Ram Bahadur, these girls are now my daughters, their every wish is your command."

"Yes sir," he said, with that particular nod of the head that Imelda would get used to in India.

All this talk of marriage was affecting Saury and Kathleen in different ways. As Kathleen listened to the joyful banter she began to realise that she was going to lose her sister, and the thought of life without Imelda was unthinkable.

Saury, on the other hand, had his own secret agenda. He was in a serious relationship with Leslie Edwards, and they had become inseparable. She loved all his eccentric quirks, and was never bothered by his constant tardiness. Saury thought Shu's marriage to Imelda would break the ice for him and make it easier for Leslie to be accepted by his parents.

Shu received his Doctorate with honours and special citations. He was almost twenty-six, and he was returning to Calcutta with high hopes and enormous optimism. He left Imelda in the care of his uncle and brother. He promised to send for her as soon as he got a job.

Shu threw a grand farewell party at Sir Dhiren's place. Along with many of his teachers, all his friends from Cambridge and Faraday House were present. They were an elite group, all graduating at about the same time with incredible career prospects ahead. Sir Dhiren and Lady Mitra, Saury, Imelda, Kathleen, Leslie and an assortment of friends came to the dock to bid him farewell. As festive as the occasion was, Shu was sad to leave England. He loved the freedom it offered him. His seven years in the country had had a deep impact on his thinking and behaviour.

Nikhil Chowdury and Bappa Mallik were returning on the same P&O ocean liner, and were sharing his cabin. Tulu Sen had returned with Barbara and their daughter Sheila a few weeks before, and Robin Mitter and Saury had another year to go.

Shu's greatest mission would be convincing his parents to accept his decision to marry Imelda. He had sworn his uncle and aunt to secrecy until he had broached the subject himself. As they set sail, he found himself exhilarated by the challenges he would be facing. One thing he knew for sure: nothing would prevent him from marrying Imelda Connor; he would do it with, or without, his parents' blessings.

15

Calcutta

There was much joy and celebration on Shu's return to Calcutta. He had been away seven long years and much had changed in the Bose household. There had been two tumultuous weddings, the first being Menu, Shu's middle sister's wedding to Suchandra Nath Mitra, affectionately known as Nalu, the son of a rich zamindar from Chorbagan.

Chorbagan was a business district in the older section of north Calcutta. This was where ambitious Indian entrepreneurs would go for loans. The streets bustled with hordes of traders, rickshaws, and bicycles weaving through horses, cows and an occasional car.

Menu was happily absorbed into a large conservative joint family. They lived in a four-storey complex built around a square courtyard. Generations from great-grandparents to grandchildren lived in the small flats around the courtyard. For outsiders, the place was chaotic; screaming, shouting children, followed by mothers, their heads covered by white saris with red borders, unlike the refined atmosphere of the Bose household.

The second event was Chotto's wedding to Nirmal Roychowdhary. The two sons-in-laws were very different. Nirmal was highly educated and worked with the elite Indian Foreign Service. He was considered a big catch, for the foreign service was known to recruit only the best and brightest of India's educated young men.

But the family had been struck by tragedy, too. Dhebu and Himanshu's son Tonu died of typhoid at the age of six. There was a pall over the family who had lost their only grandson, and the light dimmed in Dhebu's eyes. Even though her spirit was reignited a few years later with the birth of her daughter Archana, she now had a constant sadness.

The events of the last seven years had changed the atmosphere of the household. The baboochi was a little more cantankerous, but still held court over the servants, deferring only to Ashu and Boroma. The house at Harish Mukherjee Road had swelled to palatial proportions with the addition of a third floor.

Himanshu and Dhebu had half of the third floor, with a separate entrance along the east side of the building. The other half was for Saury to move into when he returned. Amarendra and Pankajini had their living quarters on the second floor, while the ground floor housed the grand hall where they did all their formal entertaining, as well as Amarendra's private office, library and bird sanctuary.

They were a typical Bengali family, and the idea that their children would move out and live independent lives was completely alien to Amarendra and Pankajini. Theirs was a generation that wanted to appear modern and forward-thinking, but whose traditional values were so deeply engrained that it was impossible for them to change. The homes had all the ambiance of the European upper class residence, but the Indian setting made many of the artifacts look contrived and out of place.

The house was bordered on one side by a courtyard and on the other by a large lawn and garden. Two large iron gates gave entry, monitored at all times by a chowkidar. The gates opened onto a wide cobblestone driveway that led directly to a six-car garage at the back of the property.

Adjacent to the garage, built like barracks, were eight to ten servants quarters. An eight-foot brick wall, camouflaged by bright flowering bougainvillea and jasmine, wrapped around the property. There was an Italian marble fountain in the centre of the lawn, with three tiers carved with intricate flowers and foliage and Venus gracing the top. The holding pool housed Amarendra's tropical goldfish. Along the wall were clusters of big trees: mango, neem and champa. These provided a canopy of shade to protect the flowers from the brutal summer sun.

From the garden, a dozen white marble steps led up to the main entryway of the house: a carved wooden double door with large brass lion-head knockers. The door opened onto an oval foyer. Here an ostentatious table with a prominently displayed guest book and an ornately carved grandfather clock greeted you. A corridor led to the Bose's expansive living room. There were two seating arrangements around separate Persian carpets. The dining area had two huge Venetian crystal chandeliers hanging over an oval teak dining table. Everything was on a grand scale; the chandeliers seemed doubled in oversized mirrors that lined one side of the wall.

Across the hall was 'the bird sanctuary,' to which only Anshu had access. There were half a dozen cages for Amarendra's birds hanging from the high ceilings and numerous circular stands with attached toys for their amusement. In fact, all Amarendra's personal rooms had circular bird stands in the corners. He was never without at least one bird on his person or nearby.

In anticipation of Shu's arrival, Boroma had asked Chotto to help her get a suite of rooms ready for him. She decided that they would furnish the bedroom with basic furniture, and let Shu pick his own personal pieces. She chose blue and taupe with accents of brown and gold – safe colours for a sophisticated man – and picked out a traditional four-poster bed. The posts were carved with spiralling curves and polished a dark mahogany.

The second floor had always been Boroma's domain, the control centre from where all the daily activities of the children and servants were monitored. This was where visiting friends and family were entertained. Though the floors were Italian marble, the furniture was much more casual. There were formal portraits of grandparents and family groups. Here the children took their music and singing lessons, as well as their dreaded English elocution classes. To the left of the staircase was Amarendra and Boroma's bedroom.

Up here, Boroma showed her preference for familiar Indian comforts. The four-poster bed had long bolsters and small sausage-shaped pillows. The antique dressing table had little silver containers for red sindoor, kajol and perfumed oil. There was a silver brush set with a silver hand-mirror, and a box with thin black nets and two-pronged hairpins, used to keep her bun in place.

The king-size four-poster bed dominated the room. But

it was the small cot covered with a mattress, an embroidered bedcover and a smattering of brightly coloured pillows that was Boroma's command post. Here she rested, drank numerous cups of tea, examined the fish and vetted the vegetables, watched the dhobi count the towels and sheets, all the while talking on the phone, stopping only to issue an order to anyone who walked by.

The room also contained two large steel almirahs. Boroma's many keys were tied to the end of her sari in a 'ghucha' which she wore slung over one shoulder.

The puja room was a small room off the main bedroom. Here on a low table, Boroma had set up a shrine to the goddesses Durga and Kali.

Her day began with an oil massage from a young girl, thin as a rail, with arms of steel. After a quick bath, Boroma prepared for her day. She sat on a cushion placed before the shrine. First she bathed the gods, then arranged the freshly picked flowers, and lastly lit the wicks of the diyas. The kids were expected to go in and bow before the shrine every day but it was a rushed formality. Fruit or sweets were placed on a plate, and passed around as 'prashad' or blessed food, for everyone to eat.

When Shu returned to Calcutta after seven years abroad, his mother reverted to treating him like a child, peeling his fruit and cutting his toast into quarters.

"Ma," Shu went into her room one morning, a little exasperated, "I don't want my oranges cut up into minuscule pieces and apples chopped and peeled. Don't you have better things to do?"

"Okay baba. I forgot."

"And I'm sick of omelettes and aloo chops. Can't the baboochi make anything continental?"

"So you've become an English sahib? Baboochi has cooked for you all your life so don't get high and mighty with him. He is very sensitive and I don't want him to get upset. It would ruin our meals for the rest of the week." Nevertheless, his mother sent for the cook.

"Partho," Shu started tactfully, "you know the only thing I missed in England was your cooking."

"Thank you sahib," the cook replied.

"Can you get bacon or ham, or sausage? Maybe baked beans?"

"Pujalal, that chap who works for Beasley Sahib, can show me where to by those. Also chicken stew."

"Good! Once in a while I would like a ham sandwich."

"No pig or beef in this house! Have you seen what they eat? What will all my friends think?" Boroma moaned.

Shu was growing anxious as he waited for the right moment to broach the subject of his marriage to Imelda. He decided to wait until after the big homecoming banquet that was being arranged in his honour had concluded. All his relatives and friends had been invited, with special attention to families with daughters of marriageable age. There was an extra buzz of excitement as people ran around cleaning and shining every inch of the house.

"Hey, Ashu, what's going on? Why all this bloody fuss?" Shu casually asked.

"This bloody fuss is for the Princess of Harish Mukherjee Road," he replied hissing through his teeth.

"What's wrong with you? Haven't I told you not to say the word 'bloody'?"

"You say it, so it should be okay."

"No, not okay! Don't try to brown-nose me with all your bullshit or I'll bring your wife into town," Shu huffed angrily.

"I'll choose the most phorsha one for you."

Shu was not amused at Ashu's jokes: he knew they had a ring of truth in them. He went looking for his mother.

She was going over the menu with one of the chefs. Gravely, he pulled her aside. "Ma, I want to talk to you, privately."

She excused herself and followed him into the next room.

"I haven't been back more than a couple of months, and I believe you are inviting all your friends who have daughters of a marriageable age tonight?"

"What rubbish. Has Ashu been telling you these lies? I have invited *all* our relatives and friends. If some of them have daughters, shall I tell them not to come? Anyway, what's the harm in meeting a few girls; maybe you will find someone…"

"That's my personal life. It's got nothing to do with you."

"Do you want to upset me before the big event?"

"I don't much care. I'm going to talk to Baba, this nonsense has to stop."

He stormed out, leaving her standing in the middle of the room grumbling.

"Personal life! Who does he thinks he is?"

Shu was dismayed that his parents seemed unaware of how inappropriate this appeared to him. He did not have a job. He had not even talked to his parents about what he wanted to do with his life.

Gathering courage, he knocked apprehensively on the heavy teak door of his father's study.

Amarendra was relaxing and smoking a pipe surrounded by

mahogany bookshelves filled with law books and Indian and English Classics. Shu was again struck at how impressive his father appeared in the luxurious ambiance of his study. Next to his armchair was the stand for his favourite white cockatoo, Shona. The bowl of nuts on the table was to encourage the temperamental bird to talk and dance. He had Shona on his desk; Ruby, the red and blue macaw, on the stand; and on a leash was Bhalu, his beloved black panther.

Shu made small talk about the new cockatoos.

"They are macaws and parrots," Amarendra corrected him.

He reminisced about the time he had persuaded his father to buy Ruby.

"Biggest mistake of my life. That bird hasn't shut up since."

"Care for some tea?" Amarendra asked.

"With some of the fresh shondesh and murmurra?"

"Murmurra?" Amarendra laughed. "Always your favourite."

"I thought Bhalu and Kalu were going back to the zoo."

"Sadly I have to give them up, can't put them back in the forest, they have no fear of humans." Amarendra was eyeing Shu closely. There was an uncomfortable silence as both father and son sized up the situation. Then Shu took a deep breath.

"Baba, I have been told that this home coming party is really a camouflaged bazaar, set up for me to pick out a prospective bride."

"Has Ashu been doing his usual pot-stirring? I want my son to be introduced to society: what better way than a banquet held here in the grand hall?"

"What a relief. Well, maybe this is as good a time as any to tell you that I have met an Irish girl who I intend to marry as soon as I find a job."

"And when was all this decided?"

"Mama babu has met her and given his approval."

"You were sent to England to study. There was no talk about you deciding to marry some girl we know nothing about."

"I was waiting to get a job before I asked for Ma and your blessing. My intention was to concentrate on my studies when I was abroad, but sometimes things happen over which we have no control," Shu tried to explain.

"One always has full control over the direction of one's life. I don't want any histrionics over this."

"There won't be any histrionics from me. I am telling you this because I want your assurance that you will talk to Ma, or I will not attend and make a fool myself."

Amarendra raised his voice slightly in controlled anger. "What do you mean you will not attend? Do you think I spent a fortune sending you to the best colleges in the world to have you return and tell me what you will or will not do? You will attend the banquet on Saturday. Your mother and I have made a great effort to invite all our friends and relatives. Surely, you don't seriously think we can accept you marrying someone without knowing anything about her family background? I'm the head of this household, you will need my approval to get married. So end this foolish talk: my decision is final."

Shu felt a slight flutter in the pit of his stomach, his temples throbbed as he slowly stood up and, in a voice that even he did not recognize, repeated, "Your decision is final? YOUR decision?" The words were spat out, dripping with sarcasm. "You will decide who I marry? Where I work? Where I live? Who declared you to be an omnipotent all-knowing god? Forgive me if I seem insolent," he bowed in mock obeisance, "but I thought you had sent me to England to be educated, to be independent and not to – I think your exact words were – 'follow the mindless herd', so forgive my confusion. Let me make myself clear, Baba, my decision is as final as yours. I will attend the party, but only because it is too late to back out. It will be the last of your parties that I will attend. And only I will decide who to marry."

He strode from the room a liberated man. He had stood up to his father! He passed Ashu bringing in a tray with tea and snacks. "I'll have them in my room," he snapped as he picked up the bowl of murmurra without missing a step.

Amarendra couldn't hide a smile when a worried Ashu peeked inside.

"Come in, Ashu. My son has become a man. I should be very proud."

16

London

"I'm not sure I can do it," Imelda confided to Kathleen. "I can't imagine my life without you."

Kathleen had gone through this conversation many times. Without Shu's constant reassurance, Imelda was starting to waiver about her decision to join him in India.

After Shu left she felt so alone, as though a part of her was always missing. Shu had not only taken her heart with him, but also her spirit. Her vibrant personality was subdued by the grim reality of what lay ahead. She hardly knew anything about India, and even less about Shu's family.

In the movie theatres, the newsreels showed footage of Gandhi, "That naked brown man," as Wilson Churchill had sneered. She wrote to Shu about him.

"Gandhi is a great man," he wrote back, "listen to what he says. He is the only man that can get India its freedom without a bloodbath."

"What do you think of Gandhi?" she asked Kathleen earnestly. Kathleen did not reply.

"Shu thinks he's brilliant," Imelda continued.

"He's just plum-ugly! No other word for it, plum-ugg-ly"
Kathleen repeated.

"Don't talk like that. It's not polite."

"Well, stop asking me all these silly questions. Do you want
me to lie?"

"Suppose I catch some incurable disease and die?"
continued Imelda, morosely. "You wouldn't be able to come to
my funeral. I'll have no family at my funeral. I'll be dead and
alone." She started to cry.

"Shu will be there, he'll be family. Your body would rot if it
was sent back."

"You're not helping me one bit!"

"Why go if it's so dangerous?"

"Because of Shu. My plan is to bring him back to London.
You will come and visit us, won't you, when I send the ticket?"

"Of course I'll come. Saury has promised to send me a ticket
too, so I can come twice. Stop worrying."

"But if I do die, you must promise to bring my ashes back
and bury them next to Mother's. I want to be buried in Ireland."

"Brilliant, we'll be united in death no matter where we die,"
Kathleen retorted. "Drama queen!"

"I gave Ma my word I'd look after you."

The sisters shared a one-bedroom flat in London. Simply
furnished, the knitted throws on the chairs doubled up as
blankets and foot warmers. There was a gas meter that had to be
fed coins to keep the place warm. The only thing they splurged
on were the white lace curtains which reminded them of home,
along with the Bridget's cross, a family portrait with their
mother, and a small pot of dying shamrocks on the window sill.

Imelda continued to work at the stables and at the bar. Kathleen had a year left before graduating from school; she made money working weekends as a salesgirl for a clothing store owned by two sisters, Aileen and Nan. They adored Kathleen and practically adopted her.

Kathleen was a caring and dutiful daughter and did occasionally visit Patrick and Nancy. She also kept up with her brothers who were all working and seldom visited their father.

Patrick O'Connor became more withdrawn and isolated as time went on. Imelda was never far from his thoughts. Ever since she had left, the Irish curse took over his life. He drank like a man obsessed, spending hours every day at the local pub. It was normal for him to be thrown out, too drunk to remember the way home as he staggered along the streets singing songs about Ireland's freedom. His British neighbours, exasperated with his nightly sojourns, often hurled hurtful epitaphs after him.

"Shut up, you Irish laggard!"

"Go back to Ireland, and plough your fucking potatoes!"

When sober, he was morose. No one dared talk about Imelda.

Both father and daughter, stubborn as mules, were determined to wait for the other to make the first move. Whenever Kathleen returned from a visit, Imelda pumped her for details. She missed her home and her large family and was eager for signs that they thought about her. She yearned to belong again to that rowdy clan, fighting over the last morsel of cake. Now, she was reduced to lingering over every precious bit of information that Kathleen bought back. It always ended with the dreaded question, "Did he ask about me?", and Imelda would go to bed crying under her blanket.

"I think you should make your peace with Dad before you leave, or one of you will surely die," Kathleen told Imelda gravely.

"Well, it's not going to be me," a defiant Imelda replied.

17

Calcutta

The house in Calcutta was filled with frenzied activity the week before the gala event. The floors were polished, the fans given a new coat of paint, the chandeliers polished until they sparkled. Huge flowering plants were strategically placed to hide the entrances to the kitchen and pantry. Boroma was rushing about making sure no detail was left unattended, pacifying quarrelling caterers, directing the florists and boosting the cook's ego.

The chauffeured cars began arriving around seven o'clock. With the background music and the tinkling of champagne flutes, one had to talk loudly to be heard. Weaving their way through the guests, white-gloved waiters carried silver trays laden with mouthwatering hors d'oeuvres. Shu finally succumbed and got into the spirit of the evening. He made his entrance around eight, charming and flirtatious.

"Why Laila, when did you grow into such a lovely lady?"

"Sheila Roy, I'd have recognized you anywhere."

He helped himself to many glasses of champagne. The younger women hovered around him, hanging on his every word. He took on an extra air of importance, his accent becoming more and more British as the evening wore on. His 'oh, how maaarvlous' was beginning to wear thin as his friends looked on in amusement. The surprise of the evening was Mira, a friend of Chotto's.

"Well, look who's back. My childhood heartthrob," she exclaimed with a slight sway and an expansive smile. "I'm a famous movie star now you know," she said, spilling some of her champagne.

"That's not hard to believe."

"Still the silly joker," she giggled, as she tried to touch his nose with her finger.

As his parents looked on, the tension and acrimony of the past week dissipated. Everything would be alright.

Reality came crashing down on Shu the next morning when he found himself unable to get out of bed. His head felt like it was about to explode as he lay there with the curtains drawn, cursing himself.

Boroma, on the other hand, was elated. She knew she would be inundated with invitations for lunches and teas. She forgave her son for his threats and pointed silences.

Once he was able think straight, Shu decided on a new strategy: to make his father his accomplice.

His parents' marriage never lived up to either of their expectations. His father was an academic, a scholar and a philosopher. He wanted a wife with whom he could discuss books, ideas and world events. By contrast, Boroma's greatest aspiration was to run an efficient household. She loved Tagore. She hated Shakespeare. But most of all she hated his birds. "It's as if they shit gold," as she used to say to her sister.

It really was not so much the birds (or the panthers, or the peacocks) themselves; it was that they took precedence over her. The first thing Amarendra did when he returned from court was let the panthers out of their cage, get out the birds and relax in the garden with a cup of tea and a plate of fruit. He rarely showed his wife any such consideration.

Shu felt sorry for his parents, trapped in the sad social arrangement they had inherited. His mother was a beautiful woman, yet her limpid brown eyes seldom sparkled with joy. She always covered her head in front of her husband, never addressed him by his name and seldom looked him in the face. She deferred to his every wish, never contradicting him, for that would be considered audacious for a woman. But for all that, they had the most civil of relationships, and were the envy of many of their friends.

The evening after the party, Amarendra was in an expansive mood. He invited Shu to his study for a drink. He stood there, aloof and distant, wreathed in a haze of tobacco smoke, Bulbul the grey Amazonian parrot on his arm. Shu felt a wave of unexpectedly sympathy for the old man, so forlorn in his isolation. He was seeing his father with different eyes. There stood before him a man of immense integrity who had risen to the top of his profession through hard work and a brilliant mind. He always made his children strive for excellence, never compromising on their beliefs to attain it.

Shu slipped into a chair across from his father.

"So... was the banquet to your liking?" Amarendra began, in a somewhat stilted manner.

"It was superb. Ma really outdid herself," Shu replied enthusiastically.

"You quite charmed the guests. I received lots of compliments on your behalf. Doctor Mazumdar offered to throw in a Bentley if you were to marry his daughter."

"Why do they make it so difficult?"

They both had a good laugh, as Ashu refilled the drinks. Amarendra relit his pipe. After a few drinks a more relaxed Amarendra told his son how his friends at the Calcutta Club were sick of being treated like second-class citizens in their own country and that Subhas Chandra Bose had solicited his support.

"He scares me, that man," Shu said. "Is he related to us?"

"Only very distantly. Yes, he is a bit of a loose cannon."

"What do your friends want to do?"

"You know us, we're Bengalis first, but we are realistic. At this moment, a stable country is the priority, and Gandhi and Nehru are leading us down a sane path. This country will have to go through a huge upheaval. Bringing an English girl into our family at this time makes no sense. Her life will be in constant danger. Think long and hard before you do anything so imprudent."

Shu leaned towards his father. He felt hot tears sting his eyes not only because of what he was going to say, but because he felt so close to the old man.

"Do you really think I have not thought about that?" He looked directly into his father's eyes. "But Baba, I don't want a life like yours and Ma's. I understand your life. You get your pleasure from your profession, your pets. You have reached the pinnacle of your career, a position in society none of your sons will ever attain. But maybe we have other dreams." He stopped for a moment. "You don't know Imelda. She is every bit as brave as these people you quote and talk about. She was thrown out of her home because of me. You know, your son, 'the native'! We have faced prejudice on both sides."

He took a deep breath.

"She chose to leave everything she has ever loved to be with me. She is willing to leave her sister, her family and her home. At eighteen, she is willing to risk everything to follow me to a place she had never even heard about," his voice broke, "because what we have is very special. She's everything I ever wanted in my life. She's daring, she's bold, she's brave and she brings so much joy into my life. Give her a chance, Baba, have a little faith in my decision."

He gripped Amarendra's hands to stop from trembling, he was so choked with emotion. When he looked up, he saw tears streaming down his father's cheeks. The sight stunned him, he felt connected to his father for the first time in his life. Shu instinctively put his arms around him; the old man felt so small and vulnerable. Then he pulled away, suddenly feeling self-conscious and awkward, and mumbled, "By the way Baba, she's Irish, not British."

They both smiled, holding on to the moment.

The next evening at dinner, Amarendra cautiously broached the subject with his wife.

"Have you had any feedback about the party?"

"Oh yes! So many people have called to say how fabulous the food was. I must keep that French chef's number, his hors d'oeuvres were wonderful." She looked pleased.

"I have been offered a really good position in an reputable firm, good pay and lots of perks," Shu interjected. "I think I'll accept. It's time for me to be independent and make some important decisions in my life…" he went on but was interrupted by his mother.

"So do I. I have sixteen proposals of marriage for you. I threw most of them out. You know Mrs. Sengupta had the nerve to suggest her daughter, Shoma."

"What's wrong with Shoma? She's a very smart girl," asked Shu, puzzled.

"Smart? Did you see the size of her feet?"

Shu deftly changed the subject.

"Have you heard from Sir Dhiren lately?"

"No, why?"

"Well, it would have helped with what I have to tell you. I have met an Irish girl, who I want to marry."

"An Irish girl? She's not a maid is she?"

"There you go! Your brother has given his full approval, and so have Baba and Saury."

"Sir Dhiren, his British Lordship. Saury and Baba? So you have been sneaking around behind my back and talking to the family? And your father agreed without talking to me first?"

"Gheri only brought up the subject yesterday, your approval is essential for any final decision," Amarendra pointed out mildly.

"This is the thanks you get when you send your sons abroad. They come back and sit on your head," she walked off muttering angrily.

"Well, that went well."

"You know, Shu, if I were you, I'd humour your mother. Tell her you'll meet a few of the girls, what harm can that do?"

"What harm…? Think of how the girls will feel."

"You flatter yourself. Girls are used to meeting boys and

believe me, I hear of more rejections than approvals. I'm more resourceful than you think," his father went on. "I've been thinking about how to make this scheme of mine work. I'll give you fifty pounds for every girl you meet, no strings attached."

"That is ingenious, father. Wait! Are you actually bribing me?"

"Let's call it an incentive. Shake on it and I will book Imelda's passage to India."

"What about all those talks on integrity and character? I'll tell Ma I'll see a few girls, but first I'll have to diffuse the drama I've created."

His spirits lifted, he hurried off to outline his plan to Ashu.

He had decided to ignore his mother, staying locked in his room and refusing to eat – although both Ashu and Biswas were sneaking in food on the sly. The subterfuge began to have an effect on Boroma, and by the second week, she cracked. She knocked on his door.

"What do you want?" Shu called out gruffly.

"I want to talk to you."

"I have nothing to say."

"Gheri, don't act like a child. Give me a minute," she pleaded. "This is so foolish. I have been worried sick about you. Everyone is acting as though it's my fault."

"It is your fault! All you care about is what people will say; not a thought about me or my happiness."

"Your happiness is all I am thinking about."

"You want me to live like you and Baba and be happy?"

"No need to get personal. I've always done my duty."

"And I've done my duty by coming home… to this!"

"What do you want? Just tell me what you want," she said as tears rolled down her cheeks.

"I want you to trust me, Ma. You know I won't do anything to harm anyone in the family. If you want, I'll see as many girls as you please, but it has to be on my terms."

On the other side of the door, his mother's face lit up.

"You will? But that's all I ever asked! Of course it will be your choice, you silly boy, who else would choose?"

18

London

Imelda and Kathleen were excited as they planned their trip to Ireland. Over the years, they had been in constant touch with their aunts and cousins, and Imelda could not wait to see her beloved horse, Toby.

Kathleen had her own secret agenda. On a previous trip, she had met Percy Lacey, one of the local lads who helped out on their farm. Imelda did notice that Kathleen was in extremely high spirits.

"You're full of the blade," she said to Kathleen as they packed for the trip. "I thought you'd be a wee bit sad with me leaving and all."

"Oh, I just love to go to Ireland. It gets me Irish up. The Irish Sun, the Irish sky, the rain, nothing smells like good old Irish sod! Aren't you glad we're Irish?" Kathleen sounded as dramatic as Imelda.

"You should be a wee bit upset about me leaving," said Imelda, not a bit amused with her sister's exuberance.

"But I shurre love being Irish! 'Tis a grand thing! Now all I need is a strong Irish lad."

"That was my dream, too, meeting Shu just ruined my life. I meet this boy and I lose all my senses…"

"You do love him?" Kathleen asked, a bit taken aback.

"Is love the only thing that matters? Should I give up everything for him? I thought Ma would be guiding me, but she's left me alone – alone with an idiot like you, full of sunshine and happiness."

"Such an ungrateful sister," Kathleen said looking cross.

As Imelda's fears increased so did the recurring dreams about being abandoned by her family. One evening back in Ireland, as they sat around the kitchen table, Imelda confided these dreams to her Aunt Beatrice.

"What has happened to our family?" Imelda sobbed into her aunt's arms.

"Now, Imelda. 'Twas a different time. Enough of this daydreaming. If I hear one more sad word I'll smack some sense into you," Aunt Bea firmly told her. "You can't be living your life so afraid. If you love your lad, then follow yer heart. You're a strong girl, Mel, God will guide you, but you must have faith in yerself."

She was supported and uplifted by everyone. "Yer Kathleen's daughter," she was told, "you'll take us all to India with you!" But it was Mother Bernadine who told her she must make her peace with her father before she left. "Theirs was a grand love, don't be believing the idle gossip. Do not leave with an angry heart."

A different Imelda left Ireland. What touched her the most was to see Toby transfer his affection from her to a mare called Clare. White with large brown spots, she and Toby had become inseparable. When Imelda rode Toby, Clare galloped alongside them – much to Imelda's delight.

"I would still marry Father O'Reilly in a blink," she said smiling sadly, as she made her final visit to her mothers grave. "Ma knew all about that, didn't you Ma? You always knew all about me."

When they returned to London, there was a notice on the door of their flat saying there was a package waiting for Imelda at the post office. There was also a note from Sir Dhiren asking her to contact him. Both sisters simultaneously burst into tears.

"It's here," Imelda shrieked as she clutched Kathleen's hand.

Then she went to the post office to pick up the package. It was from Shu. The envelope held four hundred pounds for Imelda.

"You'll never believe how I earned this money," he wrote, "but I want you to go on a shopping spree on me."

Imelda felt flush and generous. The first thing she did was to rush to Camden Street Market and bought gifts for all her aunts and cousins in Ireland. Then she told Kathleen she had a surprise for her. "We are going to shop from Bond Street, through Oxford Street all the way to Tottenham Court Road. We are not going to stop until there's not a penny left. Not one blooming penny!"

"Nooooo – it's for you," Kathleen protested.

"It's for *us*. Come on, don't spoil things. Let's pretend we're rich and buy all the things we never could. And when the money is finished, we will come home."

"Can we save a bit for a steak dinner?" Kathleen asked tentatively.

"And steak dinner every day this week," Imelda declared boldly.

At first they were careful, totaling the bills after each acquisition. Then, with blissful disregard, they bought everything on their list. There were a couple of suits, a few dresses, three or four skirts with blouses.

"Oh my God, I don't think we have a penny left. I didn't even look at some of the prices. Do people really shop like this?" A jubilant Imelda exclaimed.

They arrived at their flat, heady with excitement, barely able to walk with the many packages in their arms.

"Should we go through the accounts again?" asked Kathleen worriedly.

"Don't remove any tags till we are sure." They tried on all the outfits again, then went through the receipts.

"Tell me if this is correct. We have spent two hundred and eighty pounds, and that includes the gifts I mailed to Ireland," an incredulous Imelda announced. "That means we have one hundred and twenty pounds left. Surely that can't be right."

"My Lord! Is this a bottomless pit of money? Let's go buy something from Bond Street. I didn't have the nerve yesterday," Kathleen confessed.

Bond Street had always been off limits. They had gone there once with Shu and Saury and marvelled at how comfortable the young men were with spending money. Now it was their turn. But after all the bravado of splashing out, they still couldn't help making meticulous lists of what they needed, and carefully comparing prices. The one thing they decided to splurge on were luxurious undergarments. They went to Harrod's and bought six French lace bras with matching lace underwear. Lastly, they bought two large steamer trunks in which to pack their precious things.

That evening, they met Saury and Leslie for dinner. Saury assured everybody that it would be easier for him to marry Leslie because he had a closer relationship with his mother.

"So the next time we meet it will be in India? Let's drink to that. Sláinte!" Imelda said, raising her glass.

Sir Dhiren had to use his influence with the foreign office to get Imelda's passport expedited, but that did not lesson the reams of paperwork that Imelda had to fill out at the passport office.

"I want it made clear that I am Irish," she told the passport officer.

"With a name like Imelda Connor?" he laughed.

But even with Sir Dhiren pulling strings the paperwork took so long that the ship she was originally booked on sailed without her.

A month later, the boarding pass arrived in a large brown envelope. She recognized the big P&O emblem on the left-hand corner. As Imelda was signing for it, she could not stop her hand shaking. She had lived the past six months waiting for this moment. She sat down, her palms sweaty, her knees weak. She sat motionless and stared at the envelope for hours, not daring to touch it.

She knew she could not leave England without seeing her father. She was his special child, and she was not going to let pride keep her away. He would take one look at her and every horrible incident would be forgiven; and then she would feel safe again.

The day she finally decided to visit Patrick, she was jumpy and nervous; every little noise startled her and the knot in her stomach grew tighter as she made her way towards Putney

Green. She stopped at a bar and downed a pint in one long gulp, asking for a refill before the bartender could turn around. Even her lucky white sweater could not calm her anxiety.

Standing erect and very tense, she walked down the stone path leading to the door of the cottage. She felt as though she was walking through heavy sand.

Her mouth was dry, her knuckles white as she knocked. Quietly she gave the door a few taps, and then tapped a little louder. The door opened suddenly and there stood Nancy.

"Jesus, Mary and Joseph. Will yeh look to see who's here."

Imelda sensed Nancy was much more in control than the last time they had met: she was not afraid of Imelda anymore.

"Good evening, Nancy. I've come to see my father. Can you please tell him I'm here?"

"You have some nerve to show yer face at our door," Nancy replied coldly.

"Please tell him I'm here," Imelda repeated.

"Come to break his heart again, have yeh? 'Twill be a cold day in hell fer him t'see you."

"Maybe he'll change his mind when you tell him it's me."

"And just what would you like me to say?"

"Just tell him his daughter has come to see him. I've a right to see my own father," Imelda said brusquely, her eyes brimming with tears.

"Don't be telling me what rights you have," she shot back and closed the door, leaving Imelda outside.

Imelda strained her ears trying to listen for her father's voice. She could always tell his mood by the tone of his voice. Before she could take a couple of deep breaths, Nancy was back, and by the look on her face Imelda had her answer.

"Yer father wants nothing t'do with you. As far as we're concerned, you're done an' dusted."

With that, she slammed the door shut.

Imelda stood outside for a few moments before she fully realised what had happened. Then she straightened her shoulders and walked back towards the gate. She carefully unlatched the hook, unaware of the tormented eyes that followed her every move from behind the curtains.

Imelda heard heart-wrenching sobs and realised they were coming from her. She felt totally abandoned; she felt limp, like a wet rag. At the age of eighteen, she had to make the most important decision of her life alone. She knew if her father had put his arms around her and told her he loved her and not to leave him, she would have stayed. But by the time she'd reached the station, her grief had turned to rage and then to hatred. She swore to herself she would never forgive him.

"I'll show him just how little he means to me," she thought.

She knew he loved her long hair: there had been many times he had told her never to cut it. She knew just what she would do. She delved into her bag for a pair of scissors and in a fit of childish rage, chopped off her beautiful long auburn mane. The regrets would come later, but for that instant the desire to inflict pain took over her. She stuffed the hunks of hair into a brown paper bag and wrote fiercely on a piece of paper, "This is all you'll ever see of me."

Bag in hand, she marched back to her father's house. She stood very tall and then, with a sharp breath, she flung the bag as hard as she could at the front door. It landed with a dull thud, splitting open, exposing golden glints of reflected light. Satisfied, she turned and walked away.

She had made up her mind. She was going to India to marry Shu. And as soon as she was settled into her new home, she would send for Kathleen. She would find her sister a husband among the thousands of servicemen stationed in India. This may have been far-fetched, but the hope of reuniting with Kathleen was the only way she could cope with the magnitude of her decision.

19

Calcutta

Shu had settled into a cushy life in Calcutta. He and his friends had landed well-paying jobs that assured their place in Bengali high society. They met for dinner at least twice a week at the Calcutta Club, and played cricket and tennis on the weekends.

The Calcutta Club was shamelessly fashioned after the Bengal Club and the Saturday Club, two institutions known to be exclusive enclaves for the white ruling class. But that did not dissuade these Indian 'brown sahibs' from being more British than the British. They imitated their segregated counterparts, adopting rules and regulations only a colonial mentality would allow. Women were barred from the first floor of the Club, although they were permitted to play mahjong or bridge on Wednesday afternoons, followed by a luncheon of curried lamb and mulligatawny soup. The upper floor, or 'Uppers' as it was called, had a bar and grill, a smoke room, a card room and two billiard rooms. In the main dining hall, patrons in formal wear were served by white-gloved waiters, while they enjoyed the classics played by the resident band. Saturday afternoons were for families, when the lawns swarmed with screaming children eating lemon chilly-chicken while the adults feasted on cucumber and watercress sandwiches, chicken kabobs and petit fours.

Cricket at the Club was far less taxing than playing on the maidan. The players had four runners to get the long balls that went to the boundaries, and two leisurely tea breaks. They had ball boys and bearers who offered them drinks and cool damp towels during the change-over. Life was effortless now that they belonged to India's upper crust.

Shu's friend Nikhil was a Cambridge Blue in both tennis and cricket. He was in much demand.

"I absolutely refuse to play mixed doubles," he carped, as Shu and Bappa laughed heartily. "It's ruining my game."

"Don't bullshit us. You just love being the alpha male, showing off your Cambridge blazer at every opportune moment."

"Shu, Dassi said there's a rumour floating around that you are frantically seeking a bride."

"Utter BS! I'm just keeping the home fires under control. Imelda will be joining me before the year is out," he reassured them.

"You'd better not be two-timing her, you bastard. Why are you meeting girls anyway?" Nikhil persisted.

"He's an opportunist," Bappa interjected, patting an embarrassed Shu on the shoulder.

"The pressure our families put on us is tyrannical," added Nitish.

"There's method to my madness," he said. "I'll let you chaps in on it later. Tea break's over."

Shu's strategy of meetings girls was paying off. Not only did it keep his mother off his back, he was collecting a good amount of money. Ashu was getting a five per cent cut, and made an enthusiastic accomplice, giving long critical assessments after each meeting.

Boroma was in her element. Every week she held a social luncheon where she would invite three or four families with their daughters. Her younger sister, Charulata Dutta, and Dhola Kaka were her chief advisers. The new role of arbiter empowered her with immense energy, as the parents of the girls would go to great lengths to curry her favour. Between Boroma and Charulata, the poor girls themselves did not stand a chance. Boroma always focused on the colour of their skin.

"You focus on such ridiculous things. I was so embarrassed when you asked Smita to show her feet," Shu protested angrily after one such meeting.

"Embarrassed? You? You should talk. You humiliated me by flirting with Manjula's mother. A woman of forty! I didn't know where to hide my face."

"She was smart, and much more interesting than her daughter. And I wasn't flirting, I was making conversation," Shu objected.

"Really? 'Your daughter has inherited your enchanting smile'," Boroma mimicked Shu's British accent.

"Are you quoting from memory, or are you writing down every word I say?" Shu couldn't help but laugh at his mother's comical imitation.

"I think it's time to make a decision. You write down your three favourites and I will pick mine."

"Me too," Ashu added.

Preparations for Imelda's arrival were carried on surreptitiously and with much trepidation. It had been mutually agreed that Sir Dhiren Mitra would legally adopt Imelda, so she would be considered a Hindu and therefore entitled to a Hindu wedding. Also their children would have legitimate inheritance rights. Imelda would have to sign a document waiving her right to bring up her children as Catholics, though legally, the fact that she would get married in a Hindu ceremony would automatically excommunicate her from the Catholic Church.

On her arrival, Imelda would have to stay in Sir Dhiren's house. They would have a simple Bengali ceremony at Sir Dhiren and Lady Mitra's home and, as her guardian, he would be responsible for all the necessary legalities.

Amarendra talked to Boroma about ordering a few sets of jewellery from Satramdas, the family jewellers. She agreed readily, as they would add to the collection of saris she had put aside for Shu's and Saury's prospective brides. Amarendra was getting anxious about these secret arrangements, worried that his wife would find out before the plan was successfully executed.

"Shu, bring this dreadful drama to an end. Imelda's ship is arriving in a month and your mother has to be made aware of the situation."

"Don't worry. Tomorrow I am going to tell her that Imelda is my choice."

"I think you are underestimating her tenacity," his father replied.

"I've kept my side of the deal. I've met all the girls she chose, now she has to hold up her end. I'm going to hold her feet to the fire."

"Just keep my name out of it – and don't ever mention the ridiculous fly-by-night money-scam again. It was an absurd idea."

"Why Baba, since when are you afraid of Ma?"

"Not afraid but, unlike you, I do have a reputation to uphold. Trusting you is a big leap of faith."

"You will not be sorry, there are just no words…" Shu started to get emotional when his father interrupted, patting him on the back.

"You don't need to say anything. Now go on and work on your mother."

20

Sailing to India

Brokenhearted and terrified, Imelda left Southampton on March 3, 1932, on board the P&O ocean liner, the *RMS Viceroy of India*. Sir Dhiren and his wife, and Saury and Kathleen, came to see her off. Sir Dhiren's office had all the formalities of getting on a ship. Imelda had two large steamer trunks, and Sir Dhiren brought along another trunk which he booked in with her luggage.

"Is that for Shu's family?" Imelda inquired, eyeing the large trunk.

"No, Imelda my dear. That's a little surprise for you. Your aunt and I wanted to give you a wedding gift. I won't call it a dowry, but you know we are old-fashioned and don't know the latest trends, so we recruited Saury, Leslie and Kathleen to help pick out a formal wardrobe for you. I hope you'll wear them."

"So that's why you kept disappearing."

Kathleen nodded, as the tears rolled down her cheeks and she clutched Imelda's hand.

"Imelda, don't forget my good friend Sir Lloyd George is on board," Sir Dhiren continued. "He has assured us that he'll keep an eye on you. Shu and his family will be at the docks to pick you up, so I want to see you leave with a smile."

The quayside was as chaotic as a shipyard. There were politicians and bureaucrats, and a large consignment of military personnel. Along with the hustle and bustle there was an atmosphere of merriment. Union Jacks, streamers, balloons and confetti were everywhere. A band in blue and white stripes played jaunty popular tunes to keep the crowds in a festive mood, especially the young British soldiers on their way to the colonies. Women in fur coats and fancy hats were followed up the gangway by men in grey suits. The most exciting rumour circulating was that the actress Tallulah Bankhead was on board, so everyone was on the look-out for her. Then the final call for boarding came. The ship was ready to leave.

Kathleen and Imelda clung to each other until Saury had to almost pry them apart.

"Imelda they are going to pull up the gangway! We'll be meeting in a few months – don't make it so hard on yourself." He was teary-eyed as he pushed Imelda towards the gangplank.

"I will write every day Kathleen, I promise!" Imelda shouted as she retreated up the gangway. "Take care of my sister," she yelled to Saury.

"You have my word."

"I miss you already, Kathleen," she sobbed uncontrollably.

The band played a stirring rendition of 'Ole Lang Syne' over and over again as the passengers were handed streamers to throw to their loved ones on shore. With its horns blasting loudly, the ship slowly left the port. Forlorn, Imelda stood at the railings not wanting to throw her streamer, for it would connect her again to the sister she was leaving, and the land she had grown to

love. She took one look at Kathleen clinging to Saury, her face
buried in his shoulder, and ran blindly to her cabin, making little
heartbreaking sounds that couldn't seem to get past her chest.

She lay curled up on her bed for two days, feeling nauseous
and isolated. The cabin boy who bought her some tea on the
second day offered to get her some medicine. She declined,
and had no desire to join the festivities on board. On the third
morning there was a persistent knocking at her door.

"What do you want?" she asked, annoyed.

"Excuse me, madam," came a voice. "Am I speaking to
Imelda Connor?"

"Yes."

"I have an invitation from Sir Lloyd George for you."

"Oh!" She opened the door and accepted the note. It was
an invitation for cocktails in the Arbor room at 6:30 pm, and
dinner in the main ballroom at 7:40 pm.

She sat on her bed thinking she should venture up to the
deck. The sea breeze would do her good and a little food might
help. She already felt miles away from home and they had barely
been at sea two-and-a-half days. Her contradictory emotions
were confusing, filling her mind with lingering doubts. Shu had
taken five months to convince his parents to let him marry her,
what if they disliked her? What if she could not understand
them? What if she made no friends? What if got some terrible
disease? What if… what if… what if?

She lay back in bed, her head hurting and her heart pounding
when there was another knock at her cabin door.

"Who is it? No room service, thank you," she called out.

The polite knocking continued, so she got up and opened
the door.

There was a distinguished-looking young naval officer at the door.

"Excuse me madam, I am ADC to Sir Lloyd George. He has asked you to join him in his room for a few minutes."

"Why? I mean why would he want to meet me?" she asked.

"I believe, madam, Sir George is a friend of your father's, and he has been getting telegrams inquiring about you. We have been expecting you at dinner for the last two evenings."

"Can you give me a few minutes to freshen up?"

"Certainly. I will send someone to escort you to his cabin. Sorry to have disturbed you." He clicked his heels and left.

She jumped in the tub, washed her hair, brushed her teeth and felt squeaky clean. She was ready when the escort arrived. She had put on a simple dress and tied her wet hair at the nape of her neck. Her cheeks were puffy, and her eyes red and swollen.

Imelda followed her naval escort, for the first time taking in the opulence of the ship. Its halls and ballrooms exuded grandeur and luxury. They walked through an enormous glass-domed hall that had sweeping staircases on either side giving the grand illusion of leading up to the heavens. The ships amenities included movie theatres, massage parlours and nightclubs with a variety of entertainment. Passengers were being pampered, entertained and constantly fed. Imelda finally arrived on the eleventh deck. Here the atmosphere was more formal. Solders and naval officers controlled the flow of people. Imelda had to go through two barricades of security.

Imelda, intimidated by all this attention, was staring with unabashed awe at the huge state room when she heard a deep and raspy British voice call out from the private deck, "What's a pretty girl like you doing in a place like this?" It was such an obvious pick-up line that Imelda burst out laughing. She turned and came face to face with a white-haired man of about seventy-five. Imelda didn't know if she should curtsy, bow or shake hands, so she just stood there. He struggled to stand up and gave her a warm hug.

"So you're Imelda Connor, eh? I've had everyone on the look-out for you. Where have you been hiding young lady?" he joked with a twinkle in his eye.

"In my cabin," Imelda answered.

"How old are you? You don't look a day over sixteen. I have a granddaughter your age. Sit down Imelda. So you're Irish? Ha! Love that Irish lilt. I come from Welsh ancestry myself. Let's have a bit to eat, what would you like to start with?"

Unknown to Imelda, this genial old gent was the most important passenger on the ship. A lot of the security that people assumed was for Tallulah Bankhead was in reality for him. He was Sir David Lloyd George. He had been the Prime Minister of Britain from 1916 to 1922. He had spent the last decade campaigning for progressive causes, and served the British Government as a roving ambassador. He was on his first official trip to India as Foreign Secretary, with the tough job of negotiating with Gandhi and Nehru about India's war effort.

Sir Lloyd George had a distinctive dishevelled look about him, like an eccentric old professor. The beret on his head could barely contain the long wisps of his thin white hair, while his bushy white mustache was tinged yellow from cigar smoke. Nothing escaped the attention of this wily old politician, and he had immediately noticed Imelda puffy eyes.

"Tell me, Imelda, why does Sir Dhiren refer to you as his daughter?" he inquired as they sipped white wine.

"Because I'm going to marry his nephew, and it helps if I am a legal Indian, so he's adopting me."

"Aha. Tell me all about this chap of yours. He must be very special for you to leave your family for him." He was such a lovable old rascal with a naughty sense of humour that he easily overcame Imelda's initial reluctance to open up to him.

"This should be the happiest time of your life. If I were to judge by your face, I would assume you were going to a funeral."

One afternoon, after too many glasses of wine, a homesick Imelda began talking about her fears. Her fear of not being accepted by Shu's family, her fear of catching some horrible disease, and her fear of being so far away from everything with which she was familiar. She was relieved to be able to share her qualms with a kind, gentle father-figure.

"Are you as important as Sir Dhiren?" she asked, curious about all the security constantly around him.

"No one is as important as Sir Dhiren," he replied with a smile.

Tallulah Bankhead's presence had everyone on board in a constant state of excitement. Grown men would tremble at the sight of her big wide eyes, sexy lips and sensual voice, and fought to touch her outstretched hand. She and the young studs, with their rippling muscles, had severe-looking bureaucrats and their wives swooning like teenagers. The darker whispers were that she really preferred women, and these men were red herrings.

Imelda had Sir George's private telephone number, and his assurance that if she ever needed help, all she had to do was give him a call. Happily, a week into the trip she decided to look into the trunk that Sir Dhiren had given her. She gasped as she took out the most beautiful silver beaded evening gown she had ever seen. Surely, this was meant for a movie star – Tallulah Bankhead perhaps, but not her! There was a note attached.

Welcome to our family. Our Gheri is a very lucky young man to have found love and you. We feel blessed. This is our wedding gift to you, and we want you to wear the pearls when you land in India. All our love and blessings to the two of you.

Sir Dhiren and Lady Mitra

In the satin-lined box was a double string of pearls. A second box contained a diamond and emerald pendant on a gold chain with matching earrings. Also in the trunk were: a black, off-the-shoulder taffeta evening gown, a simple black dress and a green chiffon formal dress; gabardine trousers, cashmere cardigans, and a grey silk suit with a short two-button jacket; as well as dainty silver, black, and gold evening bags and matching shoes. Imelda spread everything around the room, overwhelmed. Then she carefully put each item back into the trunk, locked it, and hid the key. Two days later, there was an invitation to the Captain's Ball, and she immediately knew what she was going to wear.

When Imelda walked into the ballroom in the beaded silver evening dress even Sir Lloyd George did not recognize her. He was used to her freshly scrubbed freckled face without a hint of make-up.

"Are you not going to say good evening, Sir George?" she joked as she put her hand out to be kissed.

"Imelda, good god! What did you do to yourself?" he asked, astonished at her metamorphosis.

"I thought I'd surprise you a wee bit. I couldn't find my tiara though," she laughed mischievously, oblivious to the effect she was having on those around her. She had tied back her hair in a loose chignon and was wearing lipstick and a touch of blue eye-shadow. All the naval officers scampered about trying to get a dance with her, and Imelda enjoyed all the attention.

There was a close sense of camaraderie among the diverse group of passengers. There were young soldiers going to join their battalions in the war zone and bureaucrats posted in remote villages in a society they barely understood. Vulnerable, they made strangers their confidantes.

Imelda had befriended a raucous group of Irish 'lads'. They were soldiers between the ages of seventeen and twenty facing their first military assignment abroad. She developed a kinship with them and was the centre of their little hub of activity.

As the ship neared the Equator, the air got heavier and thicker and everyone seemed to be slowing down. The sun was brighter and hotter, and the tropical sunsets were more vibrant.

The night before their arrival in Calcutta there was a Farewell Ball. Imelda sat close to Sir George, getting weepy at the sentimental music being played.

"Come along, Imelda," Sir George chided her, "you are the luckiest little girl in the world! Tomorrow is going to be the first day in your life's new adventure, and I don't want to see tears."

"Can I introduce Shu to you when we dock tomorrow?" she asked.

"I would love that, but I think there will be some official work for me to do. I will have you over within a week."

"A week? Oh no, that won't do at all. I want Shu to meet you sooner than that," Imelda protested.

"I have to see what meetings the government has set up for me. I am here on important work my dear, but don't worry, you'll hear from me."

Imelda was packed and ready by midnight. The stewards were going to collect the luggage by six the next morning, and the ship would dock at ten. Imelda did not sleep a wink. Her mind was racing with overwhelming thoughts.

She wondered what it would feel like to be in Shu's arms again. She couldn't exactly remember. Was he that wonderful? Or was it the imaginative fantasies of a girl in love? She was filled with so many doubts... but it was too late for all that now. How she missed Kathleen! Her mouth was dry and her hands clammy. Was Shu having second thoughts about her too?

21

Calcutta

Shu was on cloud nine at the prospect of Imelda's impending arrival. As he rushed around making all the arrangements for the wedding and reception, his friends were beginning to get worried. Unlike Imelda, he did not have a doubt in the world. Nikhil and Bappa sat him down to send out cautionary feelers.

"There is a possibility that Imelda may not like it here," Bappa gently warned his friend.

"I don't see even the slightest possibility of that," Shu countered.

"Imelda is from a different world. Joint families are unheard of over there. This may cause some serious misunderstanding. You must see that," Bappa patiently continued.

"I'm two steps ahead of you. I have hired this cook, Hari, who makes incredible western food, and have added a small breakfast kitchen next to our bedroom. And if that's not good enough we'll move into our own home, father will support it. Hey – life is one big crap shoot. The odds are in our favour."

"I refuse to argue with a fool." Nikhil walked away frustrated.

About three weeks before Imelda's arrival, Shu carefully

orchestrated a meeting with his immediate family, including his brother Himanshu and wife, Dhebu. They had retreated from most family functions after the death of their son, but Shu was close to Dhebu, and often went up to her room and listened to stories about her lost son. The two of them would just hold hands as Dhebu wept. He told her about Imelda, and Dhebu thought the two of them were 'pagol' – crazy.

Shu had already worked on his sisters, both of them firmly in his corner. Menu was all bubbly with excitement and could hardly contain herself after Shu had confided in her. Anything her brother did was acceptable to her. Chotto thought it all sounded like a romantic Jane Austin novel. "I can't believe all this is going on in my own family," she gushed dreamily.

Boroma thought that the family was going to be discussing the girls that had been seen and approved by her and Shu. She was happy all her children were home for dinner, and was busy making sure everyone's favourite dish was on the menu. After dinner, they sat around having their usual lively conversations when Shu stood up and clinked his glass.

"I have a very important announcement to make, which is why I wanted the whole family here," he began grandly. "As you all know, when I returned from England I told Ma and Baba that my intentions were to first find a good job and then marry a girl I had met in London. As expected Ma had a meltdown and Baba had some valid questions about the decision. I argued fiercely with Baba (not an easy task) and finally won him over. Ma was different – but to cut a long story short, I agreed to a comprise by meeting girls that Ma deemed suitable to be married into this illustrious family." He waited for the good-natured laughter to stop. "I think that was fair. So Ma, you were going to give us your suggestions. Who did you think is best suited for me?"

"You have surprised me, but I liked Meenakshi and Protima. Both very beautiful and smart."

"Ashu's choice I have already dismissed. So Ma, I did what you wanted and met whoever you chose, and some of the girls were very nice, thank you. But after a lot of serious thought, I still want to marry the girl I originally chose."

Boroma gasped loudly. "How can you do that? We haven't even met her."

"But you will, in exactly three weeks. You will meet her and have your chance to agree or disagree with my choice. And she will also have to decide whether she wants to stay and put up with all our nonsense."

Himanshu got up and said very seriously, "Gheri came to me and asked for my advice. He finally got over the trauma of being locked in the bathroom," he chuckled, "I told him that their life together will be more difficult than most, but if he is willing to face that, he has both our blessings."

Menu and Chotto could hardly contain themselves jumping up and down saying, "Ours too! Ours too! We support Gheri-da."

"What? Are you all taking sides against me?" Boroma asked, clearly annoyed at the show of support for Shu. "And what does your father have to say?"

"After I saw Shu's determination and commitment to this girl I have given him the benefit of the doubt. I have no fear for their future, so let's welcome Imelda Connor into our midst, and give Gheri all the support he will need."

Himanshu and Dhebu left the festivities, and Shu turned

to his mother and said, "Ma, look at them. Life holds no guarantees for any of us. We of all people should recognize that. I want to be happy, even if it is for a short while, so please smile. I've kept my promise to you. It's now your turn."

He hugged his mother as both his sisters cheered loudly. She was crying, but she recognized that the decks were stacked against her. Her devious son had worked on everyone and won.

Menu tried to comfort her mother. "Ma, Gheri-da told me she is not even English, she can't speak English properly."

"No, Menu, what I said was, she's Irish and speaks English with a different accent."

"Oh-ho. He's marrying a girl from England who can't even speak English properly. What if I said he marrying a girl from Bengal who couldn't speak Bengali properly? Would you all be dancing around like clowns?" Boroma huffed angrily.

The sword of Damocles had been lifted and Shu could be heard singing loudly as he rushed around the house fixing little things. He asked Chotto to look for a picture that had a stream or lake with trees for his bedroom, and went to the jewellers to design a ring.

Boroma now had Sir Dhiren on her list of enemies. She was convinced he was trying to destroy her family.

As protocol demanded, Imelda would stay with Sir Dhiren and his family at 16 Ballygunge Circular Road until she was married.

Shu was at constant loggerheads with his mother who now wanted to take over the marriage ceremony.

"You have had your way with the bride, now if you try to destroy our reputation with a shabby show of a wedding, I will wash my hands of the whole thing," she threatened him.

"You are driving me mad, Ma! I want to avoid a tamasha. The ceremony cannot be more than half an hour, I will not wear that marriage headgear – and nor will Imelda. Agree with that and you can handle the rest. I want a small get-together with my friends at the Calcutta Club." Shu's face was red with frustration.

The morning of Imelda's arrival, a nervous Shu came out to see a line of four cars waiting to take them to the docks.

"Aloke, why are there four cars ready?" he asked the driver.

"Boroma ordered them, sir," he replied.

"The Bentley is what we are going in, maybe the Rover can come to carry the luggage. That will be enough."

Just then Boroma and Amarendra Nath emerged from the house and immediately Boroma wanted to know why the cars were being sent back.

"Ma, we do not need more than two cars: one for us and the other for the luggage," Shu explained patiently.

"But the luggage may not fit in two cars. She must be bringing a small trousseau…"

"I told you a hundred times, she will not be bringing any trousseau. We do not live in the middle ages," Shu exclaimed exasperated.

"I've been told even European girls have a small trousseau?"

"Ma, just stop," Shu snapped.

This was not a good beginning. They quietly got into the car.

22

Calcutta

Imelda stood on the deck with her head held high, her hair a tangled mess, her face pale and her knuckles white on the railings. The passengers were told to wait thirty minutes before disembarking, as there was an official welcome ceremony for their honoured guest, Sir Lloyd George. Imelda looked down at the millions of people lining the docks.

The quay was awash with flags, decorative streamers, banners and bunting. There was a military brass band playing as decorated horses, mounted by solders in bright red turbans and red livery, marched back and forth with the Union Jack gaily waving in the breeze. The band struck up 'God Save the King' as Sir Lloyd George was escorted down the gangway to the red carpet. He was greeted with garlands, and a large group of officials. Children sang welcoming songs and then, with a cavalry escort, he was driven away through the throngs of people lining both sides of the street.

Once the army personnel and official dignitaries left the wharf, the waiting public was allowed near the passengers' ramp. Not moving a muscle, Imelda scrutinized every face carefully.

She suddenly let out a wild shriek, and the second that she saw him, she was on her way running and screaming down the gangway straight into his arms. Every doubt melted away as she hung on to him. Shu was teary-eyed and overcome with emotion. He had fought the brave fight and won: Imelda was here.

He finally pulled himself away and took a good look at her. She looked so much younger than he remembered.

"What have you done to your beautiful hair?" Shu twirled her around.

"I did a very foolish thing. You have lost so much weight."

"I missed you too much to eat," he laughed as he hugged her again. There was an awkward shuffle and a slight cough behind them. His parents were quietly taking in the scene.

Self-consciously, Shu slowly unwound Imelda's arms from his neck. "Imelda, meet my parents. They have been dying to meet you."

Saury had taught her how to look demure, put her hands together and say 'nomoshkar'.

During all her practice sessions, he would laugh hysterically, so when the moment arrived she was too embarrassed to show off her Indian greeting skills. Instead she gave them both a timid hug, and was immediately aware of how she towered over Shu's mother.

Amarendra Bose told her how he had looked forward to welcoming her into his family. His face was severe but behind those forbidding glasses, Imelda saw a kindness to which she immediately responded. Boroma was thinking about how young Imelda looked, and how white and fair she was. She was certainly not the sophisticated conniving wretch she had pictured; it would be difficult to dislike her. After some casual chitchat during which Shu firmly held onto Imelda's hand, a gesture Boroma noticed, Amarendra gently asked, "I don't want to rush things, but can we help you get your luggage?"

"Luggage. Oh gosh. Where is it?" She looked around her and then remembered that she had left her hand-luggage with all her important documents on the deck where she had been scanning the crowd.

"Don't move," she said to Shu, and turned and ran giddily back up the gangway feeling light-headed and buoyant.

Calcutta took her breath away; it was unlike anything she had ever imagined. It was lush and green, with wide avenues lined by tall majestic neem trees. The city was meticulously planned. The British had built magnificent mansions along the wide roads, interspersed with parks. These old houses with their large porticos and grand entrances were built to impress.

As Imelda slipped into the luxurious leather interior of the bottle-green Bentley, she sought Shu's hand.

She was trying to absorb everything around her. She quietly studied Shu's father. He had an imposing presence. He was wearing a distinguished grey suit and everything about him was immaculate. He had the look of a man who knew he was important. Imelda was drawn to his kind eyes: they reassured her that they would be friends.

Amarendra was a man of few words, and often appeared detached from those around him, but he took note of the minutest details. He noticed Imelda had chewed her fingernails to the quick and that one of her shoes was tied with a knot and the other with a bow. He liked her immediately: she had a simplicity and innocence about her. As her eyes sparkled with happiness, he marvelled at the daring of this young girl, crossing two oceans to be with his son.

Imelda's attention shifted to Shu's mother. She was elegant and had a motherly air to her. She must have been beautiful in her youth with her smooth skin and refined features. She had a closed demeanour, seldom exposing her softer side. She was wearing an understated beige sari with a brown and gold border. Her jewellery was minimal: gold bangles and a gold chain around her neck. Like traditional Bengali married women, she wore red lacquer bangles with a white shell bangle, and had a little red sindoor in her hair. She was not fluent in English and spoke in a slow deliberate manner. Her flat, monotonous tone contrasted with the tilt of Imelda's Irish accent.

"I'm your mother now, so you must call me Ma, okay?" She took Imelda's hand and patted it.

"Okay, Ma," she said shyly.

Despite her misgivings, Boroma responded to the warmth and happiness Imelda exuded, and she was charmed. She saw the tenderness reflected in her son's eyes as he anxiously watched Imelda's every reaction.

Everything on the wide avenues caught Imelda's attention. "Look at those big white flowers." She stuck her head out the window taking in a deep breath. "Look at that horse and boogie."

"It's bugg-ee," Shu deadpanned. "I think we'll need an English teacher for her, father."

"Nonsense. I think she is absolutely enchanting," Amarendra smiled.

Imelda was so engrossed with all the cars, carriages, rickshaws and animals on the street that when the car entered a large mansion and stopped she waited in the car, thinking they were at some official building. She shrank back inside the car when two turbaned guards saluted and opened the door. Shu came around to her side.

"Look, Imelda, we arre home!" Shu joked in his mock-Irish accent. "If there were fewer people around I'd carry you over the threshold." He tried coaxing her with a big smile and an outstretched hand.

Imelda didn't move. Who were all these people standing in line and staring at her? This was a mansion – this was definitely not 'home'. After Shu had cajoled her out of the car, she managed to whisper, "Whose home did you say it was?"

"Ours of course. Let me introduce you." Shu took her hand and laughed in a lighthearted manner, trying to make her introduction to the staff very casual. They had been waiting for over an hour and were excited to meet the new 'Bou'. Some went to touch her feet; others just folded their hands in greeting. A few children reached out to touch her. Shu radiated calm holding Imelda's hand firmly as he guided her through the eager crowd of well-wishers.

"This is Ashu – he's dad's special agent. He's been with dad before any of us were born."

Ashu bobbed his head at her, smiling broadly. "Shob boojhe," he said.

"That means he understands everything, but he'll take a couple of months to decipher your accent," Shu laughed as he casually put his arm around Ashu's shoulders.

"This is Vishnu, our gardener, and his son, Deb. They take care of the garden and the animals. Meet Partho, our baboochi or chef: the people around him are members of his serfdom. Hari is our special cook: he speaks good English and can make the best apple strudel in town. I enticed him away from the Edwards at a considerable cost."

"Welcome to Calcutta, memsahib," Hari said.

"And lastly meet Druvo, our driver who also speaks English."

Imelda walked through a blur of sounds and faces. All these faces! Some with red lines in their hair, a few with covered heads, crooked red-stained teeth, eyes outlined in black just staring at her.

Amarendra met her inside, with Shona perched on his arm. "Come on, Shona, say welcome to Imelda." He had been coaching the birds for about a month.

As Shona preened her magnificent white feathers, turning her head to study Imelda carefully, a beautiful red, blue and yellow macaw screeched out loud and clear.

"Welcome Eee-mel-da! Welcome Eee-mel-da! Welcome Eee-mel-da!"

"Good job, Rani. Shona, she beat you to it," Amarendra beaming with pride. "Imelda, this is my pride and joy, Shona. I've had her for over fifty years. And that was Rani, doing her usual one-upmanship. I have five other birds who you will meet later. The whole family is coming over this evening to meet you: I did try to keep them away until tomorrow, but I was overruled. Shu had to fight them off from coming to the harbour."

He then ordered Ashu to bring some tea and snacks.

"Can I hold the bird?" Imelda asked timidly.

"Just put out your arm. Wait a minute, let me put a towel over your nice jacket."

Shu was busy getting the luggage put away when Boroma said, "Gheri, Imelda is staying at Mama babu's house until the wedding."

"She can stay a few days in the spare room, and then we will move her. This place is so new to her, I can't let her stay there all by herself."

"What do you mean all by herself? Lotika and Bashi are there, and Sir Dhiren is arriving in two weeks."

"I think she should move in only once he arrives."

"I don't want any unnecessary gossip."

"Let me worry about that, Ma. You focus on the wedding."

It seemed unseemly to argue, but she had plenty to say to Charulata and Dhola kaka on the phone the next day.

"I have to learn all about these birds. I know a lot about farm animals, but not birds," Imelda said, wonderingly.

"Do you want to meet the others?" Amarendra immediately offered.

"I would love to."

She followed him through the foyer, past the chiming grandfather clock and into the bird sanctuary. Raja, another pure white cockatoo with an imposing yellow crown, was agitating for Amarendra to pick him up. He was so at ease with the birds that Imelda instantly relaxed.

"I know this is a parrot," Imelda said happily.

"That's Bulbul, the Amazonian grey-headed parrot. She is the wheel that squeaks the loudest to get my attention." He handed the bird a nut from a special container, to which she squawked back, "Thank you, Amar!"

Imelda laughed out loud. "This is so amazing."

Imelda entered the large living room with Italian marble

floors, sparkling chandeliers and Persian rugs. She had slipped into a world she had only read about in books.

Shu returned and gave Imelda a hug before pouring out the tea.

"I think Imelda should get acclimatized here instead of at Mama babu's, wouldn't you agree Baba?" He looked at Amarendra.

"Whatever suits Imelda is fine with me," he nodded in agreement.

"Did you have fun on the ship? Meet any interesting people?" Shu asked.

"Sir Lloyd George was on the boat."

"Did you see him?"

"I was at his table. I wanted to introduce you to him down at the pier but there was that big ceremony."

"He's the quite the bigwig here. How in the world did you get to sit at his table?" he asked, surprised.

"Your uncle knows him. He promised he would invite us over as soon as he gets a spare moment."

"I wouldn't count on that, he's here on a very important mission. Let me show you around. Father, we will take your leave and get together later on." Shu took Imelda's hand and led her up the grand staircase.

"We'll be living upstairs. I know the rooms are large, but you can change whatever you want. And don't worry, you'll get used to things. First the living and dining room." At the sight of all the gilded mirrors and glittering chandeliers, Imelda sat down, put her hands over her face and started to cry.

"Darling, what's the matter?" Shu asked flustered by the sudden onset of tears.

"I'm thinking I don't belong here; in this big house with endless corridors and staircases."

"Of course you belong here! You belong with me. You can do whatever you want. We have a separate private section, and you can make it into our home. You know, spin straw into gold. You know how to make things cozy."

"How can I make it cozy? It's half-museum and half-house! Wherever you look there are these statues. Then when there are no statues, there are huge mirrors, so you stare at yourself. The rugs are too beautiful to walk on... a... and the chairs are too expensive to throw your legs over. Everything is so cold and untouchable."

"I never saw it that way. I was born here and I guess one gets used to things. Listen, we'll get rid of everything you don't like: change all the pictures, furniture, drapes, and try to make it home."

Imelda felt ungrateful. "Oh Shu, I'm sorry. I think I am just overwhelmed. Everything is on such a grand scale, I feel so small and afraid of failing all your expectations."

They hugged for an instant, acutely aware of the many peering eyes silently watching them.

"And now to our bedroom," said Shu, his smile was wicked and his eyes twinkling. Imelda blushed.

"If you notice I have added a small kitchen through that door. It used to be a veranda."

"Oh good. I can cook here. I've learnt lots of new dishes. Cabbage, brussel-sprouts and turnips. Learnt them from my Irish aunts."

Shu reacted in mock dismay. "Thank god you don't have to cook then."

"What do you mean, I don't have to cook?"

"We have cooks to do that, you tell them how you like a dish and they do it." As they rounded a corner into the room, Shu kicked the door shut and pulled her into his arms.

"I've waited so long to hold you again. I've missed you every minute we've been apart," he whispered in her ear.

"Me too," she murmured dreamily as they kissed.

There was a slight rustle and a shuffling of feet that Imelda first heard. As she languorously pulled away she was faced with a red-faced Boroma not knowing where to look. Flushed, she quickly jumped away from Shu who reacted with controlled humour.

"Ma, are you stalking us already?"

"Your father asked me to remind you that the family is coming for an early dinner," she muttered.

"Thank you. Next time send Meera."

"Who's Meera?" Imelda asked.

"She's Ma's maid and spy Number One," Shu replied dryly.

Boroma left the couple wringing her hands in dismay, and muttering under her breath, "Chee-chee." She was inconsolable to her sister on the phone, repeating again and again the horrible scene she had witnessed.

That evening, Imelda dressed in one of the dresses Sir Dhiren had given her. She also wore the emerald pendant and earrings. She looked dazzling as Shu's family gathered around her, touching her hair, her face. It was all innocent curiosity, as Menu and Chotto sat protectively by her side. Imelda was the centre of a family love fest.

"I love your accent," Chotto gushed, "and your hair! Do you colour it?"

"Heavens, no. I wouldn't choose this colour if I did," Imelda
laughed.

"I would," Menu said admiringly, lifting and examining the
hair closely, stroking it like fine silk. "So beautiful with your
blue eyes and fair skin."

"Her eyes are green," Chotto corrected. "They match her
necklace."

"I don't care! Blue or green, they are the most beautiful eyes
I have ever seen."

Imelda had never been fawned over by so many people and
was embarrassed by the open show of admiration. Older ladies
came over and took her chin in their hands repeatedly saying,
"Such a beau-tee-full girl!"

Others squeezed her cheeks so hard her eyes almost popped,
"Such a swee-eet face, no? Our Shu is a lucky man."

No one had ever talked to her like that, or forced her to eat
until she almost puked. Shu tried to rescue her, taking her plate
away but was quickly shooed away by the elders. "So sweet! He
is protecting her from us. Go away, you can't talk to her until you
are married, you're in Calcutta now." They all had a good laugh.

"Imelda, don't bother to remember their names," Shu shot
back, "we're never going to see these people again."

Imelda felt very confident suddenly as she sought out Shu's
eyes. He was watching from a distance with an 'I-told-you-so'
sort of grin on his face.

Boroma was heard repeating many times, "Mai ta bishone
phorsha," meaning "the girl is very fair."

'Phorsha' was the first Bengali word Imelda learnt. Everyone
who met her commented on how 'phorsha' she was, and it was
meant as a compliment.

Imelda was made to feel very welcome. That is one of the strengths of a traditional Bengali family. They may argue, have different opinions, but once a decision is made, the family comes together to give their full support. Sisters, brothers, aunts, uncles, cousins and grandparents, all of them supported Amarendra and Pankajini Bose's acceptance of Imelda as their daughter-in-law. After dinner, the conversation continued in the living room where white-gloved waiters offered fluted champagne glasses to the family. Most of the older women opted for ginger ale or fresh apple juice.

Amarendra took Imelda's hand and signalled Shu to join them. The three of them went to the centre of the room where Amarendra raised his glass to quiet the chattering crowd. He spoke with an easy elegance.

"Imelda, I want to welcome you into our family. As you can tell, Shu is not the only one you have enchanted. You have won all our hearts." There were shouts of approval and loud clapping, and some tears. "My son fought long and hard for you, and now I know why. I was immensely proud as I watched you disembark the ship with your head held high. You are so much younger than I had expected. I hope all of us in this room will remember this moment. The moment you joined our family, a brave young Irish girl of eighteen who left her world to be with our son in his. May you be blessed with happiness. Let us raise our glasses to Imelda and Shu, my daughter and son."

23

Calcutta

Kamala Das, a well-known Bengali socialite and a college friend of Chotto, was pressed into teaching Imelda all the subtle nuances of Bengali society. Behaviour that was perfectly accepted in Western society had to be tempered in India. Kamala was known for her uncanny ability to transform her Indian clients into westernized memsahibs in under six months. Her course guaranteed the ability to speak and understand English. She was a professional beautician who had been to England and quickly picked up the 'dos and don'ts' of British high society. She was in great demand by newly-wed 'Brown sahibs,' for at the time, a wife who knew the difference between a fish knife and a salad fork was considered a great asset.

With Imelda, her role was reversed. This was going to be the Indianization of an Irish girl, who had to learn the unwritten rules for acceptable behaviour in her new home. For starters, anger or affection were not to be publicly displayed, and all disagreements were to be had behind closed doors: the façade of respectability had to be maintained.

The relationship with servants was also difficult to

understand. Shu seemed to have a close relationship with all the male servants that worked with the family. But Kamala warned Imelda, "You cannot become friends with the maids, they will grow to disrespect you. You can shout all you want at your maid, but the heavens will fall if she ever raises her voice to you."

"But father discusses everything with Ashu," a confused Imelda replied.

"I know this is complicated, but Ashu is technically not a servant, nor are Baboochi, Biswas, Partho and Aloke. Don't worry. You have time before any of them will understand you anyway."

Kamala took Imelda and Chotto sari shopping. First stop: New Market.

New Market through the years had become the largest shopping centre in Calcutta. It had separate fruit, vegetable, fish and flower markets, along with thousands of designer shops and restaurants – an early prototype of a modern mall. Patrons had a running credit with the shops they frequented.

In the store after an exchange of pleasantries, Kamala explained exactly what they wanted.

"Only French chiffons in shaded pastels," she said as she threw a brilliant pink sari aside.

A salesman sitting cross-legged on a covered divan would catch saris thrown from a makeshift hole in the ceiling, which he would then proceed to display with great aplomb and explain all the intricate work on each exclusive piece.

"These are in top fashion, Rajmata just bought a dozen of these…"

"We need to stay away from reds, magentas and orange.

They clash with her hair." Then, turning to Imelda, "Do you like any of these?"

"I love them all. I'm starving, we've been out for hours," she complained.

"Stop thinking about food. We have to go to Glamour, that's where Maharani Indira Devi buys most of her saris. Shopping for a marriage is serious business, Imelda. It's going to take all day. Now, back to Indira, she is the high priestess of fashion here."

"But the shop-man calls her Rajmata."

"Please do not say 'shop man'. That is so disrespectful, his name is Mr. Dutta," an exasperated Kamala explained. "Get used to the idea that how you look reflects on the whole Bose family. You have to keep up with Chotto."

"Or people will start talking," Chotto added, exhausted.

"I have to change how I dress, how I think and how I talk. Sometimes I don't give a flying fig."

If Kamala thought getting Imelda to buy the saris was difficult she had no idea what a daunting job it would be to get her to put one on and then actually walk around in it.

"Why can't I just twirl into the sari?" Imelda laughed as she spun on her heels, yards of sari flying all around her. Kamala sat on the bed, her head in her hands.

"Now it's my turn to cry. Imelda, take tiny little steps and pretend you are small and petite," she pleaded.

"But I'm not small and petite."

"I know. But don't walk like you are chasing a goat."

"That's a mean one, Kamala."

"For God's sake, don't lift the sari above your ankles. No ankles or legs please."

"But I'll trip over the pleats," poor Imelda pleaded in frustration.

The sari had to be pinned on to her at every possible juncture, at the pleats, at the waist and at the shoulders.

Amused by all this fuss, Shu passed by.

"Quack quack, waddle waddle," he laughed.

Imelda burst into floods of tears.

"I can't take this shit anymore!"

"Watch your language," he gasped between bouts of laughter.

"I don't give a damn. Takes me a bloody hour to get the bloody thing on, and then I take a few steps and it falls off, " She sat on the floor crying with the sari bunched up around her.

"Listen darling, only two more weeks. Mama babu's arriving next week, we'll get the adoption formalized, get married and all this will be history."

"I don't see *you* geting rubbed with yellow paste every morning. My arms are turning yellow, just look at them." She held out her arms helplessly. "I'm getting walking lessons, talking lessons, singing lessons, dressing lessons and Bengali lessons."

"I heard you are learning a Bengali song. Sing something for me."

"No, you'll only laugh."

"I swear I won't."

"You absolutely promise?"

"Absolutely! Not even a smile."

"Okay, look the other way."

Before Imelda had even finished a line, Shu was doubled over, hooting with laughter.

"Do you know what your mother told me today? She told me not to call you by your name, but address you as 'O-go'."

"Really?" smirked Shu. "I prefer Mr. Irresistible."

She threw a pillow at him as he ducked out of the room.

In the makeup department Kamala did an excellent job. Imelda had always just slapped on some lipstick and thought that was more than enough. Under Kamala's firm direction the young girl blossomed into a self-confident beauty.

Her Bengali teacher, Swami Anando, was a whole other story. He was a learned theologian, a skinny man, who wore a dhoti with a shirt over it. His head was shaven but for a *jota*, a long tuft of hair in the centre of the back of his head. He had pointed betel-nut-stained buck-teeth, a hawk-like nose and piercing black eyes. Imelda spent an hour each day with the Swami learning how to speak basic Bengali and identify the many goddesses in the Hindu pantheon.

When they first met neither could understand the other.

"You have a very funny accent. Where are you from?" he asked.

"From Ireland, originally," Imelda replied.

"Ah, I love islands: coconut and palm trees," he said nodding. "I feel you are very lucky, your aura is very good."

"They say I'm Irish lucky," Imelda agreed.

"You will go from Irish to Hindu in one birth, many people take many births, so you are on a quick-track, ha ha! You are on a quick-track to become Goddess Durga."

"Thank the Lord, it's not Ma Kali."

The Swami held his ears making 'tsk! tsk!' clicking sounds as he stuck out his paan-stained tongue.

"Don't say that. Big sin. Goddess Kali is a very powerful goddess."

So the lessons carried on with Imelda getting more and more confused, and punctuated frequently by the Swami's favourite refrain: "It is, and it is not. You see, but you not see."

Imelda thought Anando was hilarious. She would imitate him to Shu.

"He says 'You are the powerful Goddess Durga and I salute the Goddess within you'. Then I say, 'But master-ji, if I am the Goddess Durga, why can I not learn Bengali?'"

"You only need to know a little Bengali, just so you can communicate with the servants. They will also pick up English," Shu reassured her, rubbing her back gently.

"Shob boojhe," Imelda replied in Bengali.

When Sir Dhiren and Lady Mitra arrived in Calcutta, Imelda moved into their sprawling bungalow at 16 Ballygunge Circular Road. Arrangements were hurriedly made to go to the District Magistrate's office and formalise the adoption.

The atmosphere was tense as they sat around the Magistrate's large desk. The entire family insisted on witnessing the ceremony so he had to accommodate them with two rows of chairs. He slowly examined all the paperwork.

"Would you be kind enough to write your name in block letters?"

Imelda carefully wrote out her name.

"You have not put your good name, madam?"

Imelda was taken aback. The family sniggered nervously.

"He means your full name," Shu explained.

"No madam, I mean your *good* name."

"But that *is* my name," protested Imelda. "I don't understand, it's not good enough?"

"Sorry sir, madam, but the good name is very important in official paperwork."

Imelda ran her hand through her hair. "Well… my father used to called me the Irish Joan of Arc… what about Joan?"

"Imelda… Joan… Bose," Shu repeated. "That sounds wonderful! What do you think, Sir Dhiren?"

"Imelda Joan Bose sounds splendid," Sir Dhiren agreed.

"So Imelda Joan Bose it is. Joan is her good name." Then he corrected himself, with a slight giggle. "Not Bose quite yet."

They all thanked him, leaving him a box of sweets.

Imelda was now an official Hindu, daughter of Sir Dhiren and Lady Mitra, resident of Calcutta, with a very good name: Imelda Joan Mitra (or 'Mitter' as she pronounced it.)

While Imelda was absorbing the smells, sights and colours of her new environment, she was exhausted over the many arguments she was having with her interior designer trying to get him to understand the ambiance she wanted in her suite of rooms.

"I cannot make the man understand, I don't want it all fancy and fussy," she complained to Kamala. "He's always muttering about high teas and silverware sets. Please explain no high teas and cucumber sandwiches here. I don't want to be afraid to use my own china. I don't know where Shu picks up these people to help me…"

"At the Club. I think I will get Mira to help you. She does know where to get things."

"Mira?" Imelda replied, astonished at the suggestion.

"Yes. I know people are always gossiping about her but she gets great deals on artwork and furniture. You can't be eating off plates that even the servants won't touch, and Mira will understand what you want; good quality, simple, not ornate."

Imelda was unconcerned about the warnings of well-meaning friends, because she enjoyed shopping with Mira. With her help, she transformed the huge bare rooms into a series of smaller comfortable sections.

The bedroom they left alone with its huge four-poster bed and camphor chest. They added a few bright blue pillows to the sofa, and a standing lamp. A tall mirrored dressing table completed the room. Landscapes of lush hills with flowing streams replaced the stern portraits, adding to the ambiance of the rooms. Under Imelda's guiding eye, the whole suite was transformed from a cold impersonal space into a warm and glowing home with an air of elegant informality.

24

Calcutta

As the day of the wedding approached, Sir Dhiren floated the idea of having a Brahmo Samaj ceremony. The Brahmo Samaj movement, led by Rabindranath Tagore, was a reformist version of Hinduism, with a believe in one God, no idol worship, and most importantly, giving women equal participation in all ceremonies. Shu immediately thought it was a brilliant idea, and got no resistance from his father. Boroma, on the other hand, swore she was not going to participate if the family priest, Mukeipande Chakravarty, was not in charge. Sir Dhiren agreed to go along with his sister, but Shu was adamant about not caving in to his mother. There was an angry standoff.

"I'm sick of my mother and her tantrums. Why should we have a ceremony that neither of us believes in? In the Brahmo ceremony, Imelda's beliefs are recognized and so are mine. That's worth fighting for. As far as I'm concerned she does not have to attend."

Shu was right. Boroma tried to control their every move, and made sure they were never left alone. They would stare longingly at each other across the dining table while playing footsie underneath, Shu's mother narrowing her eyes at their conspiratorial smiles.

The wedding was a week away and the Brahmo Samaj question was still being hotly debated. Tensions were running high and Boroma was having a meltdown. Family members travelling long distances had already arrived. Rooms had been fitted with mattresses and beds; hired cooks were making meals for about fifty people a day. A large dining area had been set up outside in the courtyard under a big white tent. Garlands of lilies and tuberoses had been hung over the doors and the gates. The fountain had been filled with blooming lotus flowers, and decorated with strings of flowers entwined with twinkling lights.

According to Bengali tradition, a week before a wedding a goat has to be sacrificed to the Goddess Kali and fed to a few hundred poor people. Family members have to personally serve their guests, ladling the food from large steel buckets as their guests sit cross-legged and eat from banana leaves. This ritual officially marks the beginning of a wedding. It sets the tone, followed by daily gatherings for different rituals and pujas.

The day of gift exchanges is also important. There is a hierarchy of gifts that the family has to give to close relatives; aunts, sisters-in-law, grand-aunts, sisters, brothers and cousins. They all receive saris or small pieces of jewellery according to their place in this hierarchy. The jeweller and the sari store have running tabs and are on high alert for exchanges and express orders.

The atmosphere had calmed, as all had gone well, and family members could be heard squealing with delight as they greeted long-lost relatives. Much to Imelda's distress, Barbara and Tulu Sen could not attend as Barbara recently had a miscarriage.

One day, Shu found her in a pensive mood, sitting on the edge of the fountain looking at the beautiful lotus blossoms. He took her hand.

"A penny for your thoughts, my beautiful bride?" he asked softly.

"I was just thinking how beautiful these lotus blooms look."

"AND? You can't fool me."

"I wish Kathleen was here." Her voice broke as the tears flowed. "Everyone is being so nice to me, yet I feel so alone. I know that sounds ungrateful."

"This will be over soon… In a few days we can start our lives together."

"I know. Anyway, where were you this morning?"

"Went to choose the elephants," he replied cheerfully.

"What?"

"Elephants. Two of the most enormous elephants you've ever seen. I chose the ones with the biggest flappyiest ears."

"You're not riding an elephant?" Imelda exclaimed, her eyes round.

"Nooo! But Sir Dhiren wants them to blow rose petals as the guests arrive. Isn't that brilliant?"

"Everything looks so beautiful. Those lotus flowers are so perfect," Imelda continued as she gazed at the fountain.

"Father chose them for you himself. He says he knows exactly what you like," Shu added as he followed her eyes. She smiled forlornly.

"If only there was one teeny shamrock in the lotus pond."

Ashu was assigned to gather the immediate family into the sitting room. As they helped themselves to tea and sandwiches and an array of desserts, Amarendra Bose took the floor. He began by thanking everyone, especially Sir Dhiren and Lady Mitra. He again repeated his delight in his new daughter, Joan, and the happiness she had brought to Shu and the entire Bose family.

"You all know that we are having a bit of resistance to the Brahmo ceremony. I want a little feedback from you, Joan." He looked at Imelda.

"I just want a simple ceremony. Less tension and less spending."

"Shu, your thoughts?" he asked his son.

"I have no problem with the spending," Shu joked, "but I do want the Brahmo Samaj ceremony. It respects Joan and my wishes, and I don't understand Ma's resistance. It's a Hindu ritual – just without too much hoopla."

"We all understand that Joan and Shu have to be married in a Hindu ritual, whether Brahmo or traditional. We cannot just have a small civil ceremony, Imelda, because we want to show the world how delighted we all about you joining our family." He took a deep breath, stopped and lit his pipe, and after a few puffs walked over to where his wife was sitting. "Boroma wants our own Mukeipande Chakravarty to conduct the puja and be part of the wedding ceremony. I can understand that, he has been part of all our celebrations for the past two decades, and certainly cannot be left out. These are valued family traditions. We have family members who have joined us from all over this country and Ma wants them to recognize her as matriarch of this household. Therefore, I suggest a compromise. Purohit Mukeipande Chakravarty will be in charge of the daily rituals in this house and will assist Deb Mukherjee, the Brahmo Samaj priest, in the actual marriage ceremony. There will be a fire, and the rest of the ritual will be in keeping with the Brahmo tradition. Any objections?" Everyone agreed, and Shu went over and hugged his mother.

"See Ma, that wasn't so difficult, was it?" he laughed.

"For you, everything is easy," she replied, smiling with relief.

Sir Dhiren Mitra's house was a magical fairyland the night of the wedding. The entrance had a beautifully decorated arch made up entirely of white flowers. Hanging from them were strings of white lilies, strung at different lengths to form an oval opening for guests to walk through. Above the arch was a small box-like structure also constructed out of white flowers from which the musicians entertained the guests. The path leading to the house had beautifully decorated alpana on either side. Traditional Bengali patterns were created on the ground – swirling circles, ovals and paisley patterns made from the petals of marigolds, roses, jasmine and lilies, dotted here and there with small clay oil lamps or diyas. The trees twinkled, while the house glimmered with strings outlining its outer rim.

A huge tent was set up on one side of the lawn. Inside, from its high ceiling, cascades of green satin flowed down and were tied back with white bows. The tables and chairs were set in green satin and white taffeta. Opposite, and closer to the house, stood the marriage canopy.

It was beautiful in its simplicity. White tuberoses strung together formed a lattice, stretched between four banana trees at each corner. Lighted diyas led all the way to the canopy, where the heady scent of the flowers filled the air.

Imelda's day started early. Traditionally, a bride is supposed to fast on her wedding day, but Imelda was allowed to eat fruit, vegetables and yogurt.

There were six women in attendance, all under the supervision of Kamala. Sir Dhiren's daughters, Lotika (Monu) and Bashi, tried to cheer Imelda up.

"Remember, Imelda: last day of hell," joked Monu.

"Now you know why I will never get married," Bashi stated firmly, as Kamala shooed her out.

The day began with an exfoliating rub made from a flour paste, followed by a turmeric and sandalwood massage. Once her skin was polished and glowing, her hair was washed and put up in a French twist with white jasmine pinned along the side. Subtle sandalwood dots adorned her forehead, and kajol accentuated her blue eyes. A red liquid, alta, was painted all around her feet.

"I'd sooner elope than go through this rubbish," Monu grumbled, annoyed at all the ceremonies she had to attend.

"Can people elope in India?" Imelda asked.

"Lord, not in this family. Come on, everyone is waiting to bless you with fertility rites and god-knows-what."

The men in the family carried the bride on a palanquin to the marriage pavilion. Imelda came down escorted by Chotto and Menu and various cousins. Lady Mitra greeted her and guided her to a low chair placed on a raised dais in the middle of the room.

"Joan, this is the blessing ceremony. We have all gathered to give you our blessings and pray for your happiness, which hopefully will include children. Now, sit down on this chair, and accept the sweets in your hand. No sweets in the mouth," she warned everyone.

Then with much aplomb, an enormous fish, ornately

decorated with shiny beads and huge glass button eyes, was brought and placed before her.

"Are we really going to eat this?" Imelda whispered to Kamala.

"Only if you want to have kids," she replied laughing.

After lunch, Imelda was allowed to rest for a couple of hours before Kamala arrived to get her ready. Relaxing for the first time in weeks, Imelda had a long and luxurious bath. The water was infused with lavender, jasmine and rose. While wrapped in a towel, she had her hands and feet manicured, the beauticians insisting on reapplying the red alta. Her hair was tied back and rolled into a very sophisticated bun, entwined with jasmine and secured on either side by two diamond pins. She looked regal in her wedding finery, gold and diamond bangles on her wrists and the famous diamond star around her neck.

"I don't think I can move," she said under her breath.

"You won't have to till after the ceremony, then you can change into that light chiffon sari," Kamala whispered back.

"The one with the pearls?"

"You look absolutely stunning. Just don't trip over the pleats."

"What if I have to go to the bathroom?" Imelda asked terrified at the thought.

"That is not going to happen. Do NOT and I repeat NOT drink any water."

At seven, she was escorted downstairs to await Shu's arrival.

Shu was throwing tantrums of his own. He refused to have his picture taken with the traditional white crowns Bengali grooms were required to wear. He refused to bathe in milk, and wanted no more ceremonies at the home to welcome the new bride. He wore a simple cream-coloured silk shirt and a silk dhoti. He would only wear a gold chain around his neck and the emerald ring his father had given him at his graduation.

His friends Robin Mitra, Bappa Mallik, Nitish Roy and Nikhil Chowdury were all there dressed in silk shirts and dhotis, and had started the celebrations early by getting Ashu to bring them a bottle of scotch.

By the time they had to leave the house they were inebriated, loud, and egging Shu on.

"This is the worst bloody wedding I have ever attended. No nauch girls, no fun! Shu you better do something to liven this shit up. I'll give you a hundred bucks if you kiss Imelda in front of everybody," Nikhil dared him.

"I'll make it two," Bappa agreed.

"I'll give anything for a striptease," Robin added.

Worried about their condition, Ashu brought in cups of black coffee.

"Ashu bhai! Did they lead you to the gallows like this?" Nikhil thumped Ashu on the back.

"Don't talk bloody rubbish. Drink your coffee and keep your mouth shut. Boro Sahib is coming soon, so no more whisky!"

"Drink the bloody coffee, will you? You can't be pissed on my wedding day," Shu warned his friends.

"I vote for nauch girls!" Nikhil bellowed.

"Okay, Ashu, it's nauch girls for my friend and I don't want to hear you say 'bloody' for the rest of the evening." Shu instructed Ashu. "Now, get some nauch girls or we'll make you dance."

"Drink the bloody coffee before I throw you into a cold shower," Ashu replied, defiant to the last.

It is traditional to blow conch shells on auspicious occasions in Bengal. The best 'shank' blowers were usually the servants who were always included. Shu left the house accompanied by his parents, brothers, sisters, cousins and friends in a retinue of cars, with the sounds of conch shells surrounding them.

In the meantime, the guests had begun arriving. Two elephants with decorated headgear and brightly designed saddles stood on either side of the floral archway and gently blew petals in the air to welcome the arriving guests and dignitaries.

Lord and Lady Wellington, the viceroy of India and the governor all arrived punctually at seven-thirty, followed by the chief justice and Maharani Indira Devi of Cooch Behar.

Suddenly there was a quiet as the shehnai-players fell silent. Led by an entourage of conch-blowing relatives, Shu materialized from amid the crowd. He looked tense, as he made his way to the pandal accompanied by his parents. Imelda was already at the entrance of the canopy, with her eyes cast down as she had been instructed. He saw her standing there, looking so fragile and so lost. They exchanged garlands, as Imelda kept her head bowed.

"You can look up, it's only me," Shu said softly.

"No, I can't. I've been told to keep my eyes down," she replied hardly moving her lips.

"Rubbish," Shu replied and he took her chin with his hand and lifted it, kissing her gently on the lips. There was a slight gasp and then a titter of laughter among the crowd.

Nikhil, Bappa, Nitish and Robin jumped up and down and would not stop whooping and clapping until there was a standing ovation from all the guests. Shu, smiling, took Imelda's hand and led her to the chair.

Shu swore for years that amid all the din and commotion, he still heard his mother's disapproving "Chee-chee!"

The ritual was short, and soon they were walking around the fire seven times. With the placing of red sindoor in her hairline, they were officially married. Petals and rice rained down on them as they emerged Mr. and Mrs. Bose.

After the ceremony, Imelda was taken inside and dressed in a much lighter chiffon sari. Shu and his friends changed into tuxedos. They then were re-introduced as Mr. and Mrs. Bose and joined their friends and family for a western-style dinner accompanied by light chamber music.

After most of the guests had left, Imelda and Shu headed home. Once in the house, Shu lifted Imelda in his arms and whooping and puffing ran along the corridor into the bedroom. Their bed had been decorated with red rose petals and strings of white tuberose buds.

As Shu struggled through the door, the first thing he saw was his mother sitting serenely on a small bed and being fussed over by two maids. One was combing her hair, the other massaging her feet. He stopped so suddenly that he almost dropped Imelda.

"What took you so long?" Boroma said calmly. "I'm exhausted."

"MA!" he yelled. "What are you doing here?"

Imelda was exploding with laughter; she had to cover her mouth at Shu's outraged expression.

"What do you mean what I am doing here? It's traditional for the groom's mother to spend the first few nights with the newly married couple. I will only sleep here until you leave for your honeymoon. Thank God it's only for two nights."

Shu left the room and roared for Ashu from the top of the staircase.

"It's just so people don't gossip," Boroma explained to Imelda. The maids rushed out. Ashu came in followed by Biswas.

"Ashu, did you know about this?" Shu demanded, pointing to the makeshift bed.

"I'll take the bed," Ashu quickly signalled Biswas to help him.

"I just wanted to avoid a scandal," Boroma muttered as she got up to leave.

"Scandal? What about 'Mother Found Murdered On Son's Wedding Night'? What is wrong with you?"

"Don't talk to your mother like that! My mother-in-law slept with us for a year."

"Her mother-in-law slept with her for a year?" A bewildered Imelda repeated, as she carefully tiptoed over to the bed where she collapsed in hysterics, laughing like a maniac.

Shu was beginning to see the hilarity of the situation. He watched his mother gather up her things, struggled to look stern as he sat next to Imelda who was holding her side in pain as she tried to breathe between the snorts. As the door closed, he took a deep breath and keeled over in spasms of uncontrollable laughter. The two of them lay there shaking in convulsions until they were completely exhausted. They lay there for a while, but as soon as they caught each other's eye, they would burst again into gales of laughter. Finally, a worn-out Imelda turned to Shu, her face streaked with kajol. Seeing the mischievous twinkle in his eyes, she leapt up to check the mirror.

"Oh my God, look at my face!" she screamed.

Shu, meanwhile, was looking under the bed.

"Okay, Partho, out you go."

"No!" Imelda ran back and peered under the bed from the other side. "I can't see anyone…"

"I can," he said, suddenly serious. "I see the most beautiful girl in the world."

A quiver of excitement ran through Imelda's body. She half covered her face with the pallu of her sari.

"Shall I do the dance of the seven veils then?" She twirled around him, her eyes luminous as her sari floated about her. Shu reached out and caught the end of the sari drawing Imelda closer to him, as small pearls fell to the ground.

"Careful, darling, we can't lose any pearls."

Shu's dark eyes were burning while Imelda blushed and felt demure. Slowly, he unravelled the sari and threw it aside.

25

Darjeeling

Shu wanted to go to a quiet place for their honeymoon, where he and Imelda could relax and spend some alone time. He chose Darjeeling, a quaint hill station in the foothills of the Himalayas, where his father owned a summer home. The town sits on a crescent facing the highest mountain range in the world, where on a cloudless day the peaks of Kanchenjunga and even Mount Everest are visible. Darjeeling was loved by the British for its temperate climate, its terraced plantations and magnificent tea estates. Snowy View Lodge was a large wood-framed cottage where the Bose family spent most of their summers.

The day after the wedding, Shu and Imelda were packing their suitcases to be sent ahead of them to the Lodge.

"I thought we were going to be alone for our honeymoon," said Imelda frowning a little.

"Of course we are, my darling," Shu replied.

"Well, I heard Biswas, Mina and Hari were going to be joining us."

"Oh, the servants? We can't go without them: who's going to cook and clean the place?"

"There already is a cleaning lady and chowkidar there. I can cook too you know. I just wanted the two of us to be alone."

"Darling, we will be alone. The servants have their own quarters. The place is quite isolated, the car can only go so far on the cart road; we have to walk up a steep, narrow mountain trail to get to the lodge."

"I just want to be completely alone with you," Imelda groaned, as she went over and hugged him. "Well, I'm done my packing: pants and sweaters, nothing fancy, right?"

"You'd better take a few outfits. We will go to the club."

"Oh, Shu, you promised we would not be going out anywhere."

Shu laughed as he planted a kiss on her forehead. "The Gymkhana Club is walking distance from our place. We'll have to leave the house once in a while, for God's sake. Pack a couple of formal dresses, you never know what may come up. I'm taking a suit and a couple of smoking jackets."

The jeep, with Hari, Biswas and Mina on board, left for the long drive up to the lodge.

Imelda and Shu left the next day, and were soon on the 'toy train' known as The Queen of the Hills slowly chugging along the winding trails of the steep mountainside. Biswas was there to pick them up for the last leg of the journey, about an hour's drive to the Lodge through the crisp fresh mountain air.

Imelda immediately fell in love with the place. It wasn't so much a cottage as an elegant two-storey house. From the windows one could see the endless vistas of the Kanchenjunga mountain range, the snow-covered peaks sparkling with brilliant white light. Along the east ridge stretched the Lebong racecourse and to the west stood the big blue dome of the Government House.

Snowy View Lodge was surrounded by terraced gardens, tended by a mali and his helper. Shu had brought along a few books to help Imelda familiarize herself with the flora and fauna of the region, and read about the Gorkas, the local hill people. He carefully set these out on a table for her.

Imelda immediately busied herself with the garden, communicating with the mali by showing him pictures of the flowers she wanted, or taking him to other homes to show him which flowers or bushes she wanted planted at the lodge. Shu usually sat outside, reading and drinking beer while Imelda pottered around.

"Why don't you sit down and relax for God's sake. Can't you pretend to read a book, or at least shuffle them so they look used?"

"This is relaxing for me," she would reply ecstatically, as she went to hug him with her muddy hands. The horror on Shu's face as he shied away made her laugh. "It's only good old mother earth, silly."

This was the happiest Shu had seen Imelda since her arrival in India. They took long walks along the mountain trails. They went to the Gymkhana Club to play tennis, usually rounded off with a few gin fizzes and a light lunch. Since February was off-season, there were few friends around with whom they could socialize. Unabashed, they held hands and exchanged hugs, as passers-by smiled and walked on.

One evening, as they were walking up the mall to Observatory Hill, a green Bentley stopped and the back window rolled down.

"What the bloody hell are you doing here?" a very elegant lady called out to Shu.

"My thoughts exactly," Shu replied laughing. "Remember Joan?"

"Of course I do, darling. Bhaiya got injured so we're skipping the rest of the polo season. I'll be in touch. Ciao, darling," and with a small wave she was off.

Imelda was looking after her car with her mouth wide open.

"Is she 'The Maharani'," Imelda asked bug-eyed.

"Yes: Indira Devi of Cooch Behar; her family gave father the panther cubs, and the diamond star."

Two days later a smart-looking man in a gold-braided jacket turned up at the door. He handed a gold-rimmed envelope to Imelda.

"It's from the Maharani!" Imelda shrieked, tearing open the envelope. "She wants us over for a pot luck on Saturday evening. Do Maharanis have pot lucks? She signed it with an 'I'. That's brilliant, just 'I'!"

"They are just people. Remember Bhaiya?"

"Of course I do. Is he the King?"

"Good god, Joan, they are not called kings! He is her son, and will be Maharaja some day. Bhaiya spent most of his life abroad, you may have met him at one of Nikhil's parties. He always wanted to play doubles with Nikhil because he loves to win," Shu laughed.

"I could do that, just sign 'I', or a fancy 'J' maybe. Do you have a Bose coat of arms or emblem?"

"No, we're as ordinary as Smith over here."

As usual, Imelda had nothing to wear to the dinner. She settled for a cashmere sweater over corduroy pants.

"I don't think I'm dressed posh enough," she worried.

"It's a pot luck dinner," Shu replied.

"But it's a *Maharani's* pot luck."

Biswas knew the way to Collington, the Cooch Behar's residence in Darjeeling. A liveried guard examined their invitation before letting them in.

Indira Devi welcomed them warmly as she led them to a sitting arrangement around a roaring fire.

"How are the newly-weds doing?" she asked as she welcomed Imelda with a fleeting kiss on the cheek. "Bhaiya will be joining us shortly. Do sit down and make yourself comfortable."

Imelda did not hear a word she said. She was starring dumbfounded at the slender, long mother-of-pearl cigarette holder from which the Maharani was taking delicate puffs.

She was casually dressed in a blue two-piece ensemble with a cashmere cardigan and grey gabardine trousers, high heels and a double string of pearls.

"Dinner is very informal tonight, small and intimate. Joan, what can I get you? We have a batch of dry martinis, stirred, or would you prefer scotch?"

Imelda did not answer until Shu nudged her out of her stupor. "Martini will be fine," she said with a glazed smile.

For the rest of the honeymoon, Imelda did nothing but talk about the Maharani and her 'foot-long' cigarette holder, the tiger skins thrown casually all over the place, and the liveried butlers.

The three weeks passed all too quickly. The books were left untouched on the table, but the garden looked beautiful, and soon they were on their way back to Harish Mukherjee Road to take up official residence.

26

Calcutta

The turbulence Imelda brought with her into the Bose household was unimaginable. Everything she did had repercussions. Boroma was in constant pain with migraines and headaches, attributing it all to this new exuberant daughter-in-law. Just as she would settle down to do her morning puja, she would hear Imelda belting out a tune from the shower. She would encounter an unblushing Imelda, in petticoat and blouse, happily showing the housemaid how to dust or properly polish an item. One morning she decided to confront Imelda.

She walked into the bedroom and was astonished to find Imelda on her knees showing the cleaning woman how to polish the marble floor.

"What are you doing?" she gasped.

"I'm showing Shanti how I want her to buff the floor. I don't want phenol in the water. I got some pine cleaner and am showing her how to use it."

"Can't you just tell her?"

"She couldn't understand me."

"Next time ask Bijoya to explain," Boroma huffed off muttering, "and please put on your sari."

Next moment she was on the phone with her sister. "I'm telling you she must have been a maid. She was on her hands and knees scrubbing the floor."

"I've heard respectable girls from abroad are used to doing everything themselves," Charulata explained.

"I just hope she is not a maid – I could not bear the shame of it. Girls from good families cannot have such big feet. You should see her practising her Bengali with the servants, laughing out loud. What am I to do?"

"Everyone loves her – including your husband – so I would be smart and keep quiet."

"Even Bijoya is saying things in English, everything is *madam this* and *madam that…*"

"Pankajini-di, control yourself. If Gheri heard any of this he would walk out, so go and meditate."

Then there was the Cow Incident. Imelda had started taking an interest in the care of the cows and the calf. She made them unleash the calf and let it drink freely. Twice a day she made sure the animals were taken out in the sun and walked. She had clean bins for the hay and oats, and a separate one for water.

She took special interest in their grooming. She went shopping and bought a brush and a large sponge to teach Vinod how to wash and keep the animals spotless, brushing them in the direction of their muscles.

"I have never seen the cows in such pristine condition," Amarendra beamed.

All the milkmen from the neighbourhood came and asked

for her advice, thinking she was some sort of animal specialist. They would bring scraps of paper on which they had written questions, which Bijoya the cook would translate.

"Bijoya, tell him that the teats need to be massaged with oil."

"What mean 'teats', madam?" Bijoya asked.

She pointed to a maid's breast.

"Oh, madam!" Bijoya blushed, looked skywards seeking divine intervention.

"Fingers, good word." He hung his hand downwards to explain to a mortified milkman.

"Tell him massage the 'fingers' with ghee, and also rub a wee bit on the arse, you know under here." She lifted the tail and pointed, as both Bijoya and Vinod covered their faces.

One afternoon Boroma was resting when her maid came running to tell her to look out the window. There, in the fountain, was Imelda, happily splashing herself, in her blouse and petticoat. She had been showing a neighbouring milkman how to clean his cow, and got so hot she decided to cool off.

Boroma rushed outside with her maid carrying a towel.

"What are you doing?" she asked sharply.

Surprised at her angry tone Imelda replied carefully, "I was feeling hot, so I'm just cooling myself a bit."

"Get out immediately. All the servants can see you! You cannot do these sort of things here."

"But I'm only cooling off, it's not like I'm in my bra and panties."

"Chee-chee! Bra and panties! Hai ram, what am I going to do with you?"

Imelda came out looking like a wet rag. She was sick of Boroma constantly telling her not to do such ordinary things.

That evening she was called down to talk to her father-in-law, who was sitting out in the garden with Ma. Imelda knew she was in trouble.

"Joan, come and sit next to me. Ashu, get memsahib some hot tea."

She looked down, flushed with embarrassment. He watched her, smiling: she looked like a naughty child.

"What happened this morning to upset your mother-in-law?"

"Well, father, I was in the cowshed, when Mr. Mukherjee's milkman bought over their cow, and asked me how to take care of her."

"Yes, Mr. Mukherjee has been very impressed with the way you have spruced up the place."

"I know he is your friend, so I showed them how to clean and brush the cow. I was so hot and sweaty that I thought I would cool off in the fountain."

"Ma feels your going around in a blouse and petticoat is not appropriate," he explained.

"I find her saris thrown here and there. On the stairs. In the kitchen. Outside the shed… Is this any way to behave?" Boroma interjected angrily.

"Calm down. It seems the sari is the problem."

"Yes!" burst Imelda. "They're so unwieldy. I keep tripping up, the pleats keep coming undone…"

"Then why are you wearing a sari?"

"Because… because I thought I have to."

"You don't *have* to do anything. Shu has made that very clear. Once in a while you can put on a sari, but only if you want to."

Imelda looked astonished.

"Wear whatever makes you comfortable. Get yourself some comfortable trousers – whatever. Now," he went on, taking her hand and leading her towards his parrot's perch, "let me show you what Shona can say. I have a sneaking suspicion you have been talking to her."

Boroma who covered her head in front of her husband watched how comfortable Imelda was holding his hand. She had him wrapped around her little finger.

Imelda made quick friendships with the servants by practising her Bengali with them and helping them to learn English. She asked personal questions about their families and seemed genuinely interested. One day, she shampooed and styled Vinod's wife's hair, who did not leave her quarters for a couple of weeks after that.

Imelda did occasionally go to the Gymkhana Club for lunch or a game of tennis. She was invited to play mahjong and bridge, but found that boring. She liked being active, riding at Bhaiya's fancy stable, but her social life revolved mainly around Shu and his group of friends.

Sometimes they would go to posh cocktail or garden parties. Here Imelda had to be more discerning with her clothes, choosing jewelry and shoes to fit the occasion – often following Kamala's advice.

At home, her days were beginning to follow a routine. After breakfast with Shu at eight, she would go and check the cows and tell Vinod what needed to be done. Then she would walk around the garden with the mali, and talk to Ashu about the birds, repeating the new words. If she had a tennis game, she usually left after Shu, and ate at the club.

She looked forward to having tea with her father-in-law when he returned from work. She would rush to greet him, give him a bear hug and tell him about the day's happenings. She had a very easy relationship with him and couldn't understand why everyone was so afraid of him. If she was not there he asked after her.

Amarendra made sure she accompanied him to the garden house built on the banks of the Hooghly river. He usually visited it every other Saturday. The mali there reported to her, not only about the fruit and vegetables, but about the chickens and other animals. Boroma was becoming envious of all the attention she was getting. She often watched from her bedroom window as Amarendra and Imelda walked hand-in-hand, her cold, distant husband enchanted by this young interloper.

For her part, Imelda tried hard to befriend her mother-in-law.

"Ma, why don't you join father and me for tea?" she asked.

"I don't like to drink my tea with all those birds around. I prefer to drink my tea in peace."

"But Ma, you should spend more time with father," Imelda pressed on.

"I spend time with him at dinner, that is more than enough. Baba, you ask too many questions."

One day they were in the garden. Imelda was lying on the grass and had a flower in her hand.

"Get off the dirty grass and sit on a chair," Boroma admonished her.

"I love grass, it feels so good. Look! He loves me!" She laughed as she pulled the last petal off a daisy.

"You are such a child, why do you play such silly games?" Boroma asked shaking her head in disbelief.

"Because it's fun. Now I'm going to pull petals off this flower for you," Imelda chuckled. "She loves him, she loves him not, she loves him… she loves him not."

Boroma rolled her eyes. "Such foolishness for a married woman, go read a good book."

"See, the flower says 'you love him'," Imelda rolled on the grass, her eyes glinting mischievously.

"Chee-chee! We don't talk of those 'aushobo' things in India."

Imelda's candour about love and her open show of affection absolutely astonished Boroma. Imelda seldom saw any physical affection exchanged between her in-laws and it bothered her.

"Why is love aushobo? I love all of you."

"Can you please keep it to yourself?"

"Why? I am not ashamed of it," she persisted.

"If you don't stop talking nonsense I am going to leave," Boroma said.

"Well, I want to know. Do you ever hug father? Just one small teenie-weenie hug?"

"How can you even talk about such things? We're different from foreigners, we keep things private."

"Why? Is it wrong to hug or kiss someone?" Imelda continued badgering her.

"Low-class people talk about those things. Enough talk."

"High-class people have children too. How did you have five children?

"You western girls have such silly ideas about love and marriage. Stop this vulgar conversation." Boroma was flushed with embarrassment. "Go and check if Baboochi got catfish for dinner".

At the mention of catfish, Imelda lowered her eyes. She was afraid Boroma had been told about the Catfish Incident. Boroma eyed her over her glasses.

On that memorable day, Imelda had decided to go to the kitchen to check on the dinner menu.

"What is this?" Imelda asked the cook, pointing to a bucket in which three or four catfish were thrashing around.

"Dinner memsahib," he replied, smiling.

"Why are they alive? They can hardly move in there."

"Fish always alive. I get in bucket from market, fresh. I choose best fish for family."

"I'll put them in the fountain until dinnertime; the poor things can have one last swim…"

"No! No, memsahib, please! Boroma will be very upset."

Ignoring his pleas, Imelda grabbed the bucket and dumped the fish into the fountain with the water lilies and goldfish.

About an hour later, she heard the mali frantically banging on her door.

"Memsahib, quickly come! Fish eat and walk."

"What do you mean fish eat and walk?" Imelda ran after him. Catfish can walk on land and a couple had managed to get out of the fountain basin and escape, while the third was happily gobbling up Amarendra's exotic goldfish. There was mass panic as the servants tried to scoop out the catfish as it darted between the lily pots.

Imelda had been in Calcutta over four months and was beginning to understand the complex balance of running a family kitchen. The food was simple, but it took a lot of effort to make it that way. The only outside food allowed was mishti doi, a sweet curd, and sweets, usually sandesh or rosogolla.

What fascinated Imelda the most was the *sil-bati* and the *boti*. The *sil-bati* was a slab of stone with slight ridges. On it, spices were ground into a silky smooth paste. The *boti* was for chopping and slicing fruit and vegetables. It consisted of a curved blade set on a piece of wood that was held on the ground with one foot. Despite her protests, she was banned from using it, because of her large feet.

She had befriended her sister-in-law Dhebu and often went to her room to spend time with her. Dhebu had a parrot, and Imelda decided to clip its wings so she could be let out of its small wire cage. As soon as they let it out, the bird flew out of the window and landed on the branch of the mango tree. Imelda immediately scrambled after it, screaming for a ladder. She climbed onto the tree, inching along from branch to branch to get close to the bird. All the servants gathered at the base of the tree shouting instructions.

The mali's wife burst into tears as the bird, petrified by all the noise, sat watching Imelda inch closer. Just as she was about to grab it, it hopped casually onto a higher branch.

"You bloody little bastard," Imelda cursed, as she desperately clung to the slender branch on which she was precariously balanced. Sheepishly, she looked down at the terrified crowd.

"I think I'm stuck," she yelled, red with embarrassment. A ladder was finally found and she was helped down, still more concerned about the bird than her own scratches and bruises.

"Boudi will never forgive me if the parrot flies away," she wailed to Ashu.

"No problem. I put food and water in cage, and he will come down. Quickly change before Boroma sees you."

The straw that broke the camel's back, however, was the tale of the mischievous goat.

The family priest, Mukeipande Chakravarty, had bought one of the fattest and most noble-looking goats to offer as sacrifice for Kali puja. The goat was bought a few days ahead and kept in the cowshed. Imelda came down for her usual rounds when she saw this magnificent animal.

"Whose goat is this?" she asked as she scratched its forehead.

"Goat for sacrifice, memsahib. Kali puja in four days."

"What? We're keeping this animal here until then? Does Boro sahib know about this?"

"Yes, madam. We do every year like this for many years. Big puja, have to bzzzzzzp." He made a buzzing sound as he ran his finger along his throat.

"What sort of god wants such a beautiful animal killed?" exclaimed a horrified Imelda.

"Ma Kali drink blood, memsahib."

For two nights, Imelda could not sleep and made sure Shu didn't either.

"Why don't you do something about it? You just can't lie here and let it happen. He is the most beautiful goat I have ever seen," she pleaded.

"Forget it, you can't prevent them sacrificing a goat at Kali puja. Don't stir up any more trouble than you already have."

"Trouble? What trouble? I've done nothing... lately," she protested.

"Good. Let's leave it at that. It's the same as killing chickens; one has to deal with unpleasant things in life."

"Chickens. You don't get to know the chickens. He is a beautiful animal." She threw up her hands. "Ah, forget it. I can see that I will get no support from you." Imelda pouted angrily.

"I support you unequivocally, but sweetheart, we have to choose the battles we can win."

She turned her back to him, shaking the bed as she did so. Unable to sleep, she lay awake, her mind spinning as she thought of ways to save the goat.

The night before the puja Imelda, with the help of a reluctant Hari, brought the goat into the small room behind the study. She hung quilts and blankets across the windows to make it soundproof. She even brought in a gramophone to cover up any bleating.

She swore the servants to silence by bribing them, telling them that God would reward them for saving one of his precious creatures.

There was chaos on the morning of Kali puja. Chakravarty searched everywhere for the goat, as the servants pretended to know nothing. The priest warned of horrendous consequences. He suspected Imelda.

"Sorry to disturb you, madam, but… the goat is missing."

"Really? And why are you telling me?" she asked innocently.

"Servants say you last person feeding goat, so I thought maybe…"

"Yes, I fed him to make him nice and fat for Goddess Kali. You better go and look for him."

"Madam, you sure you no have him? Big problem for me and family if we no find goat."

"How much would another goat cost?" she asked with deep concern.

"No! No, madam. Big curse!"

"Here, fifty rupees, just go and get another goat. If the old goat returns we will use him in the next puja. Now hurry, or Boroma will get upset." She handed him the money and shut the door, relieved that her friend, the billy goat, had stayed quiet, as though he knew his life depended on it.

Poor Chakravarty ran with his bow legs to the market and got a replacement. When all the sacrifices were over, Billy miraculously reappeared.

"For sure it's a miracle!" Imelda exclaimed to Boroma.

Billy turned out to be more than a mere miracle: he became a pest of biblical proportions. He ate the prize flowers, nibbled the clothes hanging out to dry, and ate great holes in Boroma's saris. The feisty goat could not be contained. The last straw was when Amarendra was bending over his prize roses, and Billy ran up and butted him from behind. As the servants helped Amarendra to his feet, Ashu rushed to fetch Imelda.

"The goat came from back and, *pha-taak*, hit Boro sahib," he giggled.

"Oh no," Imelda gasped.

"Boro sahib fell into flower. Flower here and there. Very funny!" Ashu continued, delighted.

"Is he hurt?" a scared Imelda asked, rushing out.

"Boro sahib no hurt, no worry," Ashu called after her.

She burst into Amarendra's study where he was sitting. "Baba, I just heard about Billy. Are you alright?"

"We'll leave my pride out of it, but I escaped with a few scratches," he replied with a smile that immediately relaxed Imelda. "But your friend Billy is creating havoc, eating everything in sight, chasing the peacocks, butting the calf and now me."

"I know. He's more than we bargained for," she agreed.

"I must say, he does have spunk, butting the hand that feeds him. But I think the garden house would be a better place for him: we can keep him in the fenced area. What do you think?"

"That would be perfect; " Imelda replied.

"Are you letting them bring the live fish into the kitchen?" he asked.

"They hide the bucket from me."

"Joan," he continued, a serious note in his voice, "I know you have lofty ideals of uplifting the downtrodden, but it's one thing to teach the servants English and quite another to eat in their quarters. You cannot socialize with everyone so freely. I am bringing this up as it is a constant source of tension with Boroma."

"I just treat them as human beings," she replied.

"I know social position and class are ugly words – but they exist. I know you mean well, but you're my son's wife, and you have some prestige to uphold in this household. There's a line you yourself will have to recognize that you cannot cross."

"I will, Baba, I promise. But... can I paint the mali's room?"

"Wasn't it painted a few months ago?"

"I want to paint the windows."

"Windows? There are no windows in his room."

"Yes, I know. That's why I want to paint some in, so they can pretend to have windows to look out."

"Pretend to look out *where*, exactly?"

"Into the pretend garden that I'll paint of course," Imelda was now laughing at the incredulous expression on Amarendra's face.

As she left, he smiled to himself. He had grown so fond of

this red-haired girl. He loved the way she rushed to greet him when he returned from work, weaving her arm through his as they walked around the garden. Everything came alive around her – the animals, the servants, the guests. He didn't want to crush her spirit but she would have to learn where to draw the line. It was all about lines and she had to know when to step over, and when to step back.

27

Calcutta

Shu's social standing and career continued to rise, helped immeasurably by the cachet of having a western wife. The Boses – who were liberal for a traditional Bengali family – put very little pressure on Imelda to conform. Boroma was constrained not only by her son's attitude, but also by the implicit support Imelda got from her husband. Shu would accept no interference in his wife's activities.

The Queen's Ball at the Tollygunge Club in late October signalled the beginning of the social calendar. It was required to be seen at this event. The club, affectionately called the 'Tolly', was situated on an immaculately maintained ninety-acre golf course, rivalled only by the Royal Calcutta Golf Club, the oldest bastion for white-only members.

The Queen's Ball was followed by the Prince's Polo Ball, marking the height of the polo season. The Maharajas camped out in Calcutta with their prize horses and star players to compete for the coveted Queen's Cup. The royal families of Bikaner, Udaipur, Cooch Behar, Patiala and Jaipur led the field in these fiercely competitive matches. The undisputed star of the polo set was Jai (Man Singh), the dashing Maharaja from Jaipur. He and his beautiful wife, Gayatri Devi, had close ties to the British royal family and were one of the most photographed couples of the decade. Gayatri's Devi's brother, the crown prince of Cooch Behar Jagaddipendra Narayan, known affectionately as Bhaiya, was also a rising star. At the polo matches, the elite of India's burgeoning high society would mingle with the Maharajas and their English bosses.

Imelda and Shu were easily assimilated into this life, feeling quite at ease riding alongside the Maharaja's prize polo ponies, and being invited back to the palace for light suppers. Imelda's natural affinity with the horses and keen interest in riding led her to quickly get involved with the fanatics who met at six in the morning to ride the hundreds of acres around Victoria Memorial. She remained singularly unimpressed by the status of the elite group around her, which only made her more endearing to her close circle of friends. However, she watched the Maharanis closely, began to wear personalized jodhpurs and even bought a long silver cigarette holder. She was impressed by the sheer glamour of a gloved hand holding a long holder between the first two fingers as white smoke gently swirled around it.

The ultimate luxury for a lady of stature was to have her 'own' tailor. The best tailors were in high demand, so one would have to entice them with all sorts of special perks. It was a cut-throat business, but with some help from the ever-resourceful Kamala, Imelda secured the services of one of the best. He was a prime source of information, and helped keep her up to date on what styles were in vogue with the Vicereine or Maharani Indira Devi.

The Viceroy's Grand Ball usually signalled the end of the social calendar.

Imelda had continued her friendship with Mira, whose life seemed repeatedly drawn into a vortex of scandal. After she divorced her husband, she caught the eye of a well-known Maharaja. Their affair was the talk of the town. Kamala, Chotto, Imelda and Mira were having lunch together when Mira told them she might, in fact, marry the prince.

"When?" an excited Imelda asked.

"He has to sort it out with that hag of a mother. Maybe after the Grand Ball…" her voice trailed off.

As soon as Mira left, Kamala whispered, "The Prince will never marry her."

"Why not? She's so lovely," Imelda asked confused.

"Oh, grow up Joan! Mira knows exactly what she is getting into. These Maharajas live by different rules. For them, marriage is all about forging alliances and accumulating wealth."

The prince and his mother, the Maharani, hosted the banquet that season with great panache, but Imelda was distracted.

On their drive home, Imelda remarked, "I feel so bad for Mira."

"Why?" said Shu. "What happened?"

"She wasn't even invited to the dinner. She had all these sari blouses made, and the prince even gave her an emerald set to wear. She thought he may announce their engagement tonight."

"People like Bijoya don't marry women like Mira."

"That's a terrible thing to say."

"Sadly that's the truth. She's divorced, she's lived with who knows how many men. Maharaja's wives have to be respectable."

"The hypocrisy is disgusting. Why do women stand for it?" Imelda replied angrily.

It was becoming clear to her that behind all the glamour and glitz of the fantasy 'Royal Life,' the hidden reality was a messy affair.

28

Calcutta

The Boses were going through another crisis with Saury's impending return from England. He had eight months to finish his chartered accountancy degree, and was returning to Calcutta to check out employment opportunities.

Shu was apprehensive about Saury's future with Leslie. He realised that the opposition to a second foreign daughter-in-law in the family would be daunting. His advice to Saury was to get married in England before he returned, so that it would be more a question of dealing with a fait accompli. Saury, on the other hand, believed that Shu's marriage to Imelda would have paved the way for him and thought, with his usual cocky self-assurance, that he would easily overcome his mother's objections.

It was not to be. Both parents dug in their heels and said one foreigner in the family was enough.

The bribing began early. Knowing his son's fondness for fancy cars, Amarendra promised him the car of his choice if he married a Bengali girl. He assured him of total autonomy in choosing both car and wife. Boroma's tactics were different. Every time Saury came to talk to her, she would break down, sobbing loudly about facing everyone with two foreign daughters-in-law. Saury finally caved in to the joint pressure and agreed to see a few Bengali girls.

"I can't handle her constant crying," he lamented to Shu. "How did you do it?"

"I ignored it, told Ma to take her drama elsewhere," Shu explained. "Get Baba on your side. He was a rock with me – and he can stop Ma's sniffling in a minute. If you really want to marry Leslie you can't faff about looking at cars and see women. You're digging yourself a hole you won't be able to climb out of."

"But Ma told me you saw quite a few women…" Saury said accusingly.

"Yes, I did, but I made a deal with father that I would meet them to appease Ma. There was never any question about who I would actually choose. And don't be an idiot about the car; you know you can get any bloody car you want."

"It's not the car, Shu. Maybe I don't want Leslie to go through this ridiculous charade. The constant battle for acceptance would wear her down. Seriously, I don't know if she could handle it. Baba adores Imelda: you've won the battle right there."

The negotiations with Saury were endless, and none of the girls satisfied his high standards. The car on the other hand was easy, he chose a replica of his car in London; a Lagonda, black, instead of the winter green, and a regular four-door model instead of the coupe. He had begun to receive great job offers.

On a casual evening out to see a performance of *Gitanjali* at Ashutosh College, Amarendra was captivated by a beautiful student who opened the show with a song. He quietly contacted Bashishata Babu, a professor at the college, and invited him over. Bashishata agreed to make inquiries about the girl.

A few days later, the professor came back with all the relevant information. The girl's name was Bina Mitra. She was the second daughter of a widow who lost her husband in Burma during the war. She came from a *bhodro* family: her uncle, Rai Bahadur Dibendra Mitra, even had a street named after him. She had two sisters, Ranu and Dolly, and a brother, Kanu. She had graduated from Bellora Girls School in Bhowanipur, and was in the final year of her BA at Ashutosh College.

The professor found out where Bina caught the bus for college and suggested Amarendra take Saury to see her surreptitiously before he made any contact with the family. Amarendra happily agreed and persuaded his reluctant son to stake out the bus stop.

Saury was soon swayed. She was one of the most beautiful women he had seen: slim, fair with incredibly refined features. He immediately agreed to meet her.

The meeting was set up at her uncle's house. Boroma was in a frenzied state of anxiety, as she had not seen Bina and did not completely trust her husband's judgement.

Saury arrived, accompanied by his brothers and parents. After a traditional tea and small talk the attention shifted to poor Bina. She sat in the centre of a big sofa with her eyes downcast. Her mother sat next to her and held her hand, trying to keep her calm.

Her uncle welcomed the family, then launched into a litany of Bina's accomplishments. She was a great student, played a good game of badminton, was a leading star in the college plays, could dance and, of course, she sang like an angel.

"Would you like her to perform a song for you?" he asked. "Or dance?"

"I remember her amazing voice," Amarendra replied, "so maybe a song?"

A harmonium was carried in on cue and placed on the floor. Bina, not lifting her eyes, slipped behind it and sang as she picked out the melody on the keys. Everyone sat motionless as she sang, her rich melodious voice resounding throughout the house.

Shu bent over and whispered to Saury, "I take it all back: that girl is incredible. She's ethereal, like a painting. I'm not sure she'll choose you."

As they were leaving, Boroma went up to Bina, held her face in her hand, squinting as she examined it closely. Then, touching her mouth with her forefinger, rubbed Bina's arm. Bina did not know what was happening, as all the family stared at this strange behaviour.

"What was all that about?" Shu demanded angrily once they were seated in the car.

"I was just checking if she had white makeup on her arms."

"She may not accept a marriage proposal after this."

"Not accept a proposal from us? My son is the most sought-after groom in all of Calcutta," she huffed angrily.

"Maybe in your imaginary world, Ma," said Shu, "but believe me, men like us are a dime a dozen for a beautiful girl like her. What do you think, Saury?"

Saury was quiet, lost in his own thoughts and did not respond.

"I doubt we will find a more suitable girl for Saury," mused Amarendra, "but the decision is his to make." They drove the rest of the way back in silence.

Saury and Bina met a few times, always escorted by her mother, brother and uncle. Bina was swept off her feet, she later recalled.

"It was as though Prince Charming himself galloped up on his white horse and carried me off into the sunset."

The marriage was arranged in a month, and Bina did not finish college so she could accompany Saury back to England.

As the arrangements were being made there was great exhilaration in the house. Imelda felt excluded, as Saury pointedly avoided her. He knew she was upset about Leslie and did not want a confrontation.

A week before the wedding, Ashu came into Shu's study and in hushed tones informed him that Saury had not left his room that day. Shu went looking for Saury and found him in his pajamas, in a darkened room, very drunk.

"Avoiding the world?" Shu asked, sizing up the situation. "May I join you?"

"Help yourself." Saury pointed to the bar. "Read this." He threw a piece of paper at Shu. "Should make you happy."

Shu leisurely poured himself a whisky, carefully added the soda and slowly gave it a stir. Then he picked up the paper: it was a telegram from Leslie.

Dearest love,
I completely understand your dilemma and stand by your decision. Our time together will always be cherished by me. You will live in my heart forever. I wish you and your wife every happiness. Leslie.

Shu re-read it, his voice cracking. "She has class," was all he could say. He sat with his head down, silently watching Saury.

"Why should this make me happy?" he asked.

"Because that's what you wanted, all of you. You let me drown. You let me drown without throwing in the rudder."

"You mean paddle."

"Fine. Go ahead make fun of me. I know exactly what you think, you and your coterie of friends: Saury, the poor bastard with no guts. You're my *brother*, I relied on you. You just watched me drown."

"Saury, you're drunk."

"Of course I'm bloody drunk, so what? When the chips were down where were you? All that talk of support, huh. Where was all that bloody support?"

"I told you and am telling you again: if you don't want to go through with the marriage, I'll talk to father."

"It's too late. Leslie wouldn't have me back anyway. She thinks I'm a bastard too, just like the rest of you."

"It's not only about you. You're too bloody boozed up to understand. You cannot go through with this, not only because of you … you're ruining a beautiful young girl's life."

"See, there you go again. What about my life? Does it have no value?"

"You dumb bastard, you did this to yourself. I would drag you to father's room now and tell him to call the whole thing off, but you are in a drunken stupor and I don't want to embarrass you. Damn it, we will talk to father tomorrow. Stay in bed and do not touch another drink. I'm taking the damn bottle."

"You fool. Do you think that's the only bottle I own?" Saury slurred. Shu opened the bar and took out three other bottles. He was shaken by Saury's condition and realized he had done nothing to help him.

That night, Shu could not sleep, and early the next morning went to talk to his father. Amarendra was puzzled. "He suggested an early marriage so that Bina could go with him to England and now he's changed his mind? Is your mother aware of the situation?"

"Father, you know Ma. She is not only aware of it, she created it. She's just too wrapped up in this whole marriage circus to care."

"You are always so hard on your mother."

"Who does one turn to? You hide in your ivory tower. This train-wreck is moving too fast for any of us. We have to consider the girl and her family."

"Disaster. This is going to be a disaster. What is the matter with your brother?"

"Oh, he's the only one to blame now, is he? Interesting how everyone jumps off the sinking ship. What happened to 'we can't have two foreign daughters-in-law'? It really made the one foreign daughter-in-law you have feel appreciated, you know. Remember her? The one who waits for you every evening just to spend time with you and your damn menagerie?"

"That kind of language is uncalled for. I adore Joan, so don't bring her up."

"Your youngest son is in trouble, and it does not help to see you put all the blame on him. There is plenty of that to go around. I take some of it, I should have spoken up much earlier when you were piling all that pressure on him. You came down like a ton of bricks. Poor fellow didn't know what hit him. He didn't stand a chance."

"Why didn't he say something? Didn't we sort out your problem?"

"Well, despite all his bravado, Saury is a much better person than me. I was not afraid of the consequences and not affected by Ma's drama. Saury does not want to disappoint the two of you. The ball's in your court now."

Shu was angry with his father, and realized that Saury was right about him. Amarendra paced the floor of his study, talking in muted tones to Ashu. Saury was called in as soon as he woke up.

He was subdued and embarrassed and explained he was too drunk to remember what happened. However his behaviour was no indicator of what he really felt. He didn't think Leslie could survive in Calcutta. He did not want to put her through the drill. His mind was made up, he saw great potential in Bina and was willing to take on the responsibility of marrying her. He felt going to England would be beneficial, especially with Lady Mitra and Sir Dhiren there to guide Bina. The marriage preparations were continued as planned.

The wedding went off in great style. Illustrious people from all over India were present. Bina was the most beautiful bride. She seemed as delicate as a porcelain doll. Every morning, she was massaged in cream, and Imelda watched in awe as her thin wrists and small feet were gently rubbed. Boroma was in mother-in-law heaven telling this new Bengali bride what to do, and making the bevy of servants run round in circles fulfilling her every whim. Two weeks after the wedding, Saury and Bina left for a honeymoon in Paris and later settled in London where Saury completed his studies.

29

Calcutta

The weather was beginning to get unbearably hot. Imelda, like the rest of the people in Calcutta, lapsed into inertia. She would either soak in a tub, or lie wrapped in a wet towel beneath the punkah, as it was pulled back and forth by a servant.

The windows were covered with chiks, heavy matted blinds made from straw which were kept damp so that the air blowing through them was cooled, providing some measure of relief. The city was like a furnace. The Central Government shut down and its bureaucrats moved to hill stations like Darjeeling, or to the new official summer capital, Simla. Imelda and Shu followed suit, moving to Darjeeling for the summer months with the rest of the family.

They returned to the city, with the monsoon hard on their heels. Dark clouds raced down from the hills just before the monsoons and came towards the city in tumultuous waves. The torrential rains followed, pouring down in sheets, accompanied by deafening thunderclaps.

The arrival of the monsoon rains was celebrated with dancing in the streets. After the rains came the flooding, when life was again held captive by uncontrollable forces. The rains brought in their wake the inevitable yearly cycle of sickness and disease. Typhoid, cholera and malaria ravaged families indiscriminately, killing the old and the young, the rich and the poor, the weak and the frail.

The rain permeated everything. Clothes bloomed with mildew and insects came indoors to escape a watery grave. Little cups filled with disinfectant were put under the legs of cabinets to keep white ants away.

Terrified of malaria, Imelda would lie for hours under her mosquito net waiting to kill the one mosquito that always managed to get inside.

Imelda and Shu were vacationing in the seaside resort of Puri when Imelda began to have giddy spells. They cleared up once they got back to Calcutta, but when the nausea came back she decided to see a doctor. This was the much awaited pregnancy the Bose family desired. After the devastating death of the first grandchild, Tonu, the news of an impending birth brought unbounded joy.

Imelda was under strict instructions not to leave the house and not engage in any physical activity. A chef was hired to make special meals for Imelda, and the hunt was started for a suitable nanny.

Boroma had nothing to do but harass Imelda about the baby. "Be careful about what you eat, everything you eat affects the baby. Do not eat begoon (brinjal) or beets, it will make your baby dark. Stay away from sweet things or you will have a girl," on and on. Imelda finally went to Shu.

"Please tell your mother that I am not sick! She had a fit this morning when I left for tennis."

"Just ignore her," he replied nonchalantly.

"No, Shu, you have to talk to her. She wants me strapped down and force-fed Horlicks every hour on the hour."

"Don't worry darling, Saury and Bina are arriving next month, all the attention will shift. Come here and tell me about your day. You have to be happy, we don't want a grumpy baby, now do we?"

Bina and Saury returned and settled into the upstairs flat and as Shu predicted, the attention shifted to poor Bina. Boroma was constantly interfering with everything she did, choosing her saris, taking her shopping and picking her friends. It was as though she had finally found a sweet Bengali girl she could groom and mold, having struck out twice with Dhebu and Imelda.

Imelda busied herself getting the nursery ready. As her pregnancy advanced, her desire to see her own family intensified leading to periodic bouts of depression.

It was in her third trimester that she and Shu made their way to the Three Hundred Club for a gala hosted by the Governor General. Dressed in all their finery, along with Bina and Saury, they were going in style: riding in a hired horse-drawn carriage. As they passed the race course they found themselves drawing alongside another carriage holding their good friends Tuku and Sunny Balm. Tuku, the princess of Kakinaga, a small principality, was one of Bina's closest friends.

The two groups shouted insults at each other, comparing

horses and carriages. Imelda suddenly yelled for the driver to stop. Thinking it had something to do with her pregnancy, both carriages stopped. She rushed out and climbed up beside driver grabbing the reins from his startled hands.

"Race you to the club," she yelled excitedly as she swung the whip in the air, barely missing the driver's head.

"Are you out of your mind?" Sunny Balm yelled.

"Let's go!" she shouted back.

"Joan, you can't do this in your condition," an alarmed Shu cried.

"Do you know how sick I am of those words? In my condition, I can do anything. Whoa! Giddy up! Giddy up!"

They raced through the cobbled streets, the carriages neck-and-neck as startled crowds dashed out of the way. Imelda's carriage pulled ahead as they entered the club. Exhilarated, she clambered down. "I haven't had so much fun in ages."

"Very unbecoming for a lady-in-waiting," Saury sniffed as he straightened his bow tie. "I wouldn't be surprised if our membership is revoked. Next time we will drive separately."

"We won!" Imelda laughed. "Doesn't that count for anything?"

"That was inappropriate behavior for a lady in any condition," Saury reprimanded her as he ushered a flustered Bina inside.

In all the ruckus, Imelda was afraid to mention the contractions that she was beginning to feel. Besides, Shu and Saury were ignoring her after her embarrassing behaviour.

Early next morning she was rushed to the hospital when her water broke. Amarendra and Boroma accompanied them. As the contractions continued, Imelda's groans got louder and louder. This was in stark contrast to the other Indian women in labour: their rooms were silent. Shu bustled about not knowing what to expect. He joined his father outside the delivery room. Both pretended to read the newspaper.

"Not as much fun as I had anticipated," he said under his breath. "How much longer will it take?"

Amarendra shrugged his shoulders, "I always came home after it was over. In retrospect, much more pleasant."

Boroma hustled out of the delivery room, her face red with embarrassment. "Oof baba! That wife of yours. You'd think she is the only girl in the world to ever give birth. She wants to see you."

"Should I go in?" Shu asked apprehensively.

"You better, or she'll scream the roof off."

He nervously slipped into the room and hurried to Imelda's side.

"Where have you been?" Imelda yelled.

"I was just outside the door. Ma was with you. Are you alright?" he asked quietly.

"*Alright?*" she wailed. "You have the balls to ask if I'm alright? Can't you see I'm in bloody agony! And it's all your fault, so don't try to sneak out again." Her groans amplified.

"It will be over soon, right doctor?" Shu asked nervously.

"Over for who?" yelled Imelda, "It's not over for me, so don't you even *think* of leaving."

As the time of delivery neared, Imelda's screams could be heard all over the hospital. Boroma covered her face in humiliation while she whispered to Amarendra, "She should have her mouth washed out after this. Chee-chee! I had five children and never let out a single sound."

Shu was asked to leave amid loud protests from Imelda.

Scared and shaking, he went out for a smoke. Even in the parking lot he could hear her. He paced the corridors, the moans following him everywhere. Then they suddenly stopped. In the deafening silence the thought came to him that Imelda may have died. Heart pounding, Shu ran back towards the delivery room. Boroma and Amarendra were standing at the door transfixed.

"It's a boy," Boroma whispered. "I have a grandson." She just stood there and wept. Shu saw his father's tear-streaked face.

"Have you calmed down?" he asked half-jokingly as he pushed open the door.

Imelda's hair was drenched in sweat, but she looked radiant as she smiled and handed the baby to him.

"Let me give my brave wife a hug first."

"Brave wife," Boroma muttered under her breath. "Where has *he* been?"

"He's seven pounds, one ounce. Isn't he beautiful, all seven pounds of him. He is perfect, ten little fingers and ten tiny little toes."

Boroma came over and gently took the baby from Shu.

"He's so fair! We will call him Arup, a face like a god."

"I wanted to name him Peter. It's my favourite boy's name."

"His name will be Arup and his good name will be Peter. Arup Peter Bose," Amarendra declared, and that was that. Imelda O'Connor had delivered the Bose heir.

Boroma examined the baby carefully. "He is the image of Shu."

"Surely after all that trouble he looks a wee bit like me?" Imelda protested.

"Ma, I think he looks just like Joan, he's got her nose and mouth," Shu said, but Boroma would have none of it.

"He is completely a Bose!"

What a difference a boy made. "I should have arrived here pregnant," Imelda kidded as she thoroughly enjoyed her new-found respectability. The birth of a boy cemented her position as a bonafide member of the family.

The biggest transformation came in Boroma's attitude and tone towards her. She usually talked about her daughters-in-law in a derisive manner, referring to Dhebu as 'the Rani bou,' Imelda as 'the foreign bou' or 'the red-haired bou,' and Bina as 'the Bangal,' meaning from east Bengal and looked-down-upon by those in the west.

Peter's birth changed the status of 'the foreign one,' to 'Major Boudi.' All decisions were now deferred to her, including meals and outings.

For Imelda personally, the change was immediate and profound. There were small perks, like the inherent right to get the newspaper first with her morning tea. The baboochi came in first thing in the morning and discussed the menu for the day. The driver would ask her when she needed the car, and last but not least, Ashu was assigned to put aside the fruit for Imelda while selecting fruit for Amarendra and the birds: you could not get more important than that. The grumblings and back-biting would start later, but for now Joan Bose was Queen of 84 Harish Mukherjee Road.

Amarendra immediately changed the name of the garden house to 'Arup Nagar' and gifted it to his grandson. Peter was an adorable baby, playful and naughty, learning early how to manipulate his doting grandparents.

Boroma was obsessed with Peter. She called him Petu and

wanted a minute-by-minute account of every little thing he did. His every move was discussed over and over again, with her sister, with her friends and with her husband.

For Imelda, it became a challenge to see her own son. Every time she asked for him she was told that he was with Boroma or Boro sahib. She gave the nanny strict instructions to put the baby in his own crib for his afternoon nap, but these instructions were overruled by Boroma. The subtle fight for control had begun, and her mother-in-law was edging ahead.

When the third nanny quit because of too much interference from the grandmother, Imelda finally cracked. "Now Mrs. Crawley has resigned because of your mother! Shu, I am not taking any more, you have to speak to her."

"Why do we need a nanny anyway?"

"Because they know how to bring up a child with some discipline," Imelda replied.

"I actually found Mrs. Crawley quite annoying, always telling us what's right and what's wrong. She had the nerve to tell me I was holding Peter incorrectly."

"We are out so much, I feel better knowing there's someone in charge who knows what to do."

"Joan, darling, let Ma enjoy her grandson. She was so devastated after we lost Tonu... just relax, things will fall into place."

"I am the baby's mother, Shu, and your mother needs to understands that. Peter is my child. Mrs. Crawley told me that Ma told her specifically to bring Peter to her if he cries. And that 'evil eye' black spot is ridiculous! I have to wash it off before I show him to my friends."

"I'll go and talk to her. Don't you have that tea party today?"

"God, yes, I almost forgot. I wonder where Bina is? I have to go, darling, it's for Claudia Griffon, Saury's boss's wife. I've invited Mrs. Holmes too; she is chairman of my riding club." She gave Shu a quick peck on the cheek and ran off to find Bina.

Her sister-in-law was making her way down the stairs. She looked very pale.

"Are you okay?"

"I feel awful," said Bina. "Everything makes me want to throw up."

"You're pregnant," Imelda exclaimed joyfully. "What fun! Peter will have someone to play with, and with Dhebu's little girl we will have our own children's play group." Imelda hugged Bina.

Peter was growing up fast; he loved to visit Amarendra and feed the birds. They all recognized him, shrieking loudly, *"Petu, come here,"* and he would clap his hands together, jump up and down in giggles. "No, you come here."

Nine months later, Bina and Saury had a son named Abijit. To the family, he was known as Tutu, and he and Peter became inseparable as they grew up. They were as different as night and day. Peter was gentle and fragile, shy and soft spoken, while Tutu was rambunctious and loud. Peter avoided disagreements with Tutu and was also a manipulative mama's boy, letting Boroma win all his arguments for him.

While Peter giggled, Tutu laughed out loud. While Peter barely hit the ball to the boundary, Tutu sent the balls sailing over the fence and into the neighbour's house. Peter would carefully steer his pedal-car around the tables and chairs, never hitting anything, while Tutu was fearless as he rammed *his* car into walls and furniture. Peter's obviously had fewer bumps and scratches, so Tutu would crash his car spectacularly and then demand to drive Peter's. Rather than stand up for himself, Peter would go running to Boroma and complain.

"Ma, Tutu is taking my car again! He bangs into me all the time!"

Boroma always took Peter's side. "You can't take Petu's car and drive it like a junglee," she would scold Tutu.

"Why not? Joan-Ma told me Petu has to share with me and not be a sissy."

"Don't call your brother a sissy."

"Well, Joan-Ma says only sissies tattle-tale, and he always tattle-tales."

"Mummy also says not to bang your car into the walls," Peter added solemnly.

Five minutes later they would be best friends again.

Peter loved wearing hats. His favourite was a khaki topi without which he would never go out. His second love was his black dog, a springer spaniel called Blackie. There would be Peter in his hat, Tutu brandishing a stick and the dog, running, jumping, chasing, shouting and screaming all through the three storey house. Tutu was stronger and more athletic than Peter, but beneath his tough exterior beat a very gentle heart; he never hurt Peter, and never let him feel he was the stronger of the two.

"You can do it," he would say as he helped a tentative Peter to slide down the banisters. Of course when Peter crashed into Ashu or broke an antique vase or statue, he was quick to disappear.

"Tutu made me do it," was Peter's standard answer for all his bad behaviour.

Imelda was the one person Peter couldn't use to get his way.

She loved Tutu's devil-may-care attitude and secretly wished Peter was more like him. "I don't want to hear another word," she would say, when Peter came whining to her. "Fight your own battles."

Dhebu and Himanshu's daughter, Archana, watched from a safe distance. Unlike her cousins, she was quiet and well behaved. Her ayah always kept her safely away from the boys' roughhousing, but if Tutu or Peter so much as touched her, Archana was not afraid to give them a good push.

When Peter was around two, Imelda had another boy named Namtu. He was a cuddly bundle of joy. Both Imelda and Shu vowed to cut down on their social activities and take a more active role in his upbringing. Imelda wrote in a letter to Kathleen.

"Oh Kath, I wish you could see Namtu. He has your twinkle in his eyes and has the same dimple in his cheek. I am going to give him more attention. I just have to stop going to all those foolish teas and lunches. All the ladies talk about is how uppity the servants are getting, demanding a day off. So silly! Aunt Bea says you are seeing a young man in London called Eddie Cryan, any truth to that? What happened with Percy? You were planning a wedding the last time you wrote. I would love for you to visit me here. With all this war going on I wonder when we can meet again. I miss you so much, at times my heart actually aches."

Peter was initially unhappy with the addition of a brother – it took some of the attention off him – but Namtu was such a happy gurgling baby that he soon won over Peter and Tutu and they would take turns pulling his carriage behind their cars to make him laugh.

Despite Imelda and Shu deciding to stay at home more, the social whirl of Calcutta was hard to resist. There were two full-time nannies to look after the children, with Boroma in charge. Imelda did try to keep more control over Namtu, and it was easier because Boroma was consumed with Peter. There was slight friction between the sisters-in-law, as Bina began to resent the freedoms enjoyed by Imelda. She could order any meal and wore evening gowns instead of saris with no resistance from the in-laws. Boroma was just happy to be supervising Peter, and her obvious favouritism was not appreciated.

Politically, it was a very exciting time. The Quit India movement led by Gandhi was gaining momentum. One day, Bina and her mother were getting ready to attend a rally led by the great freedom fighter Sarojini Naidu, and Imelda, who was now pregnant with her third child, wanted to join them.

Boroma put her foot down. "You're pregnant and a foreigner, you can't go."

But Imelda was adamant: she wanted to be part of the movement. Bina's mother, a strong Congress supporter, encouraged her. "They will welcome you with open arms." She was right. Imelda was warmly included, and at the end of the rally when Bina and her mother took off all their gold jewellery to donate to the cause, Imelda took off her own bangles and added them to the pile.

The third baby was due mid-March when Shu was stationed in Bareilly to finish a project. Imelda and Namtu joined him with Hari and a nanny. Shu was supposed to return to Calcutta the first week of March, but as usual the project was delayed. Imelda was secretly hoping the birth would be March 17th: St.

Patrick's Day. The day dawned – but there was still no signs of contractions. She called her doctor.

"I must have the baby today: it's four days past my due date."

The doctor would have none of it.

"Joan, I don't meddle with nature. When the baby is ready, and your body is ready, it will happen naturally."

"To have a baby on St. Patrick's Day is very auspicious for me. Besides I have the names all picked out. Patrick for a boy and Patricia for a girl. Patrick is my father's name."

That night, Shu heard loud sobs coming from the bathroom. He rushed in to find Imelda in the tub crying her heart out.

"Oh my god, darling, what's wrong?" he gasped, scared witless.

"This bloody baby won't come out," she howled at the top of her voice.

"Shall I call the doctor?" an alarmed Shu continued.

"The bloody doctor won't lift a finger. I've sat in a warm tub for hours. I've stretched and pushed all day long and for what? Nothing! Now I won't have the baby on St. Patrick's Day."

"Is that why you're crying?" Shu sat down, then began to laugh uncontrollably. "That is insane! I can't believe it."

"All I wanted was the baby on St. Patrick's Day. Is that too much to ask?" She burst into a fresh round of sobs.

The contractions began later that night and on March 18th, 1942, Shesha Milty Bose was born. What happened to the name 'Patricia' is anyone's guess.

A year after Milty was born, Saury and Bina had a daughter named Shoma Mithu Bose. Saury and Shu's elder sister Menu had, by this time, had four kids – Krishna, Ranjana, Anjana and

Shivaji. They were the Mitras, and when they came over it was a mad house.

Boroma had little patience with her grandchildren, except for Nalu and Menu's eldest, Krishna. Krishna had what Boroma called 'pagga nakh' meaning pug nose. Poor Krishna would sit patiently and let her grandmother pull her nose to make it grow. Peter sat by and observed the process intently, saying, "I think her nose is good now. I think it has grown a whole inch."

Peter was very fond of his Krishna-di: she was sweet, gentle and quiet, and let him have anything he wanted. She would go with him and feed the birds and not scare them. She would let him brush her long black hair and pin flowers in it. Whenever Menu and family came over there was chaos and total havoc in the house, with the boys playing cops and robbers and chasing each other on bikes and cars all over the place. Peter would play for a while but escape the noise and madness by slipping away to play quietly with the girls, especially Krishna.

Peter, though adored and spoiled by all those around him, was a slightly detached child. Too much noise and activity bothered him, so he used to find quiet exploits to entertain himself. He loved to follow his grandfather around as he inspected the garden, examining the flowers, talking to the birds and checking out the cows. Petu would watched him closely, gravely observing all his mannerisms, which he would then mimick to perfection. His shoulders hunched, and his hands held behind his back, he would walk around the garden in his topi issuing detailed instructions to the mali's son.

"Make sure these flowers are cut back, send them to my mother. Why are there dead flowers on this bush?"

"Very busy, sir. Too much work."

"Get to it."

"Yes sir."

"The white peacock has been losing many feathers."

"Yes sir. Peacock lose feather all year."

"I saw Milty-baby chasing the peacock. Make a note to talk to her nanny about it. Also I saw Milty-baby pull the feather on Shona's head. Don't let her play with the birds. Namtu is better behaved, he can touch the birds. Those are my orders."

"No no, sir. Milty-baby never hurt birds."

"I have an important meeting now. I will meet with you tomorrow for further discussions."

"Yes, sir."

Boroma used to watch adoringly from the window. "He's going to be a great leader one day," she'd say.

30

Calcutta

In the 1940s, Calcutta, the capital of India and the crown jewel of the Victorian Empire, had an energy and exuberance unequalled anywhere else in the world. Calcutta society was a fascinating mix. The glitzy life of the rich contrasted starkly with the squalor of the poor and downtrodden. Eccentric English officials and zealous missionaries; regimented generals and idealistic soldiers. Not only was the city bursting with British officialdom, it had the largest US military base in the Eastern region. It was from Calcutta that American soldiers were deployed to Burma and Thailand, and Calcutta was their first port of call when they returned on leave.

Shu and Imelda relished this hectic lifestyle. With her outgoing personality, Imelda had an active social calendar, as did Shu – in many ways the epitome of a 'brown sahib', for whom nothing could be too British. They were privileged members of exclusive clubs, and Shu didn't see the irony of waiters serving guests with white gloves, while back at home his mother was hand-feeding his children as their English nannies clucked disapprovingly.

They were surrounded by like-minded people. There was Saury and Bina, Chotto and Nirmal Roychaudury, Robin and Pushpa Mitter, Bappa Mallik and his wife Chitra, Nikhil and his many girlfriends and of course Connah and Suraj Das.

Connah and Suraj had a love affair that was legendary. Connah was the beautiful daughter of a well-respected Bengali family. As an only child, she was pampered and protected by her doting parents. She met Suraj Das, a brilliant Punjabi businessman, when he delivered a package to their house. They fell in love, meeting surreptitiously at Victoria Memorial, driving in circles around local parks. When her parents found out they were furious and objected strongly, threatening to marry her to some rich Bengali boy. The strong-willed Connah ran off and married Suraj, something unheard of in those days. Connah and Bina became inseparable, and their children grew up as one large family.

There was also the dashing Brigadier Protul Lahiri. The story was that Protul was almost court-martialled for escorting a British General into the men's toilet at the Gymkhana Club and threatening to flush his head down the toilet when the General made an inappropriate remark to his wife.

Their lives were full and happy until the typhoid epidemic hit Calcutta in 1944. Despite every precaution Namtu became listless and quiet.

Death struck like a viper, unseen and immediate. He lay dead in his father's arms three days later. Dazed and bereaved, Shu carried his baby to his grave. Such a short and unheralded life: they hardly knew this little child, left in the hands of nannies and ayahs. The baby who was always gurgling and smiling, so excited to see them, was gone. He left the world with so small a footprint.

Shu kept everyone at arm's length and whispered prayers for forgiveness. Imelda stared vacantly unable to take in the sudden loss, not understanding what had happened. Shu was a different man after the death of Namtu. He brooded alone, isolating himself from Imelda in his grief, while Imelda was too distraught and too young to grasp the depth of his despair. She wrestled again with that same feeling of complete helplessness that she felt at her mother's death. The horror of seeing her dead son in her husband's arms never left her.

Together with their two remaining children, they sought refuge in the tranquility of Darjeeling. They spent many hours alone, walking along secluded lanes deep in the forest, lost in their unfathomable grief. It was time to re-evaluate their lives.

Peter and Milty clamoured for attention, constantly asking about Namtu and where he was. Peter sensed something terrible had happened in his parents' lives and wanted to get back to the security of his grandmother's care. He also missed his animals and his boisterous cousin Tutu.

He loved to tell her to eat anything disgusting. There was bark, worms, leaves or flowers, or even vegetables he did not like, and without hesitation she obeyed until the nanny stepped in.

"I shall report you to your mother."

"She's my sister, not yours," he shot back.

Of course, if Boroma had been there she would have rushed to his defence.

At dinner, there were constant tantrums about the food. Peter would not eat the chicken or the lamb and relentlessly asked for Boroma's special treats.

"I want kheer. And I want my butter shaped like an elephant."

"I will ask the cook to make kheer tomorrow, and we do not have the butter molds," Imelda replied tersely.

"You said that yesterday. Boroma always makes food that I like. This stupid cook can't even say fish, when I ask him what's for dinner he says, 'It's phish, baba'. I'm not baba or baby, I'm chotto sahib."

"You are a spoiled brat. Don't you dare ask to be called chotto sahib or Peter sahib. Who do you think you are, calling Hari stupid and telling Nanny not to call you by your name? Brat! You are to be called Peter."

"I hate it here, I want to go to Calcutta," he yelled back.

"Say that again and I will send you back," Shu replied in measured tones.

"Good. I'll leave tomorrow morning. And I'm taking Milty with me."

"Peter, stop this now," Imelda said bursting into tears.

Next day, Peter told Milty he was leaving her with their terrible parents and going back to Calcutta. She wanted to go with him rather than stay with her depressed and withdrawn parents. She wanted to go back to be with Namtu.

"I am too small to look after you, but I will come back with Boroma and pick you up. Promise." He gave her a big hug, then went to his father and demanded that the driver take him back.

"And how will we get back if you take the driver?" Shu inquired.

"Boroma can send the other car for you."

"Okay, leave, and don't come back," Shu replied.

Peter meticulously packed his bag, making Milty hand him his clothes one by one.

"If you are good, I'll leave my car for you," he said as he

handed her a small red racing car. She nodded eagerly, but howled when he said goodbye.

With a determined look of a boy ready for a long journey, he put on his topi, balanced his suitcase on top of it and strode out to the rickshaw that took them around Darjeeling. He got in and ordered the rickshaw puller to take him to Calcutta.

"Don't worry, my Boroma will pay you with gold." He sat back comfortably, placed his suitcase by his side, waved goodbye to Milty and the nanny, and said with great authority, "Chalo! Let's go."

Shu watched his defiant six-year-old through the sitting room window. He smiled despite himself: Peter had his mother's spunk. The image of his son leaving, with his suitcase on his head, was seared into his memory forever. He and Imelda talked about how spoiled their children had become, and vowed to take a greater interest in them, especially Peter, now that he was going into first grade.

They all returned to Calcutta together. For Imelda and Shu, it meant facing the reality of Namtu's death. To everyone around them, it seemed that Shu was more affected. He retreated into his books, and his personality had noticeably dulled. He began drinking a little more, laughing a little less and his sarcastic humour took on a bitter edge.

Imelda, on the other hand, handled her pain like she handled her mother's death: by focusing her attention on all the work that needed to be done. She was constantly active. The more things she had to think about, the less time she had to think about Namtu. So, along with her riding and playing tennis she busied herself with the children, and with the garden house.

She took a great interest in acquiring special brown Leghorn hens that produced large brown eggs. She was going to use them for eggs and food, but the 'food' part never did quite work out, and soon the farm was overrun by chickens, and Imelda became known as 'the egg lady,' who sent baskets of eggs to all her friends.

One day, she was in the kitchen talking to the cook and happened to ask where the family's rice came from: she knew it was not from the market, and yet they always had a steady supply. The cook explained that it came from a farm the family owned in Krishnagar. Amarendra leased the land to tenants who paid 'in kind' instead of cash. Imelda was intrigued and asked her father-in-law more about it. He explained it was technically not farmland, but had acres of mango and guava trees, rice paddies and a few dozen cows. The cows belonged to the tenants, who basically lived off the land, selling the rice and milk in the neighbourhood.

The farm was a three to four-hour ride from the city, and seeing Imelda's interest in it, Amarendra suggested that she could help Sarkar babu take care of it. Sarkar babu was the family accountant who took care of paying the employees and collecting money from all Amarendra's property. Thrilled, Imelda began by taking interest in their cows. She did her usual cleaning out of the sheds, organizing the stalls so that hay oats and grass had separate bins, and connecting a pipeline to the only well on the property.

The people were very happy, especially the women who, before the pumps were installed, had to walk long distances to carry the water back in heavy clay pots. They cooked her a feast and garlanded her.

'Joan-ma,' as she was called, became a much-loved person. All the children used to run around her when she arrived; giggling women watched her show the men how to brush and clean the cows, amazed that a woman could handle animals. Imelda would encourage the older girls to help her, for they were not sent to school. The work invigorated her and she slowly began to regain her self-worth. She showed the girls new hairstyles, brought saris for the women and learnt to cook simple Bengali food.

Joan-ma's Bengali improved significantly as she interacted with the local villagers. There were a few English words and lots of hand gestures. There was head nodding, hand signals and many hugs. Her naturally affectionate demeanour won their hearts. She took Peter down to meet the villagers, but he was skittish and shy as they showered him with affection, calling him 'Petu babu.'

Milty, on the other hand, felt at home with the women in the village. She had spent a lot of time with the servants so understood Bengali, and was used to eating the servants' food. She ate everything they offered her, reaching out her hands, and pointing to food with her favourite word, "hum."

Imelda would go down with Sarkar babu every month, and if she missed a visit, the locals would send her food and home-made delicacies.

Shu noticed Imelda's growing self-confidence and energy return as she got involved with Krishnagar and the garden house. She had returned to her roots: farming, animals and honest hard-working people. He, on the other hand, struggled with intermittent depression.

Imelda talked about her new interests with him.

"I don't understand how you can communicate with them," he asked amazed, as she repeated the stories of their lives.

"Why? They are just people like you and me. Maybe they are not as lucky as we are, you know with our cars and houses, but they have the same hopes and fears and dreams."

"I know. But what do you talk about? None of those women have even been to school… you cannot possibly understand their lives. I just don't get it."

"Really, Shu! Your education, or whatever, has cut you off from simple people. You don't even notice all these servants around you. They slave to make you happy but have you ever thanked them?"

"Have you ever heard me show any disrespect? And I do appreciate them. Half the servants have been here for over twenty years. If they were not happy, they would have left."

"All I'm saying is you need to take some time to ask about their lives. They have families, sick mothers and fathers and children who also die."

There was pin-drop silence.

The one thing the two of them never mentioned was Namtu. They changed the subject quickly, talking about Peter's school, and how much he missed his cousin, Tutu, who had moved away to Kurseong, where Saury was now posted.

The only person who constantly talked about Namtu was Milty. He had been her playmate, they had shared the same bedroom and used to babble at each other and throw toys into each other's cribs. If one cried, the other did as well.

Peter had his own bedroom where he slept with his dog Blackie, his car, and an assortment of 'grown-up' toys. Milty and Namtu were seldom allowed into Peter's room, and it was a special treat when Peter was away at school to go into his room and touch his 'things'.

It was Namtu who played with Milty, sharing his toys with her. Peter was about six years old and was too busy with school, his cousins and his doting grandmother. When Namtu suddenly disappeared with his crib, it was Milty who missed him the most. She looked for him in the garden, behind the cowshed, under the beds and in all his special hiding places. She went to Peter and asked, "Petu, let's look for Namtu."

"Shush," he admonished her, "don't talk about Namtu. Everyone will get upset."

"Where is Namtu? Where is Namtu?" She drove her family crazy, and was brushed away with no answer.

To everyone's dismay, she named her special stuffed toy bear after him. She took the bear everywhere, sleeping with it, talking to it, playing with it and eating with it. One day the bear disappeared; she returned from playschool and went straight to her bed and there was no bear. She cried for days, asking the servants again and again to help her find it, but to no avail. Like Namtu, it too had gone. Like Namtu, it was as though it never existed. Like Namtu, it came and it went, and no one seemed to notice except her.

31

Calcutta

Christmas was nearing and Saury, Bina and their children returned to Calcutta to celebrate. They had a new addition, a baby girl named Sushmita, or Mita. Milty and Mithu greeted her arrival with great enthusiasm. However, they soon learnt this 'sweet, adorable baby' with curly black hair could let out a curdling screams and grab onto the hair of whoever was next to her. Both Milty and Mithu had chunks of hair missing, as they tried to unclasp her ferocious fist with her razor-sharp nails. Archana kept a safe distance, while Peter and Tutu stopped their pedal-cars once in a while to eye this new novelty.

Since Imelda's arrival, Christmas was celebrated at Harish Mukherjee Road with as much enthusiasm as Durga Puja and Holi. It was the only Christian holiday fully embraced by the Bengali family, and it reminded Imelda of home.

Imelda and Shu took all the children to help pick out a tall Christmas tree. The pine trees came from the mountains around Darjeeling and were sold in little lots all around the city. The kids were excited as they helped pick out the perfect tree. Once they had got it home, the chosen tree was set up at one end of the hall in Imelda and Shu's living room on the second floor.

The tree was decorated with ornaments and glass balls bought from abroad, as well as home-made knick-knacks made by the kids under Imelda's watchful eye. All the decorations were brought out in boxes as the gramophone played Christmas carols. The kids worked excitedly on the tree, arguing about where to put each decoration as they sipped apple cider, warmed and scented with cloves and cinnamon. The culmination of the festivities was watching Imelda as she balanced on a ladder and carefully placed the star on the very top. After that, all that was needed were little bits of cotton, strewn along the branches to look like snowflakes.

As Christmas drew closer, gift-wrapped boxes would pile up under the tree as the children tried to guess what was in them, each child counting the number of boxes that had his or her name on it. Christmas cake was ordered at Firpo's, as was the Christmas pudding. There was always Christmas lunch at the Gymkhana Club with lots of games and presents for the children. Fairy lights were strung up all around the house and from outside one would think it was a Christian home. Christmas carols were sung at all the clubs, and Park Street was aglow with Christmas trees twinkling green and red lights.

One particular Christmas Eve, after the songs were sung, dinner eaten, mince pies carefully nibbled around the edges, and parents gone to the Gymkhana Club, Tutu and Peter got Bahadur and Ashu to stick some real candles onto the heavier branches of the tree. The younger children watched from a safe distance as the big boys took care of this dangerous project. Somebody lit a candle, which fell over, and in a flash the dry pine needles and cotton flakes caught fire and burnt to the floor. The children scattered while the servants poured water on the burning cinders, each blaming the other. Once everything was under control, they stood in despair around a pile of burnt ashes. Tutu ordered everyone to go to bed and pretend they knew nothing about what happened.

"You want me to lie?" Peter asked wide-eyed.

"No," Tutu reasoned, "just say you don't know what happened. I didn't see anything, did you?"

"Yes, I did." Peter nodded very definitely, looking accusingly at Tutu.

"Then, let's just go to bed before they get home, and don't say anything."

Imelda, Shu, Saury and Bina returned from the Gymkhana Club laden with presents only to find a wet blackened stump where the glorious tree had stood.

Another year, Tutu had a brilliant idea. His mother had received a big box of expensive French powder – which looked just like snow. The box was distinctly expensive looking, tied in gold thread and embossed with the Eiffel Tower. Both boys had a great time pouring the powder on the tree, around the tree, and then around the room. They made a white powder skating rink on the already slippery marble and went sliding from one end of the room to the other. All the children cheered: this was like real Christmas with real snow! They slid on their stomachs, like penguins. They crashed into each other, and smeared their faces with this wonderful smelling white stuff. Even the servants were amused as they watched the crazed children, laughing hysterically as they rolled on the floor, swallowing and coughing out little puffs of white dust. They had powder in every nook and cranny of their bodies. The laughing servants mysteriously disappeared when Bina came storming in and found her empty powder box. Her scream was heard all over the house.

Most memorable of all was the year Imelda was gifted a live turkey by an American friend of theirs. She decided to fatten it up for Christmas dinner. Tom the turkey had a perfect fan for a tail and a bright red neck. Amarendra was fascinated by this beautiful bird, taking time to feed him and introduce him to the birds. As he grew fatter, the bird's confidence grew, as did his assumed ownership of the garden. It was amazing to watch the personality of this mild and submissive bird change the minute Amarendra's car drove through the gates. During the day, he ignored the harassment of the cockatoos, quietly moving alongside the bigger peacocks. The minute Amarendra walked out into the garden, he would change completely: he would chase the peacocks, the children, the dog, even Ashu, anyone who would try to touch Amarendra. No one was safe.

Amarendra grew very fond of his turkey friend and told Imelda in no uncertain terms that Tom was not to be the Christmas meal: he was now a family pet. Tom the turkey spent many years alongside Amarendra and became the most feared watchdog of Harish Mukherjee Road.

Peter was now in third standard. His school uniform was grey shorts with a white shirt to be worn with a green and gold striped tie. On special days he wore his dark green blazer which had an embroidered lion's head on the pocket. He loved to show off his uniform as he walked around the house with a stick and topi.

Imelda helped dress him in the morning while Boroma brought in his breakfast, usually a plate of cut fruit, some toast and milk. He ate what he wanted, coaxed by Boroma to always take one more bite. Milty watched with envy from a distance as they all fussed over her older brother. The driver and the ayah drove him to school.

Once Peter left, Milty would be taken down to her grandfather, whom she called Dadu. She would have a small silver plate and silver mug placed next to his large one. The first thing she did was help herself to fruit, yogurt, luchi and potato sabzi, or whatever was on her Dadu's thali. She always helped herself to more than her share.

"Miltu, is this half and half? Dadu has no grapes or mango."

Milty spent hours talking to the cockatoos, screeching with delight when any of them repeated her name, or a word she had taught them. She was allowed to feed them nuts and to walk around with one of them on her arm. The problem was that she would sneak in and take a bird and sometimes forget to return it to its perch. This drove Ashu crazy, as he had to rescue birds from bathrooms and playrooms, and he feared that Blackie, the dog, would hurt a bird by trying to play with it. One morning, he found Shona squawking for help in the upstairs hallway. Milty had taken the parrot from its perch, got distracted and forgotten all about it. Ashu, who got more and more cranky as he grew older, found Milty and pulled her ear, warning her not to touch the birds again.

"Dadu, Ashu pulled my ear today," she complained to her grandfather when Ashu was out of hearing.

"Why did he do that, Miltu?" Amarendra asked, pretending concern.

"I don't know," she lied.

Amarendra called in Ashu to scold him.

"Why did you pull Milty-baby's ear? She is very upset with you. Say sorry to her." Milty nodded her head vigorously in agreement.

"Sorry? Huh! When we find a dead bird then who will be sorry? I'll pull *both* her ears next time."

"Ashu is a grumpy old man," her grandfather whispered after Ashu had stormed out.

Not satisfied, Milty went to Peter. He loved to pretend he was the boss.

"Petu-da, Ashu was mean to me today. He even pulled my ear," she protested with her 'poor me' face.

"He did? Did you tell Dadu?"

"Yes. And Ashu told Dadu he will pull *both* my ears."

"He better not try that when I'm around or I'll fire him, okay?"

Everyone knew who was the real boss around here, and Milty was happy to follow his every whim.

Peter revelled in his sister's complete adoration. He had grown very fond of his slave, quietly proud of her small accomplishments. He was especially happy when she ate things he did not like off his plate and learned to keep it a secret. When all the older cousins visited he was delighted to be master of ceremonies and made her perform in front of them.

First, it was the dog's turn. "Sit! Paw! Lie down! Bark! Roll… Good dog!"

Then came one of the birds – whichever was the most cooperative at that point – and lastly came Milty. Milty, shy in front of so many older cousins, hid behind her ayah, Surya.

"Now you are going to sing for our show," commanded Peter.

"I don't want to," she replied her face buried in Surya's sari.

"I sing with you," Surya said, ending up singing the song by herself.

On weekends Amarendra took the children to the zoo to visit Bhalu and Kalu. He would sit next to the enclosure as the panthers purred loudly and rubbed against the wire to get as close to him as possible. At other times, they would go to the garden house on a boat, or to the Victoria Memorial to eat murmurra. In the evenings, Boroma and Dadu took them for walks along the Hooghly where the children ran around catching fireflies in glass jars. Peter always filled his jar and gave it to Milty and she would squeal with delight, running around and holding the jar high above her head.

Once, as he watched her run around with her jar full of light, he turned to Boroma and said, "It takes so little to make her happy. If I gave her a jar with grass in it, she'd be happy."

"That's because you are her hero."

"I know," Peter replied, smiling.

32

Calcutta

The political climate of India in the mid-1940s was tense. The struggle to oust the British was at its height. Muhammad Ali Jinnah, the leader of the All-India Muslim League, was agitating for a separate state as Gandhi campaigned relentlessly to keep independent India united.

In the midst of this turmoil, Jagaddipenddra Narayan, the Maharaja of Cooch Behar – otherwise known as Bhaiya – decided to host a shikar, or hunting party. He invited a host of local politicians, the British Commander as well as the Viceroy Lord Archibald Wavell.

Bhaiya was friends with both Shu and Saury, but he was particularly fond of Imelda. They shared a great love of horses, and she had become a regular in his stables. He knew she hated his hunts as she had told him many times in no uncertain terms. Nevertheless, he rang her up to try and persuade her to come.

"It will be good for Shu to be seen there. Come on, it's only four days, you need to show your support for the troops."

She reluctantly agreed. "I'll come only for the parties, not for the hunts."

A long caravan of cars drove slowly up the winding roads to Cooch Behar, to the foothills of the Eastern Himalayan range. The palace was decked out to greet the many important dignitaries. Guards lined the long entrance hall, while mahouts sat on ornately decorated elephants at the gates.

Indira Devi, Bhaiya's mother, was standing inside the main entrance hall where a twelve-piece orchestra played. Bedecked in brilliant green emeralds, she greeting guests with that long gold cigarette holder held high between her fingers.

The main lawn in front of the palace was covered with a large white tent, flying the prince's colours. Four or five smaller tents flew the flags of visiting maharajas. The Viceroy and other important dignitaries stayed in one of the many guest rooms inside the palace, while other guests were assigned a small tent pitched on the back lawn.

At five-thirty the next morning, gongs were heard summoning the guests to breakfast. Restless elephants stood around, shifting from foot to foot, waiting for the hunt to begin. Imelda slept in.

The bloodthirsty revellers returned before sunset with tales of shooting leopards, panthers and wild boar, and hearing the forest reverberate with the roar of tigers as the elephants made their way through tall grass.

The next evening, Imelda was having an early cocktail with Shu's boss, George Worthington. He asked her to join in the evening's hunt, where they would shoot from a machaan. His wife joined in, "We wouldn't dream of going without you, my dear, it will be such fun. The Vicereine is joining us."

Later that evening, a very anxious Imelda joined the euphoric group of hunters. Bhaiya did a double-take when he saw Imelda dressed in boots and hunting gear. They were helped onto the elephants that carefully took them through the tall grasses to the high trees where a series of wooden look-out platforms had been built.

Long double-barrelled rifles were taken out and handed to eager participants. Once they climbed up the rope ladders, the elephants returned to the base, and everyone was asked to be quiet as the ladders were pulled up.

The atmosphere was tense. Loud drums could be heard in a distance. The beaters formed a circle around the trapped animals and were driving them out of the tall grasses and into the clearing in front of the waiting hunters. The forest reverberated with the yelps of hyenas, the excited cries of monkeys and the occasional roar of a tiger. The hunting party shivered with anticipation.

Imelda had her eyes shut and murmured quietly to Saury, "I hate this."

"Hush," Saury whispered back. "Voices carry in the forest."

The drums got louder and closer as they closed in. Suddenly Imelda heard the frantic bleating of a baby goat.

"What's that?" Imelda said loud enough for her group to hear.

There was a chorus of 'shhhh's'.

Mrs. Worthington leaned close to Imelda and whispered, "It's the bait, my dear. They have it tied where the hunters can have a clear shot."

"Oh my god, that is barbaric," Imelda exclaimed, making no attempt to keep her voice down. She was quickly silenced by stern looks and fingers on lips. She sat back for a while, her heart racing as the growls grew closer and the goat's bleats more frenzied. Suddenly, Imelda shouted as loud as she could, "Stop this now! I can't stand it. All of you waiting to kill a poor trapped animal. And you call this a sport."

There was a gasp from the machaans. Shu hid behind Saury, who tried to calm Imelda.

"Put the ladder down. I'm leaving." She grabbed the rope ladder and threw it down the side of the tree. Then, to everyone's shock, she started to climb down the rungs.

"No, no, madam! There are wild animals close by." A sharpshooter in her machaan tried to hold her back.

"You want to be killed by a tiger?" hissed Saury.

"I don't care. I don't want to be part of this cowardly act. I'm going to get the goat." As she continued to climb down, she heard Shu's sharp command. "Joan! Stop!"

She looked up, the tone of his voice startling her.

"Get up here now."

She stopped midway and started to cry.

"The hunt's over," Bhaiya announced. "Call in the elephants and stop the beaters. Everyone stay quiet and calm and we will be safely returned to the palace."

No one talked as they waited for the elephants. The shikaris, who knew all the nuanced habits of the wild animals, built fires to scare away the tigers or panthers. Imelda had never seen Shu so angry. In fact everyone in the group was furious with her. She had ruined their tiger hunt, probably the first and last for many of them.

She was also mortified by her own behaviour. It was too late to take back her outburst: she had just wanted to leave, not cause the hunt to end. Driving back to Calcutta with Shu, Saury and Bina, she was subdued and dejected.

"I hope you won't get fired," she said quietly to Shu.

"Shu get fired? What about me?" Saury added angrily. "You endangered everyone's lives. Such irresponsible behaviour."

"I hated every minute of it. You know very well I hate hunters, all of them. I made such a bloody fool of myself. I must have embarrassed you."

"Don't worry about me. You embarrassed yourself more than me," Shu replied coldly.

Imelda burst into tears. "I don't care. You were as blood-thirsty as the rest of them!"

They drove home in silence with Imelda occasionally wiping tears from her eyes. This was their first real fight and feelings were deeply bruised.

That week, they avoided each other as Imelda busied herself with Krishnagar. She didn't go on her usual morning rides.

On the third morning, a call came from Woodlands, the Maharani's home. "Joan, darling, why weren't you at the ride this morning?" Indira asked in her imperial tone.

"I'm too embarrassed to face you all," she replied truthfully.

"Nonsense, darling. We all had a bloody good laugh. I want to see you back in the saddle tomorrow at seven sharp. Ciao."

Things had got so bad between Shu and Imelda that they were not on talking terms when they went to a fancy dress ball at the 300 Club. Shu was wearing a black cloak which, with the addition of fangs, made him Dracula, or a pencil moustache made him a Sheik. This year he decided on the Sheik. Imelda was a nauch girl, with pearls in her hair and a veil across her face.

She was talking to her group of riding friends, ignoring Shu, when Chotto suddenly came over and grabbed her hand, dragging her out onto the veranda. There was Shu, slow dancing with Mira, who was giggling and flirting. Imelda was stunned.

"Oh, there you are darling," he slurred. "Mira was telling me I am the best-looking Sheik at the ball."

"I'm just having my duty-dance with the sheik," Mira said, laughing awkwardly. Imelda turned on her heels and walked away, while Chotto grabbed Mira's arm and jerked her aside. "You'd better not try any of your tricks with my brother," she hissed.

"Shame on you, dada," she said to Shu, and then turned sharply and left.

Imelda left the party in tears and went to stay with their close friends Robin and Pushpa Mitter.

Chotto, quite scandalized by her brother's behaviour, woke up their parents and told them the whole tale. Pale with rage, Amarendra waited for a very drunk Shu to return home. Ashu guided him to the study where his father, sister and mother were waiting.

"Well, what have we here? A welcoming committee?" he said in mock disbelief.

Amarendra spoke quietly and sternly in his impeccable English. "I want you to go upstairs, pack your clothes and leave this house before sunrise."

"Leave my own house? Over such a frivolous incident?" Shu asked, trying to regain his dignity.

"I refuse to waste my time explaining my actions to a drunk and stupid man," Amarendra said turning to leave.

"Where is Joan? She left me at the ball."

"How dare you humiliate my daughter-in-law. I want you out in an hour, or I'll have the chowkidar throw you out."

Shu looked to his sister and mother for support. They turned away.

"Ashu," Amarendra continued, "throw the bum out, and tell the chowkidar that Mrs. Mira Mukherjee is not to set foot in this house again."

As Shu sat dejectedly staring at the floor, his father returned.

"I had hoped for so much more from you. I thought you would be that exceptional one, I was wrong." His voice cracked as he left the room.

Ashu escorted Shu outside, and instead of throwing him out, let him sleep in his bed while he slept on the floor.

"Hey Ashu," came the mumbled voice in the dark, "will you fix your bloody bed? How d'you expect me to sleep on this shit?"

Ashu ignored him.

The next morning Amarendra went himself to pick up Imelda. She was remorseful and cried copious tears as she repeatedly told him the whole story of the failed hunt.

"I made a complete fool of myself in front of his boss and everyone."

He listened patiently, and then put his arms reassuringly around her. "Why are you so upset? I am so proud of you. I tell all my clients about your bravery. To trap and kill these beautiful animals is criminal. It's a blood sport. The odds are ninety-nine to one against the poor animals. I would hold my head up high if I were you. You put them all to shame."

Imelda stared at him, bewildered.

"I even called Indira and told her how incredibly proud I was of you, and she grudgingly agreed with me, so let's go home where you belong. It is your home, and I want you to never leave it again. I have thrown that bum out."

Quietly she came home, and had another bout of crying with Boroma, Chotto and Bina.

Shu moved into the Gymkhana Club. He couldn't believe the vengeance with which his own father had turned on him. So he got a little drunk and danced with Mira – all this drama was so unnecessary. He sent chocolates and roses with long explanatory notes to Imelda telling her how much he loved her.

Imelda immediately melted and forgave him, visiting him secretly at the club. It was Amarendra who was unbending and unforgiving, so it was up to Imelda to plead on his behalf.

"Baba, he is really sorry. Talk to him. He has promised never to get drunk again."

"That's not good enough for me. Talk is cheap, it's action that matter. Drunken debauchery is not to be tolerated, ever. You have to be tough, Joan: this must never happen again. Let him twist a little longer."

Imelda looked dismayed, and he smiled and gave her hand a pat, "Trust me on this."

The lure of the clubs was getting less enticing for Imelda. She now spent a lot more time with Peter and Milty. She planned her daily social activity around the children, but Boroma still controlled many of Peter's activities. When he came home from school, he would change and go straight to her room for his snacks. Milty would follow him and sit cross-legged on the floor, happily watching Peter being fawned over by their grandmother. It was always Peter who called her to come and share his favourite kheer.

"Come, Miltu, sit by me." That was what she waited for,

darting up immediately and rushing to his side. It was finally her turn to get his attention.

Imelda never forgot her home and longed to return to Ireland to be with Kathleen and her aunts. Kathleen had married Eddie Cryan in England and moved back to his family farm in Sligo, Ireland. They had two sons. The eldest, Michael, was a few years older than Milty, and her second son was a beautiful blond-haired boy named Thomas.

Her father, Patrick, had died a few months before Milty was born. Imelda had never reconciled or communicated with him, and the loss had left a big hole in her heart. The sisters kept in touch, writing long, emotional letters to each other, pouring out the details of their vastly different lives. Imelda wanted to live Kathleen's simple life, cooking, cleaning and taking care of her family with no servants or in-laws around, while Kathleen envied the glamorous life of her sister. With the war in England and Europe, and India in turmoil, it was impossible to plan a trip, but Imelda promised her sister that she would be over with her children as soon as it was safe.

33

Calcutta

The heavy monsoon rains had lifted, leaving the city invigorated and infused with a lushness only found in the tropics. Milty was growing into a little girl. She was a happy child, striking with dark brown hair and hazel eyes. She loved to watch her mother ride and to sit on her father's lap as he read to her. His profound serenity soothed her. She kept herself busy with all the animals, and had gained Ashu's trust enough to be allowed to hold one bird at a time as she roamed around the old house. After a few choice pecks on the nose, Blackie now kept his distance.

Ashu began padlocking the almirah that stored the birds' nuts. He discovered that not only did Milty sneak in and help herself to them, but would hide handfuls in her pockets to share with the servants' kids and to bribe Tom the turkey who would tolerate her when her grandfather was not around.

Imelda enjoyed taking her daughter on trips to Krishnagar and the garden house, accompanied by Surya, who kept an eye on Milty as she played with the other children.

After her brother, Milty's favourite person was the cook,

Partho. She had a little silver mug she carried around the house, always filled with fresh orange juice, nimbu-pani or coconut water. She would hold it out and say to Partho, "*Baboochi hum.*"

Peter, a finicky eater, was very concerned.

"You know, Mummy, Boroma was telling me that Milty must have been born in the jungle, because she's always begging for food." Imelda laughed as she hugged him.

"She's always eating or drinking, it's '*Baboochi hum*!' '*Surya hum*!' '*Ma hum*!' Did we adopt her?"

"Yes. We found her under a bush."

"See? I knew it. Some poor person must have left her there."

"We kept her because she looked like you," Imelda went on.

"Everyone thinks she is really my sister." He giggled in glee: this was their special secret.

It took Milty a long time to understand the concept of hide-and-seek. She thought if she hid her face nobody could see the rest of her.

"Miltu, that's not hiding. I can see you." Peter would go and tap the back of her head.

"But I can't see you," she would reply, crushing her face deeper into the pillow.

The days were long and humid, so when Peter returned from school one day acting listless, nothing much was made of it: he was given a cold bath and put to bed. The next morning he had a high fever and the family doctor Dr. Amar Sen was called. He was not alarmed. "It's something that's going around. Just make sure he has plenty to drink and stays in bed. It will pass," he said.

"Are you sure it's not… typhoid?" Boroma could barely get the word out of her mouth.

"To you, everything is typhoid. Chances are very slim that Peter has anything that serious, right Petu? You're a strong boy."

Peter flexed his skinny arm. Fear immediately gripped Imelda's heart.

"Let's take him to a hospital, he'll be safer there."

"No, no. We can get the best doctors to come here. The hospitals are full of infections, and Peter will be much more comfortable at home."

The arguments went on as Peter's condition deteriorated. When the test results came back, he was diagnosed with typhoid. Peter had apparently bought some ice pops from a street vendor when the chowkidar had been sent on a chore. Specialists were consulted, every doctor gave different medical advice, and the terrified family tried to do everything they were told.

Peter grew weaker: he could barely get out of bed. Milty was constantly trying to get him to play with her, bringing him snacks to entice him, and her toys to play with him. When he slept, she would pretend to read books to him. She and his dog had to be sent away to allow him to rest.

"If I die, what will Miltu and Blackie do?" one day he asked his mother out of the blue.

"Don't you ever say things like that again, it will bring bad luck." Imelda said, her voice shaking.

His words reverberated in her head. Imelda started thinking the unthinkable: maybe it was happening again. Peter too could die, like her mother, like Namtu. She could not bear the panic taking over her mind. Alone and desperate, she sneaked out of the house and made her way to the church on Chowringhee Lane. She prayed and prayed as hard as she ever had, bargaining her life for his: *Please, please, please God, don't take him.*

A young priest watched as she wept into her hands. After a while, he came over and put his arm around her now skinny frame.

Imelda's voice cracked as she told him about Peter.

"I will come to the house and bless him. Don't worry, his sickness has nothing to do with you leaving the church. Children are strong. Have faith."

He accompanied her home and baptized Peter, holding the boy's hand as he prayed.

Later that night, Imelda went to the bathroom. There, standing still as a ghost, was Dhebu, her eyes wide and wild, and her usually immaculate hair falling untidily around her face.

"Dhebu, you scared me! What are you doing here?"

"I come every night to pray for him," she said as she put her hands on her sister-in-law's shoulders. Tears streamed down her face. "Take him to the hospital or they will kill him... all these doctors! You must get him away from here."

"I can't, they won't let me. I'm so afraid." Imelda broke down, sobbing into her arms.

In the morning, Imelda told the family she wanted Peter moved to a hospital. There was an outcry.

"He is too sick to move."

"We have all the doctors coming here."

"Why move him into a strange environment?"

"His fever is down today, he is on his way to recovery."

"I am his mother," she said steadying her voice, "and I want him treated by one doctor. Every doctor is telling us to do different things, and nothing is working. Shu, please, we have to take him to hospital."

Shu was shaking with anxiety. He did not know what to do and was terrified of making the wrong decision.

"You are right: we are getting too many different instructions from all these doctors. Why don't we keep him home but only have Dr. Sen attend to him?"

"I want him to go to hospital," Imelda almost screamed.

"Joan, control yourself. We all want what's best for Peter," Amarendra said calmly.

"But Baba, Shu, can't you see he's getting worse?" She fell to her knees, her hands folded. But she was afraid to go against the wishes of the rest of the family and Peter remained at home.

Peters' sickness had taken a toll on Imelda: she was pale and had lost a lot of weight. She watched Peter's roller-coaster fever drop and rise for no apparent reason. Just when the fever had broken and he was on the way to recovery it would spike again, leaving him trembling and a little weaker than before.

She wrote a letter to her sister.

Kathleen,

Oh how I wish you were here with me, I feel so alone. Shu, poor darling, has retreated into himself as we all live in this terrible state of fear. It's been a month now and Peter shows no signs of improvement. I've set up my own kitchen so I can cook for him. The feeling of being powerless is overwhelming as I watch him grow weaker every day. Milty tries so hard to keep his spirits up, poor little girl. Pray for him Kathleen, and for all of us.

Your loving sister,
Imelda

The temperature surges devastated Peter's body. Weak and frail, he managed a feeble smile when Milty danced and performed for him. She would pick Blackie up by his front legs and hop around with him, or sneak up Shona or Rani and make the birds say his name. When he got tired of that, she tickled his feet and made funny faces: anything to get a reaction from him. She would get into bed next to him and slip her arms around him.

To focus on Peter, it was decided to send Milty to Kurseong to stay for a few weeks with her cousins. Milty threw a tantrum as she clung to Peter's bed.

"Milty stop it, you are upsetting Peter. You will come back in a few days when Peter starts feeling better," a haggard Imelda explained.

"I'll get well if you let her stay, promise." Peter pleaded in a weak voice.

"We need to give all our attention to you, sweetheart. It will only be for a few days."

"But if I die, I won't see her again."

Imelda's knees buckled. His words bored straight through her heart. "Peter, promise me you won't ever say that again. Promise Mummy, please. Never again, promise?" She was shaking from head to toe.

Milty was sent to be with her cousins Tutu, Mithu and Baby in Kurseong.

Peter took a turn for the worse. He couldn't keep any food down. Imelda and Boroma were reduced to feeding him teaspoons of broth and water to prevent him from dehydrating. When his fever spiked he suffered violent convulsions.

Imelda sat by his side for days feeding him a teaspoon

of soup, a teaspoon of water, a teaspoon of soup, a teaspoon of lemon water. Blackie refused to eat or leave his side, even Boroma did not object to the dog anymore. Peter moved ever so slightly pointing to the ceiling, and saying in a barely audible voice, "Lights, Mummy, more light, it's getting so dark." Imelda turned all the lights on until the room was bathed in brightness. She ran around hitting all the switches, they were all on. Her face was frantic as she looked at Peter. His head was turned to one side, his face was still. He was finally at peace, his skinny arms were limp as Blackie licked his hand and she knew he was gone.

The joy, the hope, the light of this household had left.

Imelda sat huddled like an apparition on the cold marble floor. She was alone. She was alone in this room full of people, and could not move to get away.

The only person that was not there was his little sister. She was miles away, happily playing with her cousins, making paintings and picking up special rocks to bring back to him, unaware that her whole world had crashed and fallen away.

Shu carried Peter all the way to the grave like Namtu before him. He wouldn't let anyone touch him. The son he loved so much but had so little time to play with. He couldn't bear to look at Imelda, her pain was so palpable. He wanted to tell her he had died too. Clouds of guilt engulfed him. He saw a little boy with a suitcase on his head, defiantly leaving to get away from him. If only he had taken him to a hospital. If only he had not bought that ice pop. If only he had taken more time off. If only, if only, if only was all that was left.

The house was like a morgue. No one moved from one room to another unless absolutely necessary. Imelda was lost in the many corridors of her mind. They seemed to be closing in on her, getting narrower and narrower. She became distant and transfixed. Shu stayed isolated, shut up with his books and poetry, oblivious to his young wife's descent into madness.

She would stand, transfixed, in a corner of Peter's untouched room, feeling his presence, watching him kick his ball around the room, race his car around and around his table, rearrange his schoolbooks, and put on his favourite topi. When daylight began to fade, she knew it was time to take the candles to his grave: he was afraid of the dark. She would not leave him alone in that dark, dark coffin.

Local people near the cemetery began to recognize her. Some street vendors called her 'pagli' or madwoman, but there was an outpouring of love for her. The women felt her pain. Many cried openly as they watched this distressed young woman rush past them. The street children stopped their games, respectfully making a path for her. Someone always brought her a cup of tea, women would come and join her vigil, some doing their own pujas, others weeping alongside her.

Imelda got to know the woman singer who had lost her daughter to typhoid, for she would sing with tears streaming down her face, and Imelda would listen transfixed. Then there was the toothless old woman, bent over with arthritis, who would come every night and bring her a luchi with some vegetables rolled in it. She was a widow, thrown out of her own house, who brought her one meal to share with Imelda. She would pat her gently on the head, blessing her, and coaxing her to take a few bites. These women saw this foreigner not as an outsider but as one of their own: a young girl, alone, distraught and heartbroken. They took her into their hearts, keeping a watchful eye over her.

Yet, behind closed doors there were unkind insinuations, whispers of fate and destiny. There is a stigma attached to a widow or the mother of a dead child, the belief that she was responsible for her own bad luck. There were a few superstitious women who would step out of Imelda's way, for they believed that bad karma could be transferred, and that children, young brides and pregnant women should be kept away.

But the outpouring of love and acceptance overshadowed the few hurtful instances. Imelda could not remember a day that someone did not stay with her until the first rays of the morning sun.

34

Kurseong – Calcutta – Gopalpur

Up in Kurseong, Milty was agitating to return home. She had been there over three weeks and was missing her life back at Harish Mukherjee Road.

"I want to go home to Mummy," she cried to her Bibi-ma, as she was putting her to bed.

"Don't you like being here?" Bina asked softly.

"I love it here, but I miss my brother, my dog, my birds, my baboochi, my cows, my turkey, my Dadu."

"You'll be going home soon, and then you will miss us too." A heartbroken Bina called to ask what to do. In their sorrow the family had, while not forgetting Milty, just thought it better to leave her out of the house as long as possible. Who would break the horrible news to her? What would they say? They could not even hint at it among themselves, always referring to the terrible event in coded language.

The car was sent to pick her up. After many hugs from her cousins Mithu and Baby, she happily left to return home. In the car she babbled incessantly about meeting everyone. "Petu is well now, that is why I can come home," Milty explained to Surya.

As soon as the car stopped inside the gates of the house she rushed toward the house and immediately knew something was terribly wrong. The baboochi and other servants gathered around her as they hugged her, crying, sobbing, preventing her from going inside.

"Why is everyone crying? Where's Blackie? Where's Mummy and Petu?"

Milty pushed past the circle around her.

Imelda was in the bedroom staring past the window grilles. She was a shadow of her former self. Her red hair was dishevelled, casually knotted at the nape of her neck, her face pale and empty: she looked like a ghost.

"Mummy, Mummy! I'm home," Milty yelled as she rushed to her, hugging her tightly.

There was no reply: her mother's body was cold and taut.

"Mummy are you alright? I'm home," she repeated hugging her harder.

"Did you have a good time?" Imelda asked, her voice barely audible.

Its flatness made a startled Milty look up to see if this was her mother talking. She did not recognize that face, the eyes were hollow and lifeless with deep, dark circles around them. Her cheeks were sunken, there was no wonderful smile on the face to welcome her back. Imelda looked right through her daughter without a hint of recognition.

Blackie came bounding out wagging his tail, jumping on her and licking her face. He too had become scrawny and thin.

"Where's my mummy?" she bawled.

"She is there," Surya said, looking at Imelda.

"Mummy is not in there," a desolate Milty wailed.

She went howling to Boroma's room to look for her brother. Instead, she found her grandmother huddled on her bed. The room was filled with pictures of Peter. On the chair next to her bed was a framed picture of him, with clothes around it and a plate of fruit in front. There was a life-size portrait of Peter garlanded with thick braids of sweet-smelling jasmine on the sideboard. In front of the picture, two lighted diyas.

Milty was only four, not old enough to understand the concept of dying, but she knew some horrible accident had taken her precious brother away. She remembered another little brother who had just disappeared, and no one looked for him. She was not going to let this happen again. She ran to his bedroom and flung open the door. All his favourite things were there, his red car, his scooter, his stick, and his topi just the way he liked them. She knew then he would surely return.

Her heart lightened and she breathed a sigh of relief. She picked up the topi and put it on.

She wore it and walked out. There was a sharp gasp and then a voice from through the window. "Put that hat back right now. Don't touch anything in Peter's room."

Her mother had never talked to her in that cold and impersonal tone. Her spirit crushed, her shoulders slouched, she walked slowly towards her grandfather's office. Ashu saw her sad broken face.

"Come Miltu-baby, I take you to your Dadu." He picked her up in his skinny arms.

"No Ashu, take me to Petu, where is he? Boroma says he has gone away. I have so many paintings to give him, and stones."

"No painting for me?" Ashu's eyes filled with tears.

Milty went running into her grandfather's arms. He, too, was gaunt and looked much older.

"I have been waiting for you, my little princess. You have been away too long." Milty grabbed onto his neck and sobbed and sobbed as though she would never stop. He stroked the back of her head for hours, rocking back and forth. He wondered how to tell a little girl she will never see her big brother again, How much pain can a little heart endure?

Amarendra was the only one who seemed happy to see her. She clung to him desperately, and when he went to put her to bed that night she would not let go. Surya tried to pry her off, but she became hysterical.

"I want to sleep with Dadu," she screamed.

From then on, Milty slept in her grandfather's big four-poster bed.

Every evening, after eating in the kitchen, she had a bath, got a few toys for herself, a book for him, and went into the net-enclosed bed and waited for him. She was happiest listening to stories about his house in the Sunderbans, and how he saved little baby egrets from the scary gharials in the water. She never got tired of those stories, which she made him repeat again and again and again, until Boroma, sleeping in her own separate bed, threatened to move out of the room.

Boroma, a life-long animal hater, had an extraordinary conversion in her relationship with Peter's dog Blackie. All of a sudden, he was the noblest of animals, allowed to sit by her side during her morning puja. She even had a bed made up for him in the bedroom.

"Petu's spirit will stay with me when he sees me taking care of his dog," she explained to shocked relatives. She even gave him the special orange kheer she had first offered to Peter's picture. She swore the dog prayed in front of the photograph. No one was allowed to eat until the picture was fed.

After a few weeks of sleepless nights, Amarendra told Milty she could only sleep in his bed if he put a long bolster between them.

"Why?" Milty wanted to know.

"Because I can't sleep with you clinging to me."

"But I want to hold your hand, I feel scared at night," Milty protested.

One night, when they lay side by side her grandfather said to her, "Why are you so scared? Every night you wake me up crying."

"I don't want to disappear like Peter or Namtu," she said quietly. And then she whispered, "I am so afraid of God. Is he in the room now?"

"They say he is everywhere," Amarendra replied cautiously.

"Tell him to send Peter back. He will listen to you. Everyone listens to you."

There was a long silence.

"He has left all his favourite toys in his room."

"He watches us from the stars," Amarendra said.

"I know, but I want him to come home."

It had been six months since Peter's death and Imelda's condition had deteriorated further. Sir Dhiren and Lady Mitra were alarmed at the change in their adopted daughter. They wanted to send her to England to be with Kathleen.

"She cannot travel in her current condition," Amarendra confided to them.

Shu decided to take Imelda to Gopalpur, a resort by the sea – far from any memories of Peter. Imelda refused to leave, but Shu insisted, securing a maid to continue the vigil at their son's grave until they returned. Sapped of all energy, Imelda could barely protest.

The air in Gopalpur was invigorating, and Shu would insist Imelda eat breakfast and lunch with him. In the evenings, they would go for long walks and he tried to talk about what had happened. She would listen with a distant stare and occasionally her face would suddenly contort as she burst into tears.

Shu was feeling less suffocated just by being away from all the constant reminders of Peter. The long walks cleared his head; he did not have the luxury to be consumed by his own grief. He realized that he and Imelda had become strangers, two people who had been willing to fight the world to be together.

One evening, Shu was returning from a long walk on the beach. It was dusk and he was absentmindedly listening to the sound of Vedic chants from a nearby temple when he noticed a commotion on the beach. As he got closer, he could see a group of five or six men – locals who acted as impromptu lifeguards for bathers – dragging something from the water. Probably a large fish, thought Shu. They rolled the figure over onto its back and two of them frantically tried to pump water out of the body, while others screamed for help.

In a split second he recognized the body. Horrified, he rushed over and found Imelda lying unconscious on the sand.

Everyone was talking at once, but the story emerged that this lady had just walked into the water. One of the lifeguards saw her and realized she was not even trying to swim. He called for help, and they all rushed to pull her out. They managed to get her to a nearby hospital, where they pumped her stomach and stabilized her condition, while Shu looked on in utter dismay.

Imelda was semi-conscious, moaning as she moved her head from side to side,

"Let me die. Just let me die."

This is what complete annihilation feels like, Shu thought. He knelt by her bed and sent up a fervent prayer: *Oh God, please help me. I have nowhere else to go.*

When Imelda regained consciousness, she was confused. Her eyes finally settled on Shu, watching him for a few moments, sitting in profound grief.

"Shu?" she said in a barely audible voice.

Pushing his despair aside, he took her hand and held it to his trembling lips.

"Why didn't you let me die?" she asked, her eyes filled with so much pain he had to look away.

"Because I love you." he said.

"I have no one," she whispered.

"You have me."

"You left me."

"I never for a moment left you. I… I nearly let us be destroyed. But we have to survive, we still have each other… we have another child."

"No. I'm bad luck. I'm cursed. You must keep Milty away from me."

He bent to kiss her forehead and saw that this lucid moment had passed. She again had that glazed look, that distant uncomprehending stare. But Shu's spirits rose, for he saw she had been perfectly coherent even if it had been for a short while. He was going to take charge and there was no room for failure.

He nursed her back to health, not leaving her side for a moment. He kept this incident a secret from his family. He decided he would take her far away. Away from the memories, away from the despair, for only if they left this life behind could his family be healed. A line from Emily Brontë's poetry echoed in his head:

Have I forgot, my only Love, to love thee?

35

Calcutta – Simla

When they returned home, Shu made some hard decisions. He resigned his job and feverishly scanned the newspapers for opportunities to move as far away from Calcutta as possible. Harish Mukherjee Road was suffocating Imelda: he needed to get her somewhere up in the mountains where the air would be invigorating and cooler. He knew she loved Darjeeling, but it was too close and too full of memories. He settled on Simla. The Central Government needed an engineer to take over its Central Power and Water division. That was right up his alley.

Shu waited until he got a letter of confirmation before he called a family meeting. He told them about his planned move. The one thing they all agreed on was he had to get away from Calcutta.

"Why not someplace closer?" his father asked. "Siliguri, Kalimpong, maybe Darjeeling? You have a house ready and waiting there."

"No, Baba, too many memories of Peter at Snowy View."

"You will always have memories of Peter, you can't run away from them. There are closer places in the North East; Shillong's called the 'Scotland of the East'. Simla is a three-day train ride. My concern is Milty, she could stay here with us and join you on weekends if you were closer. I think snatching her away from everything she knows and loves is not a good idea."

"Good god, Shu, the pay will barely keep you in cigarettes. Be realistic," Saury cautioned.

"I know the money is abysmal, but when you've had to bury two sons you realize that money and social acceptance mean nothing. Joan has fallen apart before our very eyes: money has very little to do with it."

"Alright," his father conceded, "but I would suggest you leave Milty here until you set up the house and settle in. You need to focus on Joan, she does require your undivided attention. Then, if you feel Milty should join you, either we will bring her up, or you can return and take her back. That makes the most sense to me."

"Good try, Baba, but Milty needs to be with us – and we need her. We have to heal as a family. Don't worry, she will spend plenty of time with you."

"Then you'll have to take Surya, and maybe Ali also. He can make good western food," Amarendra offered.

"I was thinking of Hari, but he has too many children. I think all Ali's children are grown and married. His wife can help Joan too. I'm concerned about the Muslim situation up north. We may have more of a problem up there."

"We will contact Sir Dhiren. He is in close contact with all the movers and shakers in Delhi. I will agree on one condition only: that I take care of the servants. I'm not letting my granddaughter and Joan live without a support system from here."

"Thank you, that would be greatly appreciated."

Amardendra left the room, his shoulders drooping, his eyes brimming with tears.

"I didn't realize the old man was so attached to Milty," said Saury.

"You need to come over more often," Shu said forlornly. "Ma is going nuts with Peter's picture. Won't eat, sleep or leave the house without it. It's insane."

"We are all floundering. Tutu is badgering me constantly to come and visit Peter. At some point I have to tell him the truth. We are thinking about putting him in boarding school for more discipline and a better education," Saury continued. Then he awkwardly put his arms around his brother. "Shu, if there is anything I can do…"

The next morning, Shu began planning in earnest. He talked to Sir Dhiren about where to stay in Simla. His uncle suggested a government suite at the Grand Hotel, which could be rented on a monthly basis until a suitable house could be found. Then he waited for the right moment to raise the topic with Imelda. A group of women from Krishnagar had just been to see her, and they had lifted her spirits. Shu walked in as they were leaving.

"You do remember we are making plans to leave Calcutta and go far away?" he began.

"To Ireland?" she asked wistfully.

"No, not Ireland: Simla. It's up in the hills, it's cool like Darjeeling, lots of trees, and we will find a nice cottage there."

"Are we leaving Peter?" she asked despondently.

"We will never leave Peter. He will be with us forever. We will take his memory and Namtu's and start a new life, far away from this place."

"I will never leave Peter alone in that dark grave, never. You know how afraid he is of the dark."

Shu arranged for a Catholic priest to come and talk to Imelda. Father O'Dea came every afternoon and talked to Imelda about the spirit and soul, convincing her that Peter's soul was up in heaven, with her mother and Namtu, not buried in the ground.

"His soul does not need light," he told her, "it *is* light."

"How beautiful," Imelda thought.

Milty was very excited, she thought she was going on a holiday, and her grandfather would be joining her. At first she said she would not go unless her Dadu came along, but after some bartering, she grudgingly exchanged him for Blackie, Surya and Ali.

Anyone who has lived through the pandemonium at Howrah Station will tell you it cannot be described, only experienced. After a harrowing ride over the Howrah Bridge, one arrives at Howrah Station, teaming with people and buzzing like a gigantic beehive. The crush begins as soon as you enter. A relief is finding the official coolies with their red jackets and silver number plates to carry your luggage. Sometimes the boxes are piled three tiers high. Vendors sell everything from hot tea, cool drinks, potato crisps, masala fries, salty snacks, magazines and water. Enormous black steam engines hiss and splutter clouds of smoke as they are filled with water, and soot-faced men shovel coal into their bellies. The stationmasters in their khaki uniforms look like they are constantly on the verge of a nervous breakdown. The smell of urine, sweat and food is overwhelming.

The compartment reserved for the Boses had been scrubbed with carbolic soap and water from the ceiling to the floorboards, then wiped down with Dettol. Khaki bedrolls were carefully laid out on each berth, with pillows and sheets. There were water flasks, sandwiches and fruit to snack on and a special box just for Milty, filled with all the things she loved, including her silver mug and plate.

There was Shu, Imelda, Milty and Blackie in the compartment. Ali, his wife Sardana, and Surya had second-class sleeper tickets. Imelda looked confused and a little dazed as they settled in for their three-day journey.

The Howrah-Delhi Express whizzed past rice and sugar fields, its engine huffing as it flew past green lights, small villages, unknown towns, and crossed rivers on bridges that felt at times too frail for the weight of the train. The landscape changed from lush emerald rice fields to tall green sugarcane, then to dancing golden fields of wheat and barley.

Shu got down and walked about at all the larger stations to buy local specialties and newspapers. Children bought whirling windmills made of shiny coloured paper and held them out the windows as the train chugged along, watching them swirl in the wind. Bearers in white uniform offered a continual array of snacks in-between the stops. Imelda spent most of her time lying on her bedroll. Every time Shu and Milty went outside she would get nervous.

After a two-hour stopover at Delhi, they continued their journey on to Kalka, the last stop at the foot of the mountains.

At Kalka, they had to change again to the Himalayan Queen, that would haul them up the winding two-gauge track on the last leg of their journey.

The train chugged along, huffing and puffing its way around the sharp mountain ridges and deep river gorges, blasting its whistle as it entered one of the hundred pitch-black tunnels. Past sparkling waterfalls and treacherous ravines, it cut through forests of oak and pine, with vivid splashes of purple rhododendrons and red flowering azaleas.

The air became brisk as the train climbed higher and the passengers pulled on sweaters and shawls. There were unexpected sights: a family of wild pheasants racing the train along a perilous edge, and a troupe of defiant monkeys heckling the passengers to throw their last banana at them.

Shu breathed deeply as he held Imelda's hand.

"What do you think, Milty? Isn't this exciting?"

"Who feeds the monkeys?" she replied.

"Come, sit here and I'll tell you," he said, patting his lap.

She pointedly ignored him.

"You're going to be very happy here. Mummy too. I promise."

The Himalayan Queen reached its destination, the pristine summer capital of British India, Simla.

36

Simla

Simla was a quaint family station modelled after British hill stations back in the old country. The city was built around an upper mall and a lower mall, where no cars were allowed. Above both malls was the ridge, dominated by Christ Church, with a magnificent bell tower overlooking the entire town. This place had an energy all of its own. There was a well-established race course and an active theatre group. It had a Monkey Temple on Jakhoo Hill and boasted the only natural outdoor ice skating rink in India.

Imelda, Shu and Milty settled into a suite at the Grand Hotel.

India was in a state of high exhilaration. World War II was over and England was making good on its promise to hand the reins of government back to the people of India. But along with Independence came Partition, the bloody and painful birth of two very different nations, in which nearly one million people were killed and millions were left homeless in the greatest migration of civilian populations the world had ever seen.

Anarchy and brutality ran rampant. Fear stalked the land, as the army took control and a curfew was imposed.

In Simla, the Grand Hotel was a secure zone, protected by the army as many important officials had been moved there for security reasons. But, like the rest of the country, Hindus and Muslims were wary around each other.

The Boses' cook, Ali, and his family understood the dangers and did not leave the safety of their rooms. It was Imelda who occasionally would get disoriented and sneak out at night looking for Peter's grave. Shu told everyone not to let Imelda out of their sight: he was afraid someone would attack her as a British occupier. He was also worried about Mohammed Rehman, a Muslim neighbour of theirs.

Rehman was a trained psychiatrist who had been educated in England. He met Shu at the civilian support meetings and they hit it off right away. His son Arif was the same age as Milty, and Shaina, his wife, often brought him over to play. The two families became close friends. Shu talked to Rehman about Imelda's condition and Rehman, a specialist in treating depression, spent many hours with her, trying to break through the barrier she had built around herself.

The Rehmans were frequent dinner guests, so when Mohammed arrived unexpectedly at dinner time one evening, Surya let him in.

"Rehman, what a nice surprise! Care to join us for dinner?" Shu asked as he rose to greet him.

"Don't move!" Rehman pulled out a gun and aimed it at Shu.

"What the hell?" Shu laughed nervously.

"My brother and his entire family has been murdered in Allahabad," he said. "My three nieces and my nephew, butchered like animals."

"Good God! People are going mad," Shu got up to console him.

"I said, don't move! Don't make this more difficult. I have to avenge my brother, his death cannot be in vain." He rambled on incoherently. Imelda watched without moving a muscle: it was a quick-thinking Surya who scooped up Milty and ran into the bedroom, locking the door.

"Listen, Rehman," an alarmed Shu continued, "we're friends... from Cambridge, for God's sake. Surely we are not going to stoop to the level of these rabble rousers?"

Unknown to Rehman, Ali had quietly slipped in from the kitchen, a big kitchen knife in his hand. He suddenly grabbed Rehman from behind and held the knife to his throat. "If you move a finger, your head will be on the floor," Ali said through clenched teeth.

"Leave the room, Joan," Shu ordered.

"Ali bhai, we're brothers. We are sons of Allah. Have you seen what the Hindus are doing to us?" Rehman pleaded, disoriented by the sudden ambush.

"Sahib is my brother. You are a traitor, and Allah will deal with you," Ali replied keeping the pressure steady on the knife. Carefully, Shu approached Rehman and took the gun from his unresisting hand. Shu was devastated when he had to fill out a report that sent his good friend, his wife and son to jail.

After Rehman had been escorted away, Shu sat down, suddenly shaking.

"Ali you saved my life, I can never repay you."

"Arrey sahib, you are my family. I only had one choice. You would do the same thing for me."

"I don't think I'm so brave. I was afraid to touch the gun. Bloody thing was so heavy I nearly dropped it." They both were laughing when Imelda rushed in and threw her arms around Shu.

"Oh darling! You were so brave, I was so afraid for the two of you!"

"Me, brave?" Shu threw an amused glance at Ali as both their eyes filled with tears. This was the first time since Peter died that Imelda had shown any emotion unrelated to her son.

On August 15, 1947, Jawaharlal Nehru took over as the first Prime Minister of India.

With Lord Mountbatten and Gandhi in the audience, a sombre Nehru addressed the country and the rest of the world, at the stroke of midnight.

> *"Long years ago we made a tryst with destiny, and now the time comes when we shall redeem our pledge…. At the stroke of the midnight hour, when the world sleeps, India will awake to life and freedom."*

Simla

The political change was immediate and profound. English soldiers were immediately relocated to other parts of the world, and in Simla that meant lots of houses were being vacated. Shu and Imelda were allotted a bungalow in the desirable sub-division known as Bemlow.

Bemlow was a beautiful secluded neighbourhood with over two hundred spacious bungalows built around a large sloping hill. Shu was allotted bungalow number B9. It was below the cart road and cricket field, and had one of the larger terraced gardens. It was a mock Tudor two-storey house, with a steeply pitched roof. The porchway led to a wood-panelled sitting room, a dining room and a large kitchen with an even larger pantry. Each room had oak floorboards and a brick fireplace. The ground floor had large bay windows looking out over the garden. The garden itself was full of flowering azalea, hibiscus and hydrangea shrubs interspersed with apple, apricot and plum trees. The terraced garden on the other side was dotted with seasonal flowers: dahlias, sweet peas, hollyhocks, sunflowers and lilies. The houses were separated by tall pine trees and linked together with meandering unpaved lanes.

A creaky wooden staircase led to the three bedrooms on the first floor. These rooms had high, sloping ceilings with wooden beams and brick fireplaces. During the cold winter months, a chimneysweep came in at six o'clock in the morning and started fires in all the bedrooms, so by the time the family woke up, the rooms were warm.

In spring, the fruit trees burst into a bouquet of pink and white blossoms which attracted swarms of pollinating bees and many species of birds, who built their nests deep among the gnarled branches.

For Milty, it was paradise, with trees to climb, slopes to slide down, horses to ride and plenty of children to play with. The only problem was the language. The locals spoke mainly Hindi or Punjabi and did not understand Bengali.

Imelda was still fragile and Milty learnt to be careful around her. She never mentioned Peter, for she knew that would bring on a withdrawal that could last for days.

Milty was now five and old enough for school. She was enrolled in The Chalet, a preschool run by the Loreto order of nuns. She rode to school and loved to stop under the apricot trees overhanging the road and pick ripe fruit.

Barbara and Tulu Sen had also left Bengal as Tulu had joined the army and was posted in Northern India. Barbara had two daughters, Sheila her oldest girl, born in London, and Kumkum, who was a year older than Milty. They had met a few times in Calcutta when Barbara came to visit, and Milty and Kumkum had become the best of friends. Barbara called to say that she and the children were coming to Simla.

When Barbara arrived she was shocked at Imelda's condition. This was not the fierce and feisty girl she had known for years. She ended up staying the entire summer. She took Milty under her wing and took Imelda to the tailor to order warm blazers and jackets and to the Chinese shoemaker for shoes. Every evening, she and Imelda went for long walks, sometimes with the kids and other times alone. She reminded Imelda of how happy she and Shu had been in London and how she and Kathleen had always looked to Imelda for strength. When she brought up Kathleen's name Imelda broke down, saying how devastated Kathleen would be if she knew what had happened to her sister.

"And what has happened to her?" Barbara coaxed gently.

Imelda looked at her with pain-filled eyes. "I am empty inside," she said. "I always lose the people I love the most." Imelda cried softly.

"There are things we cannot control," Barbara said quietly.

"All Peter wanted was more light, and I hit and hit that switch. All I have to lose now is Shu and Milty."

"But you haven't lost them, Joan. They are here. Am I a good mother?" Barbara asked suddenly.

"Of course, you are the best. Even Milty wants to live with you."

"That's because she needs a mother. I lost a son, like you. I should consider my karma bad if I believe that rubbish."

"But you have your family."

"My family is my husband and children, and your family is your husband and daughter. You're so young, not even thirty. You can have a long happy life."

"I don't want a long happy life. I don't want a life without Peter and Namtu. I don't want to live without my children."

"Milty is your child too."

So Barbara talked with her, gently, never arguing or confronting her – just one friend talking to another. They often walked to a beautiful little country chapel which was looked after by the Loreto nuns. They would go and sit in the pews where they could talk undisturbed.

"You know, Shu wanted to get married in the church so I could go to communion," Imelda confides to Barbara, "but I said no."

"Why?" Barbara asked amazed.

"Because I never got anything I prayed for," she replied.

One evening they were having dinner when Kumkum said something to which Milty's comical reply made Imelda burst out laughing. Barbara, Sheila and Kumkum continued laughing as if it was normal, but both Milty and Shu looked shell-shocked. They could not remember the last time either of them had heard her laugh.

After Barbara left, there was a definite change in Imelda. There was a vague transition period where the overbearing grief that had been crushing her spirit began to ease, giving her periods of tranquility. Fresh winds of change were in the air. She started taking an interest in the garden, digging for hours with the mali, making him plant her favourite forget-me-nots, irises, tiger lilies, pansies and sweetpeas. She paid attention to the pruning of the fruit trees, and helped Ali make apricot and plum jam. Apples were picked and stored in baskets and applesauce was canned. She started showing interest in what Milty was wearing, making sure she wore a hat when riding to school. But the biggest change was the sudden interest she began to take in her own appearance. Her thick red hair was normally brushed and left tied in a ponytail at the base of her neck. Occasionally it looked unkempt and untidy. Imelda went to a hairdresser on the Mall and got her locks cut fashionably short, she put on lipstick and greeted Milty and Shu with a welcoming smile at the dining room table. It was a momentous step for Imelda on her delicate road to recovery.

Shu made changes in his daily routine too. He restructured his working hours so there were no more tea stops with friends. By six, he was home and had Ali serve tea in the garden. Imelda and Milty were cajoled into joining him, even though Milty protested bitterly. To entice her, he let her order her favourite snacks. After tea, he joined Milty and Surya for their evening walk. Initially, Milty objected, refusing to walk with him, either lagging behind, or walking ahead with Surya and the dog.

He persisted, and soon his stories began to intrigue her. She had him repeat the ones she liked best, usually about animals and her grandfather, preferably featuring the panther cubs, the cockatoos and peacocks, and of course Tom the loyal guard turkey. Soon enough, she began to forget her resentment, and would happily reach out to grab her father's hand.

It was now Milty who waited eagerly for six o'clock. She would run back and forth with the dog to look down the lane for her father. When they met lots of hugs and kisses were exchanged. There was always a little gift hidden in his pocket – a lollipop, a pencil or a notepad.

Saturday was their day together. They would walk along the Mall, and Milty decided where they would eat. It was here she often reflected on the unfairness of her life. They shopped, usually for books that he would later read to her. There was always some token gift 'for mummy' in the bag.

Time spent with her father became magical for Milty. Her next favourite thing was spending time with her growing menagerie of animals. She had adopted a small kitten found abandoned on the street. The hutch which Ali had made for her one rabbit now held six, and she had a large cage of blue and green budgerigars. Her favourite pet, aside from Blackie, was Henrietta, a brown hen she had received as a little chick in her Easter basket whom she vigilantly protected against the ever-present kites. In gratitude Henrietta laid an egg for her every day. She also found a way to fly up to Milty's bedroom window and made enough noise to wake up the entire household.

In the evening they all had dinner together, and Imelda joined in the conversations, although her unpredictabile mood swings kept everything a little off balance. She was seldom enthused or animated, and a good meal was one without incident. At bedtime, Shu read Milty stories and her face glowed with happiness as she cuddled with her father. Every so often, out of the blue she would ask, "Daddy, is Peter ever going to come home?"

The haunting sadness in her father's eyes and the slight quiver of his chin gave her the answer.

Shu was a different man from the dapper gentleman-about-town of his youth. That life seemed light years away. His heart had been broken by Peter and Namtu's deaths and he had lost his bearings. He didn't miss all the trappings that come with position, even though his first reaction at not being invited to the Viceroy's ball in Simla was one of utter disbelief.

The Shu that emerged was a kinder, gentler man. He never raised his voice at his wife's eccentricities, never argued with her or showed a hint of impatience. He showered her with love and attention, telling her how wonderful she was, and how much he loved her. Saying that so openly did not come naturally to him, a shy and introverted man. Often he would walk back and forth in the garden, his arm around her shoulder singing to her, 'Autumn Leaves,' or 'Smoke Gets in Your Eyes'. Whenever Shu started the singing, Imelda would interject, "Sing 'Close to you' for me." And he did, Imelda joining in on the chorus.

> *"On the day that you were born, the angels got together*
> *And decided to create a dream come true.*
> *So they sprinkled moon dust in your hair,*
> *and starlight in your eyes of blue."*

She would smile with a far-away gaze, knowing he was singing about her, and for a few fleeting moments, she felt a deep quiet happiness.

If one believes in miracles, or dharma, or angels, then one has to believe in the miracle in Imelda's life. A miracle whose name was Mother Melissa.

Mother Melissa was the school principal as well as Milty's kindergarten teacher. One day, at school, she asked the children what they thought was the most important thing about their birthday. When it came to Milty's turn, she said, "The most special thing about my birthday was that I was born on the wrong day."

"That's the strangest answer I have ever heard," Mother Melissa laughed. "How could you be born on the wrong day?"

"Because I should have been born the day before on St. Patrick's Day, and then my name would have been Patricia," Milty explained gravely.

"I think Milty suits you much better. Tell me how you know so much about St. Patrick? Do you know where he's from?"

"Of course I know. He's from Ireland."

Mother Melissa got out of her chair and hugged Milty. "I'm from there too. Is your mother from Ireland?" she asked.

"I think so," Milty replied hesitantly.

"Oh, you must bring her to school to meet me," Mother Melissa continued. "I'll write her a note."

Milty got sombre, and as Mother Melissa was writing the note, she went up to her and whispered very quietly, "I don't know if she can come here."

Mother Melissa stopped writing, thinking perhaps her mother was handicapped. She did not remember seeing her at any of the school functions. She put the letter aside, deciding she would make inquiries before she made any overtures.

That evening Milty told her father that the nun who taught her was from Mummy's country and wanted to meet her.

"All the nuns there are from Mummy's country," Shu replied. "We will take her to meet them when she feels up to it."

"That will never ever happen." Milty grumbled.

"I think you're wrong. Mummy will be going to your school very soon."

But she did not have her father's patience with Imelda. There were many instances when she would say mean things to her, then feel bad when she was alone. Recently, Imelda was agitating to have Surya contact Shu over some minor matter.

"Sometimes you have to wait, Mummy," she said quietly.

"But I need to talk to him now," Imelda protested.

"Well, that's just too bad now, isn't it?" snapped Milty, not bothering to look up as she nonchalantly continued playing. Imelda went to her room and slammed the door.

That evening to Milty's utter dismay her father brought it up.

"I got mad because she always wants to have her way," Milty tried to explain.

"Sweetheart, we all get angry, you hurt Mummy's feelings."

"Everything hurts Mummy's feelings. I'm sick of it."

It was a Saturday afternoon when Imelda decided to go for a walk. Shu had taken Milty out for their usual Saturday lunch. She ended up at the little chapel where she used to sit and chat with Barbara. She took a seat at the back and was deep in thought when she felt a soft tap on her shoulder.

"Sorry to disturb you, but I have to close the chapel for the night," said a voice with a distinct Irish lilt.

"Oh dear. I'm so sorry. I was about to leave," Imelda got up hurriedly.

"You are Milty Bose's mother?" the nun asked, looking her straight in the eyes.

"How do you know?" Imelda replied, surprised.

"I could tell. She told me her mother was from Ireland, and she has your smile. I have been dying to meet you."

Imelda looked at her and smiled.

"Which part of the Old Country are you from?" Mother Melissa asked.

"County Cork."

"I'm from there too. Where in County Cork?"

"We had a farm in Kilworth."

"I don't think I can breathe," Mother Melissa's knees gave way, as she put her hand up to her heart. "Don't mind me if

I faint, but I think you are going to tell me you are Patrick Connor's daughter, Imelda. No one else could have that hair!"

Imelda's eyes were round as saucers. "Who are you? You know my father?"

"This is surely a miracle! Mother Bernadine and Beatrice told me they knew a courageous young girl named Imelda who had followed her heart to India."

"Aunt Bea and Mother Bernadine. You know them?" Imelda burst out.

"Don't you remember me, Imelda? I am Breda O'Leary. We lived but a few farms down from you. You were the riding star who all the boys wanted to beat."

"I remember you! You had a sister and two older brothers. Douglas O'Leary was Cyril's friend. I cannot believe we would meet like this."

They sat talking for hours, repeating over and over again how miraculous this meeting was, it was definitely divine intervention. There must have been a special warm glow in that chapel that day.

"Why did you become a nun, Breda?"

"I'm not Breda anymore, I'm Mother Melissa. You know Joseph O'Keefe broke my heart, left for America without so much as a goodbye. Then I lost my brother David and my mother in a boating accident about seven years ago."

"I am so sorry to hear that."

"I just wanted to get away. Being a teacher, I contacted the Loreto nuns in Dublin and after a few years training, here I am. It has filled the big hole in my heart. Have you been ill, Imelda? You look so thin and frail. I remember you as this strong young girl with the flying red hair."

"I'm doing well," Imelda lied. "We moved here from Calcutta about eight months ago. Milty has talked about you so often."

"You have such a funny daughter. I just love her. Now that I have met you, my heart is just bursting. We have guardian angels watching over us, for sure. I had been feeling so homesick, and God send me you." Mother Melissa joyfully hugged her. Then she suddenly realized the time. "Oh no, the nuns will think something has happened to me. I was sent at five-thirty to lock up, and it's past seven already. I have to go. Come to school on Monday, we must talk."

As they walked out Mother Melissa stopped, knelt down and offered up a quick prayer of thanks.

Imelda walked home with a quizzical smile on her face. To have met Breda O'Leary from Kilworth, County Cork, in a remote chapel hidden in the foothills of the Himalayas! Life works in such mysterious ways.

She told Shu about her encounter, bubbling over with excitement.

That night she lay awake, thinking of all the people she and Breda knew. What would Aunt Bea say? Would they even recognize her? Her soul had been sucked out of her and her spirit had died. She cried for her former self. She had forgotten that brave little girl.

After that first meeting, she and Mother Melissa met often, at the chapel, at the school, at home where 'Mother M' as Imelda called her would come and have Saturday lunch.

They talked about her son's death and although Imelda could not bring herself to say his name, Mother M always did. She would say his name and watch Imelda cringe and crumble into tears. She forced Imelda to accept his life, his short but joyous life, before she could deal with his death.

"If you can't face what has happened, and accept it has happened, you cannot move on."

"I don't want to move on. Can't you understand that?"

"Put all your sorrow and pain in a safe place close to your heart. It will always be your secret place for wretchedness," she would counsel. "When you miss Peter go to it, but you must learn to leave it."

Mother Melissa knew exactly what the constant torment of pain can do. "When do you miss Peter the most?" she asked.

"When it begins to get dark. I can feel his fear."

"I want you to set up an altar for him. At dusk, light a candle for him. You will focus on the moment. This is the time for you to feel. Cry, weep, sob and experience all the pain. Then spend a minute celebrating his life. Think of a happy time; think of how much happiness he gave you, and be grateful for that time. You will feel strong and in control."

"Don't you understand, I just can't put him away? He's there when Milty smiles and looks at me, I see his eyes, his smile. Sometimes I can't bear to look at her. I just don't have the strength."

"If anyone has strength its you. You can't spend the rest of your life running away from his memory. You cannot ignore the Peter you see in Milty. He is there, accept it."

Shu had been the balm that loved and nurtured her, but he could never bring up the subject of Peter and tell Imelda what she had to do. She needed a tough person, a person she trusted to force her to accept what was, rather than what had been, her life.

Mother Melissa was Imelda's miracle. She brought back the shine in those deep blue eyes. She made the smile reappear almost as suddenly as it had vanished. Imelda's face now glowed with happiness more often than sad misgivings. And occasionally the house would rock with loud laughter as Shu and Milty would tentatively throw a quick glance at each other to re-confirm that this was really happening.

Often at night, Imelda would listen to the stories Shu would be reading to Milty. Every now and then she wanted to join them. She would wait for Shu to come down and take her hand, put his arm around her. She was always his girl with the moondust in her hair and starlight in her eyes. He never let her forget it, especially now as he saw the cobwebs slowly clearing away, and the light of the moon gently brightening her tumultuous life.

Milty had at an early age learnt to tiptoe on eggshells around her mother. She knew when to talk and when not to say anything. The conversations were always on two levels. The first was the unspoken one, where all feelings were left unsaid. The second was the spoken level. She was not afraid to show an emotion, but only if it gave positive reinforcement of her mother.

"Mummy, those are the bestest pansies I have ever seen."

"Bestest is not a word. Yes, I love them too."

"The mali says you have magic fingers."

"It's called a green thumb!" Imelda laughed. "I could always make flowers grow."

"Green thumb!" Milty put her thumbs up in the air.

"My father gave me my green thumb, did you know that?"

"Your father? Was he a lawyer or an engineer?"

"No, my father was a soldier and a farmer. His heart was in the farm. He taught me to love working with animals and to be out in green fields. He said nothing is more important than getting your hands dirty and feeling the earth, like this." She dug her fingers deep into the mud and turned it over.

"Your father was a farmer?" Milty asked, surprised. "Like the farmer in the dell?"

"Yes, and he was so proud of his farm. I'm my father's daughter, Milty, and just like you, I was always his special little girl." She smiled as she touched the tip of the little girl's nose with a muddy finger.

Milty knew not to pry deep into her mother's childhood.

"Is that a new dress you have on, Mummy?" she suddenly asked looking skywards.

"I got one for you too," Imelda answered.

Later that day, Milty tried on her dress as she twirled and danced in front of the mirror.

When Shu arrived, he greeted Imelda with a peck on the forehead. "Had a good day, darling?" Then he turned to their daughter. "Milty, I have surprise for you. But first, let's have tea."

"Tell me the big surprise, pleeese?" she cut him off impatiently.

"Dadu and Ma are coming to visit us for a few weeks."

Milty screamed, running off to tell Surya and baboochi.

"Why don't you join us for the walk? It's a beautiful evening," Shu asked casually as they sipped tea. "The weather's perfect, the birds are singing, the flowers are blooming…"

Imelda often watched Shu and Milty take off for their evening walks. Milty, animated and full of energy, usually pulling her father's hand or chasing the dog. Shu, calm and relaxed, not fazed by all the noise and excitement around him.

She looked at them carefully. Those happy people were her family, she should be with them; such a small step, yet the tomorrows kept coming.

Shu turned back to her. "See you soon," he said with a small wave.

The dog started barking and running in circles as Milty pretended to pull Shu up the slope.

Imelda felt a lump in her throat as she swallowed, tears spilled down her cheeks. She was going to do it, she was going to do it now.

"Hey, you two, wait for me."

She smiled the widest, most magnificent smile, her eyes luminous as she ran to join them. She stopped to catch her breath, then laughingly grabbed Shu's hand. He was staring at her, hesitant, overcome with emotion. There she stood, so fragile and so beautiful. She seemed to be lifted and floating towards them, her red hair blowing around her smiling face.

Milty, who was jumping around excitedly, immediately noticed the panic in her father's eyes. She ran to reassure him, and took hold of his other hand.

"It's okay, Daddy," she said, in as grown-up a voice as any six-year-old could manage, "she's back. Mummy's back."

Epilogue

January 10, 1961 was a sad day for the Bose family. Amarendra Nath Bose had died peacefully in his sleep at the age of ninety-one. Word of his demise had spread quickly and thousands of mourners thronged the streets outside 84 Harish Mukherjee Road, bringing the city to a virtual standstill. People from all walks of life came to show their last respects to a beloved old man. The High Court was closed in his honour, and Bose Park was filled to capacity with people chanting, or standing with bowed heads, paying respects to the simple man who they had grown to love and admire. Eulogies recalled the heroic trails he had blazed as a brilliant lawyer. But mostly it was his integrity, his honesty and his decency they had come to celebrate. To this day, among the distinguished portraits of chief justices in the Calcutta High Court, stands the bust of one lawyer: Amarendra Nath Bose.

Amarendra died a proud man, living long enough to see all his children achieve great success in their chosen professions.

Himanshu Bose rose to be chief justice of the Calcutta High Court. He was renowned for his integrity and professionalism.

His only daughter, Archana Deb, was professor of history at Presidency College.

Shu had enjoyed his life in Simla, but his heart belonged in Calcutta, and he always longed to return to the city. He did so in 1959 to become chief engineer at the Damordar Valley Corporation, helping to design and build the first hydroelectric plant in India.

Saury Bose became director of finance at Gilanders, and later chairman of American Express. His son, Tutu, got his degree in engineering, before he took up the spiritual life changing his name to Swami Monananda. His eldest daughter, Mithu Alur, founded the Spastic Society of India (now Action for Ability Development and Inclusion), the first school for children with cerebral palsy in India, and his youngest, Mita Nundy, continued the pioneering work by opening a branch of AADI in New Delhi.

Chotto's husband, Nirmal Roychaudury, was India's first ambassador to Pakistan, and Khanu Mitra, Menu's husband, remained a well-established zamindar.

Imelda Joan Bose was the most tenacious survivor of them all. Her recovery was slow, but in the end her indomitable spirit overcame the many dark days of her life. She loved to be among youngsters and began by helping the poorer kids in the neighbourhood play table tennis at the Calcutta Club House. She bought them racquets and balls and clothes so they could play in the local tournaments. To encourage them, she joined in the matches, and to the surprise of both Shu and Milty, returned home one evening with a huge trophy. When questioned about whose trophy she had stolen, she proudly announced she had won the championship and was now officially Punjab's number one ladies' table tennis champion. She even went on to represent the Indian team in the world table tennis championship in Ceylon [Sri Lanka].

Imelda missed her sister Kathleen terribly and had heard her brother Frank had cancer: her other brothers Patrick and Paddy had both died young. Knowing that it would not be possible for them to visit on his meagre government salary, Shu applied for a consulting job in London. He got the job, and the family moved to London in 1950 for two years. Imelda reconnected with her family and made peace with her two living brothers, Cyril and Frank.

They visited Shropshire often, to Market Drayton where Kathleen and Eddie Cryan lived. Kathleen, who had good relationships with everyone in the family, insisted Imelda meet Nancy. After weeks of arguing, Imelda finally agreed. It took a while for her to accept that the kind, gentle, grey-haired woman she met was not the evil witch she remembered from her childhood.

And as for 84 Harish Mukherjee Road, the house which once was filled with purring panthers, chattering cockatoos, majestically dancing peacocks, and Tom the turkey guarding the gates is now a small college called the Institute for Cost Accountants and its magnificent Italian marbled halls now stand divided into cubicles where students work towards their own, very different, dreams.

Acknowledgements

With heartfelt thanks to my children, Ayesha – who first planted the seed of the idea, and kept it watered – and Namita, Brinda, and Nikhil who were always so supportive and helped me to stay focused.

To my uncle, Saury Kaku for filling in so many of the details.

To my cousins, Mithu Alur, Archana Deb, Mita Nundy and Swami Monananda, who all sent me snippets about their parents, and to Tommy Cryan – Kathleen and Eddie's son – who filled me in about my mother's family.

To my friend Pami Singh who, after berating me for having a 'bag of scraps' for a book, had the scraps typed up into one cohesive document and encouraged me to keep going.

And to my close friends Mindy Pande, Shobana Lahiri, Kumkum Sen, Bonnie Upal, Barbara Mahajan, and of course Mithu Alur and Malini Chib, who all helped to keep my spirits up during an overwhelming time in my life. They never let me get too discouraged, and when I did, helped me pick myself up and keep the fire lit.